S0-BRP-320

HANDEL

HANDEL

[from a painting by Thomas Hudson in the Metropolitan Museum of Art, New York]

ML 410
H13
W27
1959

7.50

Mc Clurg

20 Aug 59

HANDEL

BY

HERBERT WEINSTOCK

SECOND EDITION, REVISED

59-7221

NEW YORK: ALFRED · A · KNOPF

1959

26368

VNYS ML 410 .H13
W27 1959 c.1
KGQ001W-2003; KGQ001Z-2003

L. C. Catalog card number: 59–7221
© *Herbert Weinstock, 1959*

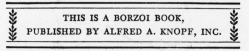

THIS IS A BORZOI BOOK,
PUBLISHED BY ALFRED A. KNOPF, INC.

Copyright 1946, 1959 by HERBERT WEINSTOCK. All rights reserved. No part of
this book may be reproduced in any form without permission in writing from
the publisher, except by a reviewer who may quote brief passages and reproduce not more than three illustrations in a review to be printed in a magazine or
newspaper. Manufactured in the United States of America. Published simultaneously in Canada by McClelland & Stewart Ltd.

Published September, 1946
Second Printing, Revised, March, 1959

Handel is the greatest of us all.

— BEETHOVEN

Handel's greatness rests on quite other foundations than Bach's. The childish observation has been made that Handel wrote a heap of indifferent works which Bach had too thorough a training and too simple an eye to pure music to do; and this has brought upon him the misunderstanding of sciolists and even of masters. But Bach himself, Mozart, and Beethoven thought otherwise; and indeed Handel, if we take his personality as a whole, stands as little below Bach as Bach is below him.

— ALFRED EINSTEIN

When he [Handel] chooses, he strikes like a thunderbolt.

— MOZART

APOLOGIA AND ACKNOWLEDGMENTS

THE FACT THAT this Second Edition differs in hundreds of details from the First Edition is justified by later research and publications.

Like everyone who now writes about Handel, I am especially grateful to Otto Erich Deutsch for his "documentary biography." And like anyone now dealing with any aspect of the history of opera, I am greatly in the debt of the late Alfred Loewenberg for the patient detective work that resulted in his *Annals of Opera.* I owe a peculiar debt to a distinguished musicologist who published a scarifying attack on the First Edition of this book: thanks to his vitriolic strictures, this Second Edition is, I am certain, better than it would have been had he been more generous.

In the First Edition I thanked for essential assistance of many sorts: Wallace Brockway, Mrs. Elizabeth C. Moore, and my mother, Edna Weinstock. The fact that Mrs. Moore and my mother are now both dead in no way diminishes my gratitude to them. I also thanked Mr. Alfred A. Knopf; my then editor, Wilson Follett; Sidney R. Jacobs, who had designed the volume; Pamela Hinkson; the staffs of the Music Room of the New York Public Library (Fifth Avenue) and Music Library (58th Street); the Metropolitan Museum of Art, which had granted permission to reproduce, for the first time in a Handel biography, its portrait of Handel by Hudson; Dr. Emanuel Winternitz and Miss Olivia Paine of the Metropolitan; and all my predecessors in Handeliana.

My sense of gratitude to Sir Newman Flower, likewise expressed in the First Edition, has been somewhat dulled. In 1944, Sir Newman sent me as a gift a copy of the abridged edition of his biography of Handel. He later threatened any English edition of my book with legal restraint because I had cited statements and opinions from the very volume he had himself sent me — and though I had painstakingly credited every such citation to him. As a result of his threat, this book has never been published in England.

I am very grateful to Mr. Alan Frank and the Oxford University Press, London, for allowing me to examine, well in advance of publication, uncorrected page proofs of Mr. Winton Dean's unique and remarkable book, *Handel's Dramatic Oratorios and Masques* (London, New York, Toronto, 1959). By this excellently organized result of massive and magnificent research, Mr. Dean has put all Handelians deeply in his debt.

To Ben Meiselman, finally, I owe a debt that cannot be calculated: he not only allowed me to read the original manuscript of this book to him as it was written (and responded with keen detailed criticism), but was also a strong arm of assistance in the preparation of the indexes for both editions.

HERBERT WEINSTOCK

CONTENTS

CONTENTS

BOOK IV

ILLUSTRATIONS

ILLUSTRATIONS

Introduction

A T the Queen's Theatre in the Haymarket an event of un-
predictable importance swelled the theatrical and musical activity of Queen Anne's London on February 24,
1711. On that day Aaron Hill presented an opera put together in
a fortnight by a young man lately arrived from Italy and Germany. Its libretto was the best a hurried hack named Giacomo
Rossi could fabricate from scenes in Tasso: the text had nothing
to do with making the date memorable. The singers belonged
to another order of things, for they included a great bass, Giuseppe Boschi, and also Nicolini, who possessed one of the sweet-
est of artificial voices. Without Boschi and Nicolini the London
audience would probably have been impolite to the new opera.
But what finally set that opera apart from every other that Londoners had heard was its music, the first complete score they
had been offered by a newcomer to their city. This young subject of the Elector of Hanover was George Frideric Handel.[1]
His name was soon as much on the lips of London music-lovers
as was speculation about who was to succeed Queen Anne and
excited gossip about a papist's attempt to assassinate the Earl
of Oxford by stabbing him with a penknife. The opera, which
was played to full houses fourteen times more before the
Queen's Theatre closed for the summer on June 2, was called
Rinaldo.

The success of *Rinaldo* was immediate and of enduring effect:
it channeled the operatic history of England for nearly thirty
years and — indirectly, through Handel's later influence on
taste — tinted the whole fabric of music in England forever. It
had other results. It launched one of the most abundant natural
geniuses of music on a singular career, first as an operatic com-

---

[1] Because the composer himself used his own Anglicization of his name
for more than half of his life, I shall use it exclusively despite the fact that
he was baptised Georg Friedrich Händel.

poser-impresario and then as the foremost creator of concert oratorios — launched him on that career and simultaneously marked out its arena. It signaled the long eclipse of music by Englishmen and set on edge the teeth of Joseph Addison and Richard Steele. What those who wildly applauded *Rinaldo* did not know was that the twenty-five-year-old Handel had patched out the newly composed sections of the score with music he had written earlier and for other purposes. Among those self-borrowings was one of the two numbers from *Rinaldo* that remain well known today: it is the stately *"Lascia ch'io pianga,"* one of Handel's greatest arias. With the likewise familiar *"Cara sposa,"* it still supplies a key to understanding the freshness and vigor that enchanted the Londoners of 1711.

The England onto whose soil Handel had first stepped in the autumn of 1710 was an agitated nation embroiled in a successful but unpopular war and intensely conscious of politics. Anne, the dull, conscientious, unfortunate daughter of James II, had been Queen for almost nine years. During much of her reign England had been dominated by the great Duke of Marlborough, Anne herself by his wife, Sarah. In London coffee houses there had been excited discussions of such previously obscure Continental places as Blenheim, Ramillies, Oudenarde, and Malplaquet. The clutch that Louis XIV had all but closed on Europe had been forced open by Marlborough. But England's greatest military leader had proved an unwise politician. In 1708, one year after the union with Scotland, an all-Whig ministry had been summoned for the better prosecution of the continuing war. But Anne was a Tory at heart. In 1710 she abruptly rid herself of Sarah, Duchess of Marlborough. When the Duke himself returned to London that winter, he faced a Tory Commons elected in support of a Tory ministry headed by Robert Harley, Earl of Oxford, and Henry St. John, Viscount Bolingbroke. The new ministers observed the old custom of waiting upon the victorious soldier, but neither the Lords nor the Commons voted him the traditional thanks. Nor was Anne likely to insist on their homage: as her most intimate companion she had replaced the Duchess of Marlborough with Abigail Hill, Oxford's cousin. Worse was to come for the man who had asserted England's military greatness but had failed to gauge the temper of its ruler and of its elected representatives. On December 30, 1711, Marlborough was to be deprived of all his offices and retired into a comparative obscurity that became absolute within a few years.

Past the middle of Anne's twelve-year reign England was still troubled by religious differences. The *cause célèbre* of 1709–10 was the trial of an earnest, addlepated, and inflammable churchman, Henry Sacheverell. Previously unnoticed, Sacheverell had preached two sermons upholding the doctrine of non-resistance to the divinely given power of kings and crying that the Church of England was in critical danger from papists and nonconformists. He charged that the Church was being neglected by the Whig ministry headed by the Earl of Godolphin, who must have known that both his sovereign and most of London agreed with Sacheverell. But Godolphin lost his head and instituted impeachment proceedings against the suddenly idolized preacher. Sacheverell's trial before the Lords lasted from February 27 to March 23, 1710. The Queen attended. Crowds cheered the vain and pompous preacher through the streets. When the Lords, having found Sacheverell guilty, passed light sentence upon him, the people interpreted the sentence as a victory for the Tories. It was then that the Whig ministry of Godolphin fell and was replaced by the Tories of Bolingbroke and Oxford. For four years the Tories were to retain power, only, by Anne's death in 1714, to lose it for all but half a century.

Anne reigned over an England not profoundly different from that of her greatgrandfather, James I, a century earlier. The population of the country, and of London especially, had increased notably in one hundred years, but a large section of it still believed in witchcraft, in touching for the King's (or Queen's) Evil, and in the divine right of kings — at least, of Protestant kings. It was a profoundly undemocratic country still: as late as 1711 Parliament could make an annual income of £300 for borough members, £600 for country members, prerequisite to a seat. The rich were enormously rich and powerful, the poor terribly degraded, the middle class small and unstable. Nonconformists and Catholics lived under intermittently crippling restrictions. On March 15, 1711, for example, following the attempt on Oxford by a French papist, Anne carried out Parliament's suggestion that she forbid Catholics to reside in Westminster or London.

Yet the burgeoning commercial England of the nineteenth century was gestating while Anne sorrowed for George of Denmark and herself sank toward an early grave. The heyday of merchant princes and a dominant bourgeoisie was dawning. It was on June 27, 1711, during the Queen's Theatre season of Handel's first English success, that a royal commission was granted for the taking of subscriptions in the South Sea Company. Within a few days, more than £4,000,000 had been invested in that Utopian blue-sky swindle. Handel himself was to incarnate and typify the final shift from the domination of blood and aristocracy to that of solid business worth, for he was to become the first great composer-impresario, to help manage a stockholders' corporation, and to experience more than one strictly commercial failure and success.

Who was this Italianate German whose *Rinaldo,* in 1711, was a three-month wonder in the Haymarket? Whence and why had he come to London? Whither was he bound? Would he remain to delight the musical among London's half million inhabitants with his eminently singable and danceable melodies? To answer these questions has been my aim in this book. I have made every effort to see George Frideric Handel's ample figure against the shifting events and forces of his era, first in Germany, then in Italy, and finally — for almost fifty years — in England. For a musical genius he was a markedly extroverted, objective man, as far removed in character from the introspective, intensely pious Johann Sebastian Bach as one artist could be from an exact contemporary. Handel left few letters and no self-examination. He lived an incessantly active long life in three countries during one of the most colorful periods in European history, and left behind him, as Sir Donald Tovey pointed out, a mass of music almost equal to all we have of Bach plus all of Beethoven. It is the story of his seventy-four years of activity that I have here tried to re-create.

HERBERT WEINSTOCK

BOOK I

I

AT the top of a page in the baptismal book of the Liebfrauenkirche [1] at Halle, a scribe entered, on Tuesday, February 24, 1685, the name of Georg
Friedrich Händel, born the preceding day to
Georg Händel and his wife Dorothea. The year 1685 was to
prove generous to music: twenty-six days after the birth in
Halle, Johann Sebastian Bach was born into a family of musicians in Eisenach, eighty miles to the southwest, while in
Naples on October 26 a son to be named Domenico was born
to the greatest practicing composer of the time, Alessandro
Scarlatti. If heredity and family environment had any influence
on a child's talent and choice of vocation, there would have
been every reason to expect a new Bach or a new Scarlatti to
grow up a better than average musician. The same influences
would have made music one of the activities strangest to the
nature of a Händel.

Georg Händel, barber-surgeon of Giebichenstein, a suburban
district of Halle, was a man of strong, unpleasantly dour character who lacked taste for art in general and patience with
music in particular. Born in September 1622, he was sixty-two
years old when his second wife, daughter to Pastor Georg Taust
of Giebichenstein, bore their second child, the first having died
at birth in 1684. Dorothea Taust Händel, born about 1652, was
no more musical than her tall, formidable husband, thirty years
her senior. They were respectable citizens who owned their
comfortable house, known as *"zum gelben Hirschen,"* on the

[1] The real name of this church was Oberpfarrkirche zu Unser Lieben
Frauen zu Halle. To the confusion of historians and readers it was indiscriminately referred to as the Liebfrauenkirche, the Kirche am Marktplatz,
the Hauptkirche, and the Marienkirche.

Schlamm. The future composer would resemble his father in nothing except longevity and unwavering strength of will. Tall and strong like her husband and her famous son, Dorothea Händel was — also like them — to live well beyond seventy years. It is no longer possible to determine her character clearly enough to say that she passed on to George Frideric more than the physical stamina needed to exist for seventy-four years in a disease-ridden, unhygienic, and generally dangerous world.

The family whose members were remarkable for the inconsistency with which they spelled their name — Händel, Hendel, Hendtler, Händeler, and other forms are to be encountered — had been severely run of the mill until its sole notable member was born. Study of such hours of its history as surviving documents preserve is neither very interesting nor provocative of useful speculation. One Valentin Händel emigrated from Breslau to Halle shortly after 1600. He married Anna, daughter of an Eisleben coppersmith called Samuel Beichling and, on March 14, 1609, became a citizen of his adopted city. He was a successful practitioner of his father-in-law's trade, and won sufficient notice and esteem from the townspeople of Halle to be elected to the local council, in which he held the post of breadweigher. Of his five sons and one daughter, the only one who mattered, historically speaking, was that Georg whose second wife, eighty-five years or so after the adventurous Valentin had left Breslau, gave birth to one of the most momentous and kinetic geniuses in the whole story of music.

Georg Händel, son of Valentin, grew up a pushing young man, determined above everything to make a solid place for himself in the small world of Halle. When scarcely more than twenty, he married a woman twelve years his senior, Anna Öttinger, the widow of a barber-surgeon who had been his employer. By hard work, which he never skimped, he himself shortly established a fine practice as a barber-surgeon. In his medical capacity he seems to have been attached, from time to time, to various bodies of wandering troops. He also achieved

appointment as surgeon-in-ordinary and chamber valet to Duke
Augustus, who, from Halle's Moritzburg, kept watch until 1680
over the archdiocese of Magdeburg for his brother, Johann
Georg II, Elector of Saxony. Aside from begetting one genius
and carrying on complicated struggles with local authority over
matters of prerogative and legal right, Georg Händel left behind him the record of only one remarkable performance
(mending a broken arm for Duke Augustus was hardly another,
though to it he owed his resounding title, *Geheimer Kammer-
diener und Leibchirurgus*).

When his son George Frideric was seven years old, he himself seventy, Georg Händel operated on Andreas Rudloff, a
peasant boy from a near-by village. He found, lodged in what
was described as a boil at the base of the patient's heart, the
point of a knife that the youth had swallowed accidentally
the previous year. On that June 18, 1692, old Händel fastened
a thread of silk to the knife — which, with its staghorn handle,
had been in young Rudloff's stomach for more than 530 days.
Disdaining the cold and hot beer, olive oil, and corrosives with
which other medics had hoped either to dissolve the knife or
to evacuate it, Händel had decided to pull it out whole, step
by perilous and painful step. The relief with which the wretched
boy, after forty-five days of this inching torment, witnessed the
success of his tormenter's wise audacity cannot be imagined.[2]
The successful removal of the staghorn-handled knife on August 2, 1692, spread Georg Händel's fame. His septuagenarian
fingers must have been phenomenally steady.

The operation was a fitting climax to a useful life. But, like
everything known of Georg Händel's career, it offers little assistance toward an understanding of his composer son. Whatever light is to be thrown on that other, more enduringly valuable life must be found in Handel's music itself, in a study of

[2] Andreas Rudloff recovered. Known thereafter as "The Sword-Swallower
of Halle," he is said to have become a military surgeon. As Sir Newman
Flower remarked, his experience might well have inspired him with an
enthusiasm for surgery.

local or Europe-wide events and currents outside the family circle, in Handel's few surviving letters and jottings, and in the most reliable and chatty memoirs and related writings of his contemporaries. He was endowed with the normal amount of filial and familial affection. It must have been all but impossible to love his severe, strait-lipped old father, but he retained a deep, if geographically remote, love for his mother until her death in his forty-fourth year. But his talent, the superior attractions of Hamburg, Italy, and finally London, and — unquestionably — pressures in himself early carried George Frideric Handel away from whatever family and childhood had meant to him. At the age of eighteen he left home, never to return but as a visitor. From that day on, he was loosed from most human ties; he became the creator and peopler of his own personal environment. Few great men in history have been so alone.

Handel was born on Monday, February 23, 1685, not quite thirty-seven years after the Treaty of Westphalia had terminated that congeries of confused religious struggles, feudal battles, and shifting allegiances since called the Thirty Years' War. The only immediate effect of the War and the Treaty on Handel was that technically he was born, not a Saxon, but a subject of the Elector of Brandenburg, Halle having been ceded to him by the Elector of Saxony under the Treaty. But their effect on most of Europe — only England, Turkey, Russia, and Poland had been substantially unaffected — and on the Holy Roman Empire in particular, was devastating, profound, and permanent. From those far-off years the names of monarchs and generals, scoundrels and ministers, may still ring romantic to our ears: Gustavus Adolphus, Ferdinand III, Wallenstein, the Duc d'Enghien, Christian IV, Turenne, Richelieu, Urban VIII, Mazarin, and the others. But poverty, disease, and stark terror had crippled central Europe for one third of the seventeenth century. The enduring results have not been wholly obliterated by three more centuries of wars.

6

The Treaty of Westphalia reshuffled the bishoprics, towns, fiefs, and small duchies into which Germany was divided. In doing so it strengthened the hands of Austria, Bavaria, and Brandenburg, and thus tended toward the simpler German map of Bismarck's Empire. It left the towns and countryside divided between Catholic and Protestant preponderance in about the ratio that was recognizable until the rise of Hitler. Halle was largely Protestant, its burghers attending either Lutheran or Reformed (Calvinist) services. It was a less colorful town during Handel's childhood than during his father's, for in the interim it had lost its distinction as the seat of a secondary, loose-lived, and not inartistic court. The Moritzburg, long the site of that court of the prince-archbishops of Magdeburg, had been largely swept away by fire during the War. Five years before Handel's birth, too, Duke Augustus of Saxony had died (his life tenure had not been disturbed despite the Treaty of Westphalia), and Halle had found itself a mere appanage of Berlin, almost one hundred miles to the northeast. Johann Adolf I, Duke of Saxe-Weissenfels, Augustus' son and successor as head of a cadet branch of the ruling Saxon family, removed himself from Halle to take up his official residence at Weissenfels, twenty-five miles to the southeast. Thereafter Halle's most notable residents were its climbing burghers, of whom Georg Händel was by no measure the least.

Georg Händel had received his appointment as barber-surgeon of Giebichenstein in 1652, when he was thirty. Thirteen years later he had purchased the house in the Schlamm. Thither he had taken Anna, his first wife, whom he married in 1643, and by whom he had six children. When the plague of 1682 struck Halle, it killed both the seventy-two-year-old Anna and Gottfried, the one of their two surviving children by whom he had hoped to see the family name perpetuated, but who left a young widow without issue.[3] Most men of sixty would scarcely have set about at once acquiring another wife and family, but

---

[3] The Händel name was actually perpetuated by the other, less favored son, Karl.

Georg Händel was a giant in strength, in stature, and in harsh firmness of purpose. He immediately courted, and in six months married, Dorothea, the thirty-two-year-old daughter of one of his few cronies, Georg Taust, Lutheran pastor of Giebichenstein. It was 1683, forty years after his first marriage. This outwardly frigid man must have nursed the flame of a perdurable urge: before his death at seventy-four he begat four children by the wife of his old age. Only two of Dorothea's children grew to maturity: a daughter and her composer son, who never married.

Pastor Taust, too, had suffered from the plague of 1682. Weak and ill, he survived until 1685. On his death, his unmarried daughter, Anna, moved to the Händel household, where she devoted the rest of her life to all manner of helpful service to her sister. The family group that the child George Frideric must have become aware of earliest consisted, then, of an aged, unbending, but not always wholly unsympathetic father, a mother approaching middle age, a maiden aunt, two sisters younger than himself (one of whom died early), and perhaps his half-brother Karl. The house in which they lived no longer stands as they knew it: the one often pictured as Handel's birthplace, the one decorated with a niched bust of the composer and plaques naming some of his compositions, is next door to the site of his real home. Even though *"zum gelben Hirschen"* must have suffered considerable damage in a fire that flamed through the central district of Halle in 1676, it was undoubtedly an impressive indication of wealth and social position. Georg Händel earned considerable sums, not only from his practice, but probably also from his appointments to royal and military service, and certainly from the wine business whose license had come to him with the house. It was this license over which he had haggled and quarreled with the Halle authorities, appealed more than once to the Elector of Saxony, and alienated many of his fellow burghers. It is likely that he did not need the income from wine, but was fighting for the letter of a legal right. When he finally won, he exercised the right for only a few years. Then, acting for once the splendid role of magnanimity, he presented the license to the town.

Everything that has ever been said or written about George Frideric Handel's first seven years has been based on more or less reasonable guesses, customarily of the most romantic sort. It is not that what facts survive are uninteresting. There simply are no documents or other dependable sources of information.[4] He was born on February 23, 1685; nothing that he himself did can be dated until February 18, 1697, when there was published in leaflet form a poetic memorial he had written to his late father. Other facts, however, can be derived from remarks he made and wrote in later years, though they cannot be dated exactly. He went to school from about his seventh year on, probably to the Lutheran Gymnasium. If the legends of his very early love for music are true, and if he attended this free public grammar school rather than some private institution, he may have found a sympathetic elder in its principal, who is known to have loved music.

Some time shortly after 1692, the year during which Georg Händel drew the staghorn-handled knife from Andreas Rudloff's body, his young son accompanied him on a visit to the ducal court at Weissenfels, to which he still held an appointment and in which his son Karl held a position as valet-de-chambre. The time-honored story that the seven- or eight-year-old George Frideric, left behind in Halle, ran in pursuit of the coach in which his father was speeding toward Weissenfels has no demonstrable basis in fact. It has, further, the fine aroma of utter nonsense. He was taken to Weissenfels and put up with either his half-brother Karl or his nephew Georg Christian Händel — also a valet-de-chambre to the Duke — because that suited

[4] Much of the romantic speculation is derived from the first book on Handel ever published, John Mainwaring's *Memoirs of the Life of the Late G. F. Handel*. Mainwaring never met Handel, and no sufficient reason for trusting his presentation of material he received at second hand has ever been advanced. The task of removing Mainwaring's unprovable statements from the Handel story was ably begun by R. A. Streatfeild and carried on by Sir Newman Flower and Edward J. Dent.

his father's purpose. Whether that purpose was to show him off as a prodigy, to give him a promised reward, or to relieve some momentarily difficult situation at *"zum gelben Hirschen"* will never be known, and is unimportant. The real importance of what is known about the trip to Weissenfels is as proof that Handel's musical bent and abilities had begun to show themselves and win recognition before he was ten years old.

As a retainer of Duke Johann Adolf's family, Georg Händel must have had certain freedoms at court, trifling liberties that would have been extended naturally to his small son. The boy's close attention to music caught the notice of musicians in the ducal employ. By accident, Johann Adolf himself became the first person known certainly to have urged a musical career for Handel. Discovering that the barber-surgeon's son could improvise on the organ, the household *Kappelmeister* permitted him to take a small part in Sunday music in the chapel. Where George Frideric had learned to play, where he had achieved any connection with music closer than that of an attentive listener in Halle's streets and Liebfrauenkirche, cannot be learned. There may have been actual events behind the legend of his clandestinely taking a portable clavichord to a room under the roof of *"zum gelben Hirschen"* and there, by night, trying its feeble tones for himself. Perhaps those who have guessed that his aunt, Anna Taust, nurtured his musical leanings have guessed well. What is sure is that before his tenth birthday he played the organ in the chapel of the ducal *Schloss* at Weissenfels so persuasively that Johann Adolf called Georg Händel to him and said that this child must have musical training.

The barber-surgeon could not have been more shocked at Johann Adolf's peremptory suggestion if the Duke had ordered him to train his boy as a beggar. He wanted the only son of his second marriage to become a lawyer. Musicians, in his eyes, as in those of most of his countrymen, were shiftless, rootless men doomed to constant impecuniousness. They were necessary to church services and to public ceremonies and celebrations, but were otherwise an immoral nuisance and a noisy drain on

respectable burghers.[5] Georg Händel would have disobeyed the
Duke had he dared. He was no longer a Saxon subject. But
any royal command was ignored only at considerable risk. Further, Johann Adolf could reasonably expect loyalty from this
man on so small a point. A frightened and probably very
irritable Georg Händel took his son back to Halle. There he
arranged for the boy's musical instruction with the most respectable musician he knew, the organist of the Liebfrauenkirche, which he himself attended. Perhaps he felt that this
useless indulgence would not harm a healthy schoolboy. The
old man was engaged in a battle that he could not win by the
sort of stubborn persistence through which he had preserved
the wine license of his house. It is senseless to blame him for
not understanding the small, strange creature he had begotten:
he had no mental means for understanding, no emotional equip-
ment for sympathy. And he was past seventy.

By selecting the organist of the Liebfrauenkirche, Georg
Händel had unwittingly done the best he could for his son's
future and the worst for his own plans. For that organist was
the most accomplished musician in Halle, the best local teacher
the boy could have had at the moment, the preceptor likeliest
to make music seem to him so attractive that all possibility of a
legal career would be banished forever. He was Friedrich Wilhelm Zachau, a man of about thirty, accomplished on other
instruments besides the organ, and a composer whose music
retains vitality to this day. Several of his choral and organ
works as reprinted in the magnificent *Denkmäler deutscher
Tonkunst* have won enthusiastic praise from modern musicologists and critics. In some details of idiom and style they adum-
brate far greater works by Handel, who remembered Zachau
always with affection and artistic respect.

Approximately three years of stiff tuition by Zachau were to

[5] Mainwaring quoted Georg Händel as saying that "music was an elegant
art and a fine amusement; yet, if considered as an occupation, it had
little dignity, as having for its subject nothing better than mere pleasure
and entertainment."

constitute Handel's entire formal music education. During them
he learned to play several instruments, including oboe, harpsichord, and violin, and was grounded severely and well in the
theoretical aspects of counterpoint and composition. Zachau
probably permitted his prodigious pupil to perform occasionally on the Liebfrauenkirche organ. The numerous student
pieces that Handel wrote out for Zachau's criticism have mostly
disappeared, but are supposed to have included more than one
hundred church services, as well as secular instrumental pieces
of many kinds. From his tenth year there survive, in the fine
Buckingham Palace collection, six trio sonatas for two oboes
and continuo. These are couched in the common idiom of the
period, their only remarkable quality being the age of their
composer. When these — or some other compositions of his
apprentice days — were brought to Handel in London long
after,[6] he is supposed to have said: "I used to write like the
Devil in those days, but chiefly for the hautbois, which was
my favorite instrument."

Zachau demonstrated his wisdom by deciding, after young
Handel had worked with him more than two years, that the boy
needed no further instruction from him. This may or may not
have meant that, as idolatrous Handelians have quickly assumed, he fully understood the genius of his pupil. In all likelihood Zachau intended by this decision to say that the boy
could now progress only by beginning to make independent use
of the techniques and knowledge he had acquired rapidly and
well. It was 1696, and Handel was eleven. But Georg Händel,
gazing down sharply from the frosty eminence of his seventy-
four years, still wanted no musician in his family. The boy was
constantly reminded that he was to enter the newly founded
Halle University as *studiosus juris,* to begin preparing himself

[6] Alexander Campbell (Hume), later Earl of Marchmont, found them.
He presented them to a Mr. Weideman, who was teaching him to play
the German flute. It was Mr. Weideman, in turn, who showed them to
Handel.

for a legal career as soon as he attained the requisite age. Whatever his rebellious internal reaction to these warnings may have
been, Handel is not known to have stormed against them or attempted to refuse. He was being allowed constant contact with
music, and he was a reasonably dutiful son.

Halle, deprived for sixteen years of the presence of a court,
was no longer a specially musical town. Church music was on
a passably high level at the Liebfrauenkirche and perhaps at
the Calvinist Dom. But secular music was wholly in the hands
of ill-paid amateurs. If the young Handel had ever heard a professional or semi-professional performance of anything resem-
bling an opera, for example, it must have been during his visit
to Weissenfels. There, in the year of Handel's birth, Duke Johann Adolf had opened an opera house in which, for about
three decades, an Italian-trained musician named Johann Philipp Krieger staged Singspiele by himself and others. But Berlin,
capital of the swiftly burgeoning Electorate of Brandenburg,
was the obvious center of music to which the attention of provincial musicians turned increasingly. Thither George Frideric
Handel was taken in 1696, whether by Zachau or by someone
else is not known. Perhaps this jaunt, like that to Weissenfels,
was by way of reward or to display the prodigy to a sophisticated audience. It would be interesting to know what persuaded
the ailing barber-surgeon to let his eleven-year-old son go so
far from parental surveillance and be exposed to so virulent a
form of musical infection. What may be taken as certain is that
he permitted and financed the expedition.

In Berlin, then a city of about 20,000 inhabitants, the Elector
Friedrich III was frantically busy. He was trying simultaneously to rival the splendors of Louis XIV's Versailles, to have
the Emperor Leopold I permit his coronation as Friedrich I,
King of Prussia,[7] and to satisfy a boundless taste for picturesque
profligacy. It was he who had founded Halle University, doing

---

[7] This coronation took place in 1701.

so partly to help the notable jurist Christian Thomasius,[8] who had been expelled from Leipzig for expounding heretical opinions. His second, and neglected, wife was Sophia Charlotte, daughter of the Elector of Hanover and sister to that Georg Ludwig whom Handel was to know well in later years as George I of England. Sophia Charlotte could find little to approve of in her husband's life, but she did share his taste for artists who would shed splendor over Berlin, and for lending assistance to Protestant refugees from France and to impecunious intellectuals in general. She had studied some philosophy with Gottfried Wilhelm Leibnitz, because of whose friendship she came, without other justification, to be called "the Philosophic Queen." More important for Handel, she had studied music to some effect with the lavishly talented Italian diplomat-composer Agostino Steffani, and had achieved enough understanding of the art to be able to conduct palace performances of opera from a harpsichord. Other Italian musicians whom the Electress patronized or befriended were the child prodigy and great singing teacher Francesco Antonio Pistocchi, Giovanni Battista Bononcini, and Corelli. It was another Italian — Attilio Ariosti, later to share musical direction of an opera with Handel and Bononcini — who had been honored by the Electress when a pastoral ballet by him had, on June 1, 1700, been chosen for the opening performance of the opera house in Berlin. Like her husband, though with more justice, Sophia Charlotte liked to consider herself a citizen of the great world.

Handel is not usually described as a child prodigy in the Mozartean fashion. Yet he undoubtedly was one, kept from a professionally prodigious career by, among other causes, the important differences in character between Georg Händel and Leopold Mozart. No sooner did Sophia Charlotte hear of his presence in Berlin than she patronized him. Whatever the purpose of the boy's visit to the Brandenburg capital may have

[8] Thomasius was a redoubtable opponent of the widespread belief in witchcraft. Frederick the Great said that, in his time, old women were allowed to die natural deaths in peace because of Thomasius' efforts.

been, he was shortly performing at court, probably on both organ and harpsichord or clavichord. The Elector heard him and, perhaps urged on by Sophia Charlotte, wrote to the boy's now bedridden father in Halle. He would take so talented a boy into his service. Further, he would send him to Italy, music's natural home, for advanced training. What a difference we can now see between Friedrich's reaction to the boy Handel and the more somber reaction, half a century later, of his more famous grandson, Frederick the Great, to the aging Bach.

Georg Händel was dying. He may still have hesitated to cross royal wishes, this time those of his own sovereign. But he would not have a musician son under any condition. He ordered the boy's immediate return to Halle. Nor could an eleven-year-old boy do otherwise than comply with his father's peremptory command. Alone — or perhaps still accompanied by Zachau — he traveled the circuitous ten days of coach stages from Berlin to Halle. The year 1697 dawned. And then, on February 11, twelve days before George Frideric's twelfth birthday, the bitter old barber-surgeon of Halle died at seventy-five. Although Georg Händel's granitic nature and the wide difference between their ages had made it all but impossible for his son to love him deeply — there is no indication that he did — the departure from his home of so forceful a personality must have made a deep impression on the ways of the boy's life.

Georg Händel had not left his widow, sister-in-law, and three young children [9] dependent on public charity. They had the substantial house he had bought. They had his professional practice to sell. Dorothea sold the practice quickly, divided the house into two apartments, rented out one of them, and settled down comfortably with her brood in the other. Life there was much as it had been before her husband's death. George Frideric either continued at the Lutheran Gymnasium or transferred to the new Latin School, opened in 1698. He continued to work at his music: Chrysander described a manuscript, dated 1698,

[9] Besides Georg Friedrich there were Dorothea Sophia and Johanna Christina, born respectively in 1687 and 1690.

in Handel's writing that included choruses, arias, fugues, and capriccios by Zachau, Froberger, Kerl, Adam Strungk,[10] and others. From time to time he played the Liebfrauenkirche organ. He became well known to the townspeople of Halle, and attracted the attention of musical visitors to the town. Georg Philipp Telemann, passing through in 1700 or 1701, and having renounced a musical career by maternal command, struck up a friendship with this boy four years his junior. "From my acquaintance with Handel, who was already famous," Telemann later recollected, "I again sucked in so much of the poison of music as nearly overthrew all my resolutions." Telemann was one of the most prolific composers on record, and Handel's later description of him as a man who could "write an eight-voice motet faster than one could pen a letter" refrains from praising him for virtues he did not possess. That the two youthful musicians developed their acquaintance into friendship is proved by Telemann's writing: "At the time the pen of the excellent Kuhnau served as my model in fugue and counterpoint; but in fashioning melodic subjects Handel and I constantly exercised our fancy, communicating our ideas both in letters and in talk during our frequent visits to each other."

The register of Halle University shows that Handel matriculated there on February 10, 1702, though not as *studiosus juris* as his father had planned. He was willing to enjoy the privileges and perhaps the boisterous pleasures of a university student, but the law was not going to distract him from the pursuit of music. He had already begun to preside intermittently at the organ of the Calvinist Domkirche,[11] chiefly, it would seem, when the regular organist, a Leipziger named Johann Christoph Leporin was too drunk to do so. Indeed, at the moment when Handel entered the University there was talk of his succeeding Leporin despite the objection that he was not yet seventeen

[10] Handel made very free use of a canzone by Kerl and a capriccio by Strungk in *Israel in Egypt*. The Kerl canzone became "Egypt was glad."
[11] Its full name was Königliche Schloss-und-Domkirche zur Moritzburg.

years old and the more telling one that he was not a Calvinist, but an Evangelical Lutheran.

Leporin's drunkenness and neglect of duty finally grew into a public scandal. The Calvinists, stung by the fun their Lutheran friends poked at them because of their drunken organist, dismissed him in March 1702. Then, overcoming the insistent demurrers of their more narrow-minded fellows, the Dom authorities gave the seventeen-year-old Lutheran a temporary appointment, dated March 13,[12] as organist. During his probationary year, Handel was to receive a stipend of fifty thalers and lodgings in some surviving part of the Moritzburg, hard by the Dom. Handel chose to go on living at home, and rented out his lodgings for an additional sixteen thalers.

As Handel became one of the foremost organists of the first half of the eighteenth century, it is interesting to know that the instrument at the Dom was both a good and a formidable one. It was erected in 1667 by order of Duke Augustus of Saxony. Dreyhaupt described it as twenty feet across and sixty-two feet high. He said that it was elaborately decorated and, for its period, very well equipped. It had twenty-eight stops making use of fifteen hundred pipes governed by two boxwood manuals and fed by three pairs of bellows. These last supplied enough air for the playing of one hundred and eighty bars of measured music (the entire Creed) without refilling. Handel had not only to perform on this organ, but also to care for it, being certain always that it was in perfect condition. His contract with the Dom specified also that he would set to music the Psalms and cantata texts proper to all Sundays and church festivals and do everything necessary to have them performed "in perfect harmony." Chrysander said that Handel assembled a voluntary choir that practiced twice a week, and that this choir became so

---

[12] Romain Rolland stated, on what authority is not clear, that the appointment was dated March 30, 1702. He added that Handel also taught singing at the College of the Reformists, there organizing a choral group with instrumental accompaniment that sang in various Halle churches.

desirable that its continuance was made an essential part of his successor's duties.

When Handel's trial period as Dom organist was up, he was rehired. But he had little desire to go on playing services, improvising voluntaries, and composing church cantatas that were confined to the Dom because no Lutheran church would use them. His eager mind had begun to fill with dreams of the far-away city of Hamburg, the cosmopolitan center of North German music. He must have discussed his dreams with Frau Dorothea and Fräulein Anna. He had passed his eighteenth birthday — and had exhausted Halle's usefulness to his career — when, in the late spring or early summer of 1703, he quit the University, resigned from the Dom, and bade farewell to whatever friends he had, to Zachau, and to his family. He set out for Hamburg, where he was determined to make a musical place for himself. Any doubt that his father's opposition and the provincial straitness of music in Halle had ever made him entertain about his vocation was left behind. Now he was sure.

II

HAMBURG had been a Free Imperial City for one hundred and ninety-three years when Handel arrived there in 1703. It had escaped the physical ravages of the Thirty Years' War, and had maintained its honored place in the Hanseatic League. It was a prosperous stronghold of the increasingly assertive middle class. For many decades it had been noted for its cultivation and support of the art of music. Preponderantly, of course, this had been church music, with special emphasis on intricate and magnificent organ-playing. At the Catherinenkirche the great Jan Adams Reincken was in the forty-fifth of his sixty-four years as organist, during which tenure his playing was more than once the object of a difficult pilgrimage by Bach. Too, Hamburg's *Collegium musicum*, founded by Christoph Bernhard, a pupil of Heinrich Schütz, provided a forum in which local and visiting composers could perform their non-liturgical works for the delight of each other and of fortunate laymen. On January 2, 1678, finally, under the sponsorship of a committee of prominent citizens, a new theater was opened in the Gänsemarkt with the performance of an opera (or sacred Singspiel), thus inaugurating Hamburg's long prominence as the operatic center of northern Europe.

That inaugural opera by Johann Theile, a pupil of Schütz and teacher of Zachau, was — as its interminable title [1] suggests — sung in German. It was intended to be morally and religiously edifying as well as textually and musically winning. But even at

[1] *Adam und Eva, oder Der Erschaffene, Geffallene, und wieder aufgerichtete Mensch.*

first the theater in the Gänsemarkt housed more than its coun-
terparts. Before 1678 was through, visitors there could have
heard two operas in which its manager, Strungk, depicted the
happy rise and unhappy downfall of Sejanus. No more sacred
Singspiele were heard there after 1692. Nor did the custom of
using wholly German texts maintain itself. Johann Sigismund
Kusser (or Cousser), a managerial successor to the musical
biographer of Sejanus, had visited Paris before his Hamburg
days and had become friendly with Lully. He began the introduction of French texts into the initially homogeneous German
Singspiel, even allowing some of his characters to interpolate
French arias into operas chiefly in the native tongue.

The future fate of the Hamburg opera arrived definitively in
1694 in the person of a twenty-year-old composer named Reinhard Keiser. This astonishing genius, spendthrift alike of talent,
money, and pleasure-producing energy, was to remain an intermittent part of the Hamburg scene for forty years. During that
time he composed almost one hundred and twenty operas, only
a few of them to wholly German texts. Most of his works were
partly or entirely Italian in both text and musical style. Keiser
began as principal composer, ascended to a co-managership as
successor to Kusser, and at last served as manager whenever
lavish and debilitating debauchery left him with sufficient energy for that position. The fact that Keiser's music is seldom
heard today is far from proof that he was not a very great composer. He was Handel's precursor and perhaps model as composer-impresario, his model even in rises to success and descents
into bankruptcy, both of which the younger man was to experience often. It was in 1703, the year in which Handel, newly
arrived in Hamburg, obtained a post as second violinist in the
opera orchestra, that Keiser's German opera *Claudius* became
the first work sung in the Gänsemarkt to include numbers in
Italian.

More important to Handel than Keiser, though by no measure
a musician of Keiser's genius, was the Gänsemarkt's leading
tenor, Johann Mattheson. Born in 1681, this longtime source

of energy was already an opera chorister in 1690 — and a soloist
in 1695. He heard *Die Pleyaden,* his own first opera, sung before he was twenty-two. But the operatic section of his very
long career was brief. For thirteen years, in a later period, he
was Hamburg's most eminent church musician after Reincken.
Then, about 1728, increasing deafness turned him from active
participation in music to writing about it. He had published a
book on the contemporary orchestra as early as 1713. Now he
became, for more than a decade, a torrent of words. Floating
on the turbulent surface of that torrent can be found not only
those many pages of largely trustworthy information about his
contemporaries which have kept his name familiar, but also
persistently advanced ideas that place him among the musical
thinkers of his era. He wrote, in his *Critica musica* (1722–5),
the earliest musical periodical worth the name. It was devoted
largely to discussions of basic musical ideas and problems
rather than to the alternately archaeological and topical matters with which most modern musical periodicals deal. Mattheson opposed all his force to the conception of music as a
science, insisting that it was an art of feeling. He consciously
addressed his books, not to his learned colleagues, but to en-
lightened musical laymen, and thus assisted the humanization
of music and music criticism. Although he was born before
Handel and Bach, he outlived them, dying in 1764 at the age
of eighty-two when Haydn had already composed twenty-five
symphonies and Mozart was a boy of eight at the Versailles
of Louis XV.

A friendship struck up after an accidental meeting with
Mattheson probably helped the locally unknown Handel to get
a berth as *ripieno* second violin in the orchestra of the Gänsemarkt opera house. Writing years later, Mattheson pictured
Handel's love of the fun that derives from fooling people. "He
acted as though he could not count up to five," was his friend's
description of Handel's behavior in the orchestra. "I know well
how he will laugh up his sleeve when he reads this, though he
laughs outwardly but little; particularly if he should recall the

poulterer who went with us by the boat to Lübeck, or Becker, the pastrycook's son who handled the bellows for us at the Church of Saint Mary Magdalene. That was on July 30, 1703; on the 15 we had been out on the water." The meeting between them is supposed to have occurred on July 9, 1703. Perhaps they soon went together to the Catherinenkirche to hear the wonders performed on the organ by Reincken's octogenarian fingers. Certainly they paid a visit to Lübeck on August 17, full of the possibility that one of them might become organist at the Marienkirche there when the ailing Dietrich Buxtehude died. Mattheson had been invited to compete for the position, but he genially permitted Handel to play the organ for the Marien-kirche authorities, confining his own display to a clavicymbal. The new friends did not remain long in Lübeck, for on the spot they learned that the man who would succeed Buxtehude must first become his son-in-law, just as he had obtained his position by marrying his predecessor's daughter. Whether Fräulein Bux-tehude failed to attract them or whether they simply boggled at marriage is not known. Bach refused the post for the same reason two years later, and Johann Christian Schieferdecker, the man who accepted it, married the girl. But Handel and Mattheson were soon back in Hamburg after what Mattheson long remembered as a very merry trip.

Handel returned to his fiddling. As his unusual abilities quickly became manifest to the Gänsemarkt management, this was soon varied by occasions when he directed all or parts of a performance from a cembalo. To augment the meager living this work supported, he also undertook some private tutoring, notably to a son of the English representative in Hamburg, John Wich (or Wyche).[2] What composing, if any, Handel did in the last months of 1703 is not known. Few unquestionably authentic compositions survive from his three Hamburg years. One of the authentic group is a *Passion nach dem 19 Capitel des*

[2] Born in Constantinople about 1632, this career administrator was long stationed in Ireland. In 1692, he married a grandniece of the diarist John Evelyn. He died in 1714.

Evangelium Johannes, which proves that he had not abandoned church music altogether on leaving the Halle Dom.

The young violinist of the opera orchestra pulled a *coup* by obtaining for his sacred composition a text by Christian Postel, a venerable poet of more than local distinction and the author of many opera librettos for Keiser and others. Postel worked up material from John, XIX, and Handel completed his setting of it in February 1704. It was sung on Good Friday, and seems to have aroused neither enthusiasm nor opposition. Many have guessed that the performance at almost the same time of a similar work by Keiser indicates the elder man's fear and jealousy of a young rival. This speculation is completely undocumented. No records survive of any repetition of Handel's little Passion. Long afterward, Mattheson criticized the work bitterly in the *Critica musica,* but the attack is valueless: the two men were no longer friends when he wrote it, and it is clear that Mattheson was in Amsterdam during the Holy Week of 1704, when the Passion had its only performance.

Shortly after Easter 1704, Keiser began to set, for use at the opera, a text prepared for him by a poetaster called Friedrich Christian Feustking. Like most Hamburg librettos of those years, this was partially translated into German from an Italian original — this time an olla-podrida based on a play by Lope de Vega — and partially left in Italian. Something distracted Keiser's unstable attention after he had set to work, and he consequently invited the young Handel to collaborate with him to some extent. Then he gave up his part in the opera altogether. Handel decided to set the text by himself. Thus he came to the composition of *Almira,*[3] first of his more than forty operas. He seems to have worked on it all during the latter half of 1704 while continuing his labors in the opera house orchestra and his tutoring of the Wich boy. He was by this time a familiar in Mattheson's father's house, where he appears to have been, for a while, a non-paying boarder.

[3] Its full title was *Der in Krohnen erlangte Glücks-Wechsel, oder Almira, Königen von Castilien.*

Mattheson, too, had been setting one of Feustking's feeble creations, *Cleopatra*. He designed it to supply himself with a fine tenor role. This opera was produced on October 20, 1704. Mattheson rang up a success as composer-tenor, and his friend Handel played the orchestral harpsichord in performance after performance of *Cleopatra*. On two or more occasions during the run, Mattheson — his role on the stage completed by death — came out, and for the remainder of the performance relieved Handel of his work as accompanist. Perhaps he did this, as Rolland suggested, so as to be on hand to receive the audience's final applause. On December 5, however, Handel suddenly refused to be relieved. The astonished Mattheson swarmed into a rage soon matched by Handel. Violent words rose, to the demoralization of the close of the performance. The fracas is said to have lasted half an hour. Nothing but a duel could salve the feelings of the two musicians, who were by this time seeing themselves as nothing less than injured heroes. Out they went into the Gänsemarkt, probably followed by the opera's patrons and surrounded by curious passersby. A duel that might have ended in a ridiculously tragic accident actually began. Then Mattheson's sword reached a metal button on Handel's clothing and splintered in his hand. The erstwhile cronies parted in bitterness.

Handel's seemingly inexplicable refusal to cede Mattheson his rightful place at the harpsichord can be explained. Mattheson was an exceedingly vain, overweening man, ruthlessly selfish and grimly determined to rise in the world. Just before the first night of *Cleopatra*, he had coolly deprived his friend of a small source of income by appropriating to himself the tutoring of John Wich's son,[4] Cyril. Only this sort of treatment could have aroused in the sometimes profane and sputtering, but never violent, Handel any feeling strong enough to lead to a fracas in the opera house and a well-attended duel. Each young man considered himself the wronged party of the affray.

[4] Mattheson held a position as *secrétaire de légation* to John Wich and, later, to his son, Cyril.

Neither made a move toward reconciliation. On the last day but one of 1704 a municipal councillor and a director of the opera house brought them together, and for a time their friendship resumed something of its previous smoothness. Handel's career might have been different if the estrangement had endured. *Almira,* scheduled for production immediately after New Year's Day, contained a tenor role so important that only the company's leading tenor could fill it; that leading tenor was Mattheson.

On January 8, 1705, Handel's *Almira* was sung at the Gänsemarkt opera. Its audience, not disturbed at all by the ridiculous story propounded partly in German and partly in Italian, gave every sign of approval. The success of *Almira* was such that it had to be repeated about twenty times in seven weeks. We are completely unfamiliar with this work of Handel's nineteenth year, which has probably not been sung since 1885, when it was revived for the Handel Bicentennial at Hamburg. It has a full-fledged overture that was later revised and prefixed to another opera, *Rodrigo,* as well as a few instrumental passages in the course of the action, these largely attempts at musical scene-painting. Already Handel commanded some skill in the creation of atmosphere and the imitation of natural phenomena by orchestral means. The arias of *Almira* have unfamiliar and, being mostly in German,[5] un-Handelian names: *"Liebliche Wälder,"* for example, and *"Schönste Rosen."* The score is preponderantly German in style and feeling, and is truly a German opera despite its Italian-sounding short title. It is at least as much German of its period as *Die Zauberflöte* was of its. Tabarco, a farcical retainer involved in the weavings of Feustking's preposterous story, has moments of being remarkably like Papageno.

In the last act of *Almira,* people described as "Asiatics" dance, incongruously, to a sarabande, the melody of which stayed a favorite of Handel's for many years. In slightly aggrandized form he used it in a cantata he composed in Italy, *Il Trionfo del Tempo e del Disinganno.* Not yet quit of it, he adapted it to still

[5] Forty-one of them are German, fifteen Italian.

other words in the *Rinaldo* composed in 1711 as his first London offering. There it achieved its last avatar as one of the most enduringly and persuasively beautiful of his arias, Almirena's *"Lascia ch'io pianga,"* in which form it has remained more than a little familiar to this day. Other music from *Almira* was drawn upon to supply parts of *Rodrigo,* an opera composed in Italy. Handel's early established habit of borrowing from himself has not caused musicologists quite the moral dilemma aroused by his equally enduring custom of borrowing from others, but it has given them work to do. Most of its results are of no interest to his biographer once the fact of its existence has been stated.

Keiser's affairs were in a state of confusion and perhaps decay when Handel won his first operatic success, and neither he nor Mattheson derived pleasure from the emergence of a rival. Whether because of disingenuous urgings by one or both of his fellow composers or because of inflammation by success, Handel acted foolishly. He grabbed up another execrable effusion by Feustking, this time wholly in German, set it in a rush, and put it on at the opera on February 25. The new work, billed as *Die durch Blut und Mord erlangete Liebe, oder Nero*, winning suffrage for only three performances, interrupted the previously unflagging run of *Almira*. Mattheson sang the role of Nero, but was probably not unpleased at the opera's failure. Keiser took steps to put his too-eager underling in proper light: he reset the two Feustking librettos Handel had used. Both of Keiser's efforts were ill received, and the irritated man began to make the Gänsemarkt a very unpleasant spot for Handel. By then, Keiser's fortunes, including those of the opera house, were definitely in one of their periodical declines. Handel did not lose much when, probably after the failure of Keiser's *Octavia* in August 1705, he left the opera altogether.

Unless Handel was able to acquire money otherwise than through teaching privately, he must have endured lean days from the time he left the Hamburg opera until his first successes in Italy about two years later. For during this time he accepted none of the small sums his mother had been accustomed, from

time to time, to send him, and yet actually saved the equivalent
of two hundred ducats [about $458]. Still, he had some free-
dom and energy for composition, for the rest of his Hamburg
stay produced several cantatas, songs, harpsichord pieces, and
one opera so long that it eventually had to be given as two
nights of opera. This double work, known as *Florindo* and
Daphne, was ordered from Handel by Johann Saurbrey, who
temporarily took over management of the opera house from
Keiser and his associates late in 1705 or early in 1706. It was
completed in 1706, and was staged as two operas early in 1708.
Handel never heard it: when it was being sung in Hamburg
he was tasting another world, the enchanting southern world
of Italy. He would certainly not have enjoyed the performances,
which in reality consisted of *Florindo* and *Daphne* altered to
suit what the manager supposed to be public taste, and lightened about midway by the presentation of an apparently ribald
farce called *Die lustige Hochzeit*. Nor can we pass judgment on
the music: it has disappeared.

Just as Handel had exhausted Halle's value to his development, he had now obtained all the useful experience he could
in Hamburg. A chance meeting with a penniless, profligate, and
artistic minor member of the rapidly declining Medici family
provided part of his impulse to find his next activities in Italy,
but none of the means for doing so. Giovanni Gastone de'
Medici [6] was in Hamburg for some time during the winter of
1703–4. Handel met him, and unquestionably was attracted by
the Florentine's glowing picture of Italy. He decided to get
across the Alps somehow. Certainly it was not with financial

[6] When Handel encountered him, Gian (or Giovan) Gaston(e) de'
Medici was the second surviving son of Cosimo III, Grand Duke of Tuscany. Originally an attractive, sensitive man, he had taken to drink and
dissipation after being forced to marry Anne of Saxe-Lauenberg, a fat
and vulgar widow who had tried to make him live in a tiny Bohemian
village. On the death, in 1723, of his father, Gian Gaston (his surviving
elder brother having died) ruled for fourteen years. On his death in 1737,
the Medici ceased to reign in Florence. When his sister Anna Maria Ludovica died six years later, the family became extinct after almost four
centuries of power.

help from the itinerant Medici, who always had insufficient
funds for his own elaborate needs.[7] The commission for *Florindo* and *Daphne* may have helped. Some royal largesse, too,
is probable. For this reason it has been suggested that, proceeding from Hamburg to Halle to visit his mother and aunt, Handel
stopped en route at Hanover and was patronized there by the
Electress Sophia, mother both of the Electress Sophia Charlotte
of Brandenburg whom he had met in Berlin and of the future
George I of England. This visit to Hanover is likely for another
reason: he could have met there the Electoral *Kapellmeister*,
Agostino Steffani. Steffani was later to be very helpful to Handel, and the story that the two men met first in Italy has been
rendered unlikely by increasing knowledge of Steffani's complicated movements around Europe as composer, papal official,
and important diplomat. This amazing man had, for a few years
from 1681 on, delighted Munich with a series of his operas. The
court theater at Hanover was inaugurated with another of them
in 1689, and Steffani continued to intersperse his other activities
with the composition of operas for twenty years more. He died
in 1728.

Perhaps Handel, having visited at *"zum gelben Hirschen"* in
Halle, went to Italy by the route through Prague and Vienna to
Venice. Or he may have followed another not too difficult route
more directly to Milan. His first Italian sojourn that can be
certified was a brief one in and near Florence. At Pratolino, in
the hills overlooking that city, he paid his respects to Ferdinand
de' Medici, the elder brother of Gian Gaston. This childless and
ailing man of forty-three had until about three years before
Handel's visit kept Alessandro Scarlatti at Pratolino to compose
operas for private performance there. It is said that after about
two years of this arrangement he found Scarlatti's music too
melancholy for his rich, elaborate taste. But the truth is that for
many years after quitting Pratolino, Scarlatti continued to compose occasional pieces for Ferdinand and to write him veiled

[7] Mattheson stated that Handel's expenses were paid by a traveling companion named Von Binitz, never otherwise identified.

requests for financial assistance. It is possible, though not provable, that it was at Pratolino that Handel first met this great
musician who so certainly influenced his own style and conception of opera. Ferdinand de' Medici had in his employ, also at
the time of Handel's visit, Bartolommeo di Francesco Cristofori,
who built for the Medici family several of the experimental instruments that were to lead him, by about 1711, to construct the
"gravicembalo col piano e forte" that can reasonably be called
the earliest piano.

Handel remained in and near Florence long enough to compose several secular cantatas,[8] possibly hearing one or more of
them sung at Pratolino. On January 14, 1707, however, he was
in Rome, for a diary entry thus dated, and clearly referring to
him, was discovered in the Archivo Storico Capitolino by L. A.
Sheppard of the British Museum working for Sir Newman
Flower. On that day "to the admiration of everyone" he displayed his astonishing ability as an organist in San Giovanni
Laterano. His by then obvious genius would have opened many
Roman doors for him, particularly as he seems to have been a
personable and socially attractive young man. But it is more
than likely that his way was further paved by letters of introduction from Prince Ferdinand, Prince Gian Gaston, or
Agostino Steffani. In Rome he composed many vocal and instrumental pieces, the latter including three Psalms.[9] One of
these last, *Dixit Dominus*, is dated at Rome on April 11, 1707,
and Handel remained in the papal capital at least three months
after its performance there on Easter Sunday.

Either while he was in Florence or during his stay in Rome,

---

[8] A preponderance of Handel's very numerous Italian cantatas — of which
about one hundred survive — and chamber duets belong to the years of
his Italian wanderings. The cantatas, little known, are in reality only
slightly less important in the corpus of Handel's works than Bach's cantatas are in his. Such a work as *"O Numi eterni"* (known as *La Lucrezia*)
belongs rightfully among his very greatest compositions.
[9] *Dixit Dominus* (revised on April 11, 1707, from an earlier piece), *Laudate pueri* (July 8, 1707), and *Nisi Dominus* (completed July 13, 1707)
all date from this stay in Rome.

someone had fobbed off on the uncritical young "Saxon" (as some Italians affectionately called him) a ridiculous opera libretto dealing with Rodrigo, King of the Visigoths, and his intricate involvements in a marital triangle, murder, and various contorted forms of battle and carnage. Using mostly new music, but borrowing a few things from *Almira*, Handel set this text while in Rome. Whatever his popularity and success, however, his opera could not be performed there. No opera had been performed in the Eternal City since, a decade earlier, the outraged Innocent XII had destroyed the Teatro di Tor di Nona, the city's opera house, as a center of immorality. Perhaps Ferdinand de' Medici had not been so ill as to have lost his longtime taste for opera, and had promised Handel a performance. At any rate, it is possible that Handel went from Rome to Florence in July 1707 bearing with him the completed score of *Rodrigo*.

Whole scenes from the openings of the first and third acts of *Rodrigo*, as well as parts of the finale, have failed to survive. What remains shows that, though this was Handel's first opera to a wholly Italian text, he was still a thoroughly German composer. The overture to *Rodrigo* is, in fact, the overture to *Almira* preceded by several highly characteristic Handelian dance movements. The opera's melodic line lacks the peculiarly Italianate grace that Handel was to achieve later, and tends to remind a modern listener of Protestant church music. Exceptional to this statement are several virtuoso passages for violin and cello. These are strictly Italianate, and rather clearly indicate study of the instrumental style of Arcangelo Corelli, whom Handel came to know personally a little later, and may already have encountered by the time he composed *Rodrigo*. No proof survives that *Rodrigo* was performed in Florence.[10] If it was indeed performed, it cannot have been repeated often, for it

[10] The fact that the martial aria *"Già grida la tromba"* ("Now sounds the trumpet") has no trumpet in its accompaniment led Victor Schoelcher to posit reasonably that the taking of the trumpet's natural place by an oboe indicates that at the time when *Rodrigo* was performed Florence did not contain a trumpeter.

would have had to be performed privately (at Pratolino or the Pitti Palace), there being no public opera house and no opera-going public in a general sense, but only invited, aristocratic, guests. Ferdinand de' Medici is said to have showed his pleasure by presenting Handel with one hundred sequins (perhaps the equivalent of $250) and a gift the young man must have found cumbersome baggage: a porcelain dinner service. Gian Gaston, still fleeing before his maddening wife, was in Florence, and may have entertained for his composer protégé.

In the late summer or early autumn of 1707, perhaps after the Florentine staging of *Rodrigo*, Handel gravitated naturally to Venice. There, when opera as a self-conscious art form had been less than forty years old, the first public theater ever devoted to it had been opened in 1637. By 1699 so many of the great Venetian families had followed the success of the Trons with the Teatro San Cassiano that the city had at least sixteen opera houses. Venice, and not Florence, the city of its birth, had become the true home of the newly viewed art of drama with music. It was an undeniable Mecca for a young composer of twenty-two whose chief desire then — and for decades thereafter — was to succeed as a composer of Italian opera.

To this exact period of Handel's life belong two of the most often retold stories about him. One of them is wholly, demonstrably false. Yet both are firmly lodged in the minds of many honest people and in the pages of many honest books, and they must be told and then looked at with a critical eye. The first story is that Vittoria Tesi sang in the Florentine production of *Rodrigo*, fell madly in love with Handel, and then followed him about, and even to Venice, gripped by a veritable sickness of passion. This is, in its way, not an unattractive story. It is impossible by any documentation to connect Handel, from one end of his long life to the other, with any love affair. He may have been sexually frigid for all the testimony (other than that of his music) that survives. Humanly, this story of Vittoria Tesi would be a bold stroke of color: she was a brilliant and beautiful contralto who blazed through the cities of Italy, Germany, Austria, and Spain, trailing lovers and broken hearts, and finally marrying a barber. But she was born on February 13, 1700.[11] It was not, then, the seven-year-old Vittoria Tesi, but a much older Vittoria Tarquini (known as La Bombace) who sang in *Rodrigo*. And she was ugly. And there is no reason whatsoever for thinking that Handel was interested in her longer than it took him to make her sing her role properly.

The other story concerns Handel's first meeting with Domenico Scarlatti, known to have taken place in Venice. This picturesque tale is set at a masquerade. A masked Handel plays the harpsichord. A masked Scarlatti rushes up to exclaim: "That is either the marvelous Saxon or the Devil!" But if Scarlatti did recognize Handel by his playing, it seems more than likely that they had met before, that Scarlatti had heard that "Saxon" touch before. He could have had no reason to suspect Handel's presence at a Venetian masquerade, communications being what they were and Handel's only notable Italian successes having been at the organ of San Giovanni Laterano and perhaps in a private Florentine theater. Still, this story may be true. Alessandro Scarlatti may well have sent his precocious son one of his flowery letters to describe some Handel harpsichord miracles heard in Florence, or even to tell him of Handel's impending visit to Venice. In any case, Domenico Scarlatti's regard for Handel's virtuosity became so intense that at a somewhat later period he never mentioned his rival in several contests of improvisation at harpsichord and organ without crossing himself.

Domenico Scarlatti, whose operas are forgotten, whose harpsichord sonatas retain their delicious freshness, being as enchanting today as when Handel must have heard some of them, was not the only good musician the German met in Venice in 1708. There was the first organist of St. Mark's, the colorful and ac-

[11] Yet so astute a musical historian as Paul Henry Láng (in his *Music in Western Civilization*) compounds this error by stating that Handel composed "the exacting title role" of *Agrippina* for Vittoria Tesi — who would (as was pointed out as early as 1889) have been nine years old when that opera was produced at Venice.

complished Antonio Lotti, one of whose madrigals was later
to involve Handel's London rival, Giovanni Battista Bononcini,
in a plagiarism scandal.[12] There was the choirmaster Francesco
Gasparini. Both these men were almost twice the age of Handel
or Domenico Scarlatti. Perhaps the young men found an easier
companion in a pupil of both Lotti and Gasparini, Benedetto
Marcello. This young nobleman was to succeed with real brilliance at both music and politics before his death in 1739. Venice was a truly musical city. Its life surged around St. Mark's,
whose very architecture had forced the evolution of a particularly complex type of liturgical music, and around the well-
patronized opera houses. Handel must have enjoyed himself,
there beside the Adriatic. It was a very far cry from the comparatively cramped and crabbed Thuringian Protestant town in
which his boyhood had been passed. How the barber-surgeon
of Giebichenstein would have felt his premonitions realized,
could he have seen his dashing young son in that setting of sensuous and richly brocaded life!

The appearance of another relatively unknown operatic composer could not easily stir a city constantly treated to its fill of
operas, including — in 1707 — Alessandro Scarlatti's masterpiece, *Mitridate Eupatore*. Handel's time for crashing the gates
of one of its theaters was not yet. He had found an intimate
friend again. He and Domenico Scarlatti were young. Perhaps
they were adventurous and a bit giddy, as young men have a
right to be. At any rate, they did not try very long, if they tried
at all, to get their works onto a Venetian stage. Shortly after
the opening of 1708, they quit the glowing seaport and went
off to Rome. It was to be nearly two years later that Handel
would first savor the sweetness of a true Venetian triumph.
Meanwhile, he had still a great deal to learn.

[12] See page 178.

III

THE ROME of Clement XI was not, when Handel returned there in the late winter of 1707–8, a happy city. Clement was a profoundly educated intellectual, admirably suited in character to his exalted position, and a discerning patron of art. His terrible misfortune was that his accession in 1700 followed by twenty-two days the death of Charles II of Spain: the new Pope thereby found himself hopelessly involved in the War of the Spanish Succession. For as long as he could, he favored the man nominated for the vacant throne by the late King. This was Philip of Anjou, a grandson of Louis XIV. But the Emperor Leopold I, opposing the French King's increasing influence, backed the candidacy of his own second son, the Archduke Charles, and finally forced the new Pope to back him too.

In this particular round of the perpetual game of power politics, Louis XIV's candidate established himself in Spain, thus preventing the Archduke from getting nearer than Catalonia to his "capital." "Charles III" had the backing of England, Holland, Portugal, Denmark, Austria and some other German states, at times of the Duke of Savoy, and at last of the Pope. But Philip V was visible in Madrid, and his backers included France, Bavaria, Cologne, at times the wavering Duke of Savoy, the Hungarian patriot Rákócsy — and a majority of the Spanish people. Philip also had the invaluable services of Giulio Alberoni. By renouncing all his rights to the throne of France, Philip was eventually to make firm his hold on that of Spain. At the end of the deal, the Archduke Charles had to be content with succeeding, as Charles VI, to a much enfeebled Imperial throne. Clement XI's involvement in this struggle was so dis-

3 4

astrous that when the War of the Spanish Succession ended in
the deliberations leading to the Treaty of Utrecht in 1713, he
was allowed no direct voice in them. The prestige of the Papacy,
indeed, ebbed lower at that moment than it had for centuries.

Clement's unequal struggle with Leopold I was approaching
its climax when Handel reached Rome late in the winter of 1707
or early in the spring of 1708. But the city was lavish and full
of music nonetheless. It resounded to every sort of music but
opera, still under papal ban. The nobility and the princes of
the Church, including several splendid relicts of the vanishing
institution of papal nepotism, lived extravagantly and fostered
literature, painting, sculpture, and music. Patrons and artists
were joined together in an academy called Arcadia, founded in
1690. At its apogee the Arcadian Academy counted about fifteen hundred members throughout Italy, each referred to by
the others by an appropriate pastoral, "Arcadian" name.[1] Its
membership rolls show the names of popes (Clement XI, Innocent XIII, Clement XII, Benedict XIII), cardinals, princes,
poets, composers, and eager dilettantes. Although Handel was
not elected to membership because he had not reached the
requisite age of twenty-four, he was immediately patronized by
Arcadians. Cardinal Benedetto Panfili, Cardinal Pietro Ottobuoni, and Francesco Maria Capizucchi, Marquis of (later
Prince) Ruspoli, three of the lordliest among them, were his
particular benefactors.

Prince Ruspoli stood high in the favor of Clement XI, who
had recently raised him from a marquisate, and was a close
friend to Ferdinand de' Medici, who is likely to have sent
Handel to him. The young German was Ruspoli's feted guest
in the palace in the Piazza SS. Apostoli, Ruspoli's borrowed residence while his own palace in the Corso was under restoration.
There, in order to carry on during the Carnival season his customary concerts and other music, Ruspoli had erected a tempo-

---

[1] Examples are Protico (Bernardo Pasquini), Driante (Benedetto Marcello), Arcimelo (Arcangelo Corelli), Terpandro (Alessandro Scarlatti),
Olinto (Prince Ruspoli), and Almiride (Princess Isabella Cesi di Ruspoli).

rary theater, having been informed that the Pope disapproved of his projected performances of comedy at his castle in Vignanello. As part of the celebration of Easter, he had Handel compose, to a mediocre text by one Carlo Sigismondo Capece, a cantata-oratorio, *La Resurrezione*, that is really a religious opera disguised to fool the Pope. Although the surviving manuscript states that *La Resurrezione* was composed for *"La Festa di Pasqua dal Marchese Ruspoli li* [blank] *di Aprile 1708,"* some have thought it more likely that the references in the Ruspoli archives to a work sung in the palace on Easter Sunday and heard by many noble guests are to another composition.

The references in the Ruspoli archives cite the payment of musicians who played, among other instruments, a trombone and four oboes not called for by the score of *La Resurrezione*, and fail to mention players of flutes, German flutes, bassoons, harpsichord, viola da gamba, theorbo, and archlute there specified. There is good reason to believe that Ruspoli would have given one composition on Sunday, April 8, another on Wednesday, April 11. It is known, for example, that he produced Scarlatti's *Della Santissima Annunziata* as short a time before as Passion Sunday, March 25. Nor is the interest of the archive entries much lessened if they indeed refer to another, unnamed work. They detail the costs of having fifty-six candlesticks made for lighting the theater salon, of serving refreshments, and of paying the instrumentalists [2] — adding up to a grand total of approximately $550. They state, too, that Corelli conducted, as he may have conducted *La Resurrezione* on April 11. They nowhere refer to Handel or *La Resurrezione* by name.

Another entry in the Ruspoli archives proves that Handel had left the palace by April 30, for it details the amounts expended during his stay for his food and for the rent of his bed and counterpanes. Where he next found lodging is not known, but it may well have been in the palace of Cardinal Pietro Ottobuoni,

[2] The musicians received stipends varying from about $2.50 to Corelli's approximately $21.

who was then in charge of the papal chapel. This archetypical product of papal nepotism — he was raised to the rank of cardinal when he was only twenty-two by his uncle, Alexander VIII — was one of the wealthiest men in Italy, an exceedingly lavish patron of the arts, and a leading figure among the Arcadians. He was an unsuccessful composer, having in 1692 witnessed the failure of his own opera *Colombo*. It was probably under Ottobuoni's aegis that Handel set several texts by Cardinal Benedetto Panfili, "Fenizio" among the Arcadians. These include secular cantatas with such titles as *Fillide ed Aminta*, *Apollo e Dafne*, and *Armida Abbandonata*,[3] just the proper fare for an Arcadian pastoral garden fete or mythological indoor entertainment. One of them — *Handel, non può mia musa* — unearthed in the University at Münster by Edward J. Dent, textually sings the praises of Handel himself. J. M. Coopersmith conducted its first modern performance, at the Juilliard School, New York, on September 14, 1939.

Most important of the Handel-Panfili collaborations is *Il Trionfo del Tempo e del Disinganno*, called a serenata rather than an oratorio. This was sung in Ottobuoni's palace, and it has been said that its unfavorable reception was one of the reasons for Handel's departure from Rome shortly afterwards. But Handel remembered it with affection: in 1737 he wooed London audiences with a somewhat enlarged version of the Italian original. Almost fifty years after its composition, too, in 1757, to an English version of Panfili's text, he arranged and composed one of his last works, *The Triumph of Time*.

One of the most often repeated anecdotes concerning Handel is said to date from Corelli's conducting of *Il Trionfo* in Ottobuoni's salon. Corelli, unrivaled as a violinist in his own Italian style, found his part in this semi-Gallic, semi-Teutonic music difficult, and conquered his shyness and natural feelings of deference sufficiently to say so. Handel, irritated by the lack of muscular dash with which Corelli had been playing, had swept

---

[3] Johann Sebastian Bach copied out this cantata before 1715, a fact that demonstrates a fairly wide distribution for Handel's compositions.

the violin from the conductor's hands and performed the passages himself. "But, dear Saxon," Corelli is reported to have protested, "this music is in the French style, which I do not understand." If the disputed passage was in the original overture, Handel's desire to replace it with music Corelli could handle with confidence would explain his having composed, to replace that original, a *sinfonia* much more Italian in style. Neither of the great musicians, however, kept any permanent resentment against the other.

Rome, in June 1708, lay in such imminent danger of siege that Clement XI had ordered several of the city's gates sealed. Probably for that reason, probably also for more personal reasons as well, Handel traveled southeastward to summer in Naples. Time-honored legend says that the Scarlattis, Alessandro and Domenico, traveled with him, and even that Corelli accompanied or followed their party. The four musicians may well have believed that the Neapolitan territories, being firmly administered for the Emperor by Austrians under the strong hand of Cardinal Vincenzo Grimani, would prove more eager for their services than was the threatened Holy City. If this was their belief, Handel was to find it justified. He was also to find in Cardinal Grimani one of the chief indirect shapers of his future.

Handel was constantly studying the craft of composition. All his life long he examined the works of other composers, extracted ideas for his own works from them, and (more frequently than some of his admirers like or than his most worshipful biographers have been happy to admit) moved whole passages from their works into his own without stating that he had done so. The entire moral question of his unacknowledged borrowings is modern and can best be left for discussion until the time when his great London rival, Giovanni Battista Bononcini, came a cropper because of a flagrant piece of plagiarism differing from Handel's practice by consisting of an entire unchanged composition. In Naples Handel interested himself in the techniques used by Lully in composing canzonets to French texts. Seven French canzonets of Lullyan character from Handel's sojourn exist in manuscripts so covered with Handel's own emendations and second thoughts in pen and pencil as to indicate that he regarded them as exercises or problems. That they have harpsichord accompaniments may indicate that he composed them with an eye toward performing them with a French singer then visiting Naples.

Romain Rolland suggested that Handel was practicing the French language with the intention of visiting Paris. "How changed things would have been there had he really come there to settle in the interregnum between Lully and Rameau," Rolland commented. "He possessed the quality that none of the French musicians possessed — a superabundance of musical material — and lacked the one they had — lucid intelligence and penetration into the true needs and potentialities of the musical drama. . . . If Handel had come to France, I am convinced that [the Gluckian] reform would have been brought about sixty years earlier, and with a wealth of music that Gluck never possessed."

After July 12, 1708, only one dependable exact scrap of information exists to tell Handel's itinerary or activities for more than eighteen months, or until December 26, 1709, when his opera *Agrippina* was produced at the Grimani family's Teatro di San Giovanni Crisostomo in Venice. More interesting than the chamber trio, *Se tu non lasci amore,* that bears his signature dated at Naples on July 12, is the serenata *Aci, Galatea* [4] *e Polifemo.* The final page of the manuscript of this secular cantata contains, besides Handel's signature and the date June 16, 1708, the words *"Napoli"* and *"d'Alvito."* This final word tends to disprove the hoary Mainwaring story that Handel composed the serenata for a Spanish or Portuguese "Princess Laura." It tends to prove that he composed it (to words, be it noted, from the

---

[4] Handel originally spelled it *Galattea.*

pen of a Spanish Princess, Cecilia Capece Minutola Enrichez [5])
for a festivity in the family of the Duke of Alvito, ancestor of
the modern Princes of Colubrano. It happens, too, that on July
19, 1708, the Duke of Alvito was married, amid tremendous
celebrations, to Donna Beatrice Sanseverino. Dent and Flower
are convinced, with what seems good reason, that *Aci, Galatea
e Polifemo* was performed as one part of the wedding festivities.
It is a slender work, lacking any instrumental introduction, in
which the three characters of the title sing seriatim continuously: the serenata is not divided into acts or parts. It is of importance in Handel's life chiefly for two reasons: it supplied
him with materials for his later English cantatas to John Gay's
Acis and Galatea, and it was probably the first of his compositions in which the great bass Giuseppe Boschi sang. This phenomenal singer, later of influence in Handel's London career,
had a very wide range; as the part of Polifemo in the Naples
serenata requires a range of twenty-nine notes [6] — quite extraordinary in a bass — the reason for supposing that Boschi
sang it is clear.

What Handel did, or where he went, from that July of 1708,
when he was visiting Naples, to December 1709, when he was
to earn his first really splendid operatic success, is not known
except that in the spring of 1709 he saw Steffani at Cardinal
Ottobuoni's in Rome. For reasons that have never been evident,
his earlier biographers decided that he remained in Naples until
the late autumn of 1709. Even if he was there, the fact that no
music from his hand survives with a Naples dateline for more
than one full year would not be more surprising than that none
with any dateline whatever is known to survive from that

[5] It was for this lady, in all likelihood, that Handel composed his only
surviving work to a Spanish text. This was published in Volume II of his
Cantate con stromenti as *Cantata spagnuola a voce sola a chitarra*, or solo
Spanish cantata with guitar accompaniment.
[6] *Nell' Africane selve*, a solo cantata for bass that seems to date from
Handel's visit to southern Italy, requires the singer to *leap* (not move by
easy stages) from the C sharp below the bass clef to the A of the treble
clef! This must surely have been for Boschi.

period. One possibility suggests itself as an explanation of this apparent inactivity (that inactivity itself being the merest supposition, for the apparent gap in his productivity may easily result from the simple disappearance of any number of compositions).

Handel was a healthy young man of twenty-four in 1709. While not one scrap of dependable evidence survives to prove that he was ever, at any time, in love, felt the most intimate pangs of romance, or even had sexual relations of any sort, it is equally true that no evidence suggests that he was abnormal in any way whatever. He was a typically fair Saxon, and reasonably handsome in a lightly sensual way. It is easy to imagine him exactly the volatile, sensitive, and physically robust young man who might attract the wandering, appraising eye of an Italian lady. And it happens that the undependable Mainwaring, Handel's first biographer, gives a circumstantial account of a wealthy lady of Naples who lent the young composer a palace complete with servants, carriages, and food. What young man, tasting a measure of worldly acclaim far from home in a foreign land — and that land southern Italy — might not succumb without struggle or protest to such blandishments?

It is difficult to believe that the composer who, time after time, was able to light up the indifferent and bad verses of inept librettists with the quintessence of romance, infatuation — passion itself — had not tasted somewhere more than a little of the heart's and the body's delights. Naples and Mainwaring's "Donna Laura" (whom later biographers tended to identify with the Spanish princess-librettist of *Aci, Galatea e Polifemo*) supply as likely a setting and partner for that tasting as any, more likely than most in view of the tremendous and unremitting public activity that gripped Handel soon after his Neapolitan sojourn.

Because Handel superscribed the Italian word *"Pifa"* on the Pastoral Symphony of *Messiah*, and because Calabrian *pifferari*, or players of a shepherd's pipe, are known to have taken an annual role in the Roman celebration of Christmas until recent times, writers have assumed that Handel must have been in Rome during the Christmas season of 1709. This sort of deduction is a writer's privilege — *vide* the preceding paragraph — but this particular piece of deduction is strained beyond the point at which it has any claim to be advanced as biography. Why may not Handel have heard *pifferari* in 1708? Why not in Calabria itself, so close to Naples, or even in Sicily? For it would be just as sensible to deduce a visit to Sicily from Handel's repeated use of the *siciliano* dance rhythm — which may indicate merely that he knew the operas of Alessandro Scarlatti, who preceded him in favoring that 6/8 beat. Or, finally, may not a fellow musician have noted down for the Saxon visitor the traditional melody the *pifferari* played in honor of the men who had watched sheep under the star of Bethlehem?

In 1708 or 1709, Cardinal Vincenzo Grimani, Viceroy of Naples, supplied the young Handel with a libretto entitled *Agrippina*, very probably with a promise that if he esteemed Handel's setting of it production at the Grimani family's theater in Venice would follow. This libretto was, if placed beside any that Handel previously had been privileged to set, a masterpiece. Drawing heavily on the scores of *Rodrigo, Il Trionfo del Tempo e del Disinganno, La Resurrezione,* and *Aci, Galatea e Polifemo,* he composed and pieced together far and away the most dramatic and beautiful operatic entity he had yet created. On the first day of the Carnival season of 1709–10 (December 26, 1709), *Agrippina* was sumptuously staged at the Teatro di San Giovanni Crisostomo,[7] and became an instant, overwhelming success.

For twenty-seven nights, on into 1710, Handel's *Agrippina* filled the Venetian theater. It is recorded that members of the audience, transported by the rich and, to them, extraordinarily full beauty of the music, called out *"Viva il caro Sassone* [Long live the dear Saxon]" and otherwise made evident the extravagance of their approval. Again Giuseppe Boschi, this time in the

---

[7] Greatly altered, the San Giovanni Crisostomo became the modern Teatro Malibran.

role of Pallante, demonstrated his great worth. Margherita Durastanti and Valeriano Pellegrini, other singers who would reappear under Handel's aegis in London, added to *Agrippina's* success. The opera's overture, much more important and imposing than the *sinfonie* Italian composers were then likely to place before their operas, failed to frighten the Venetians, who acclaimed it along with Poppea's lovely aria *"Bel piacer"* (most of which the Romans had heard as *"Un leggiadro giovinetto"* in *Il Trionfo,* and Londoners were to hear in *Rinaldo*) and a half dozen other arias and concerted numbers in the score. Cardinal Grimani must have been doubly pleased, with the success of his libretto and with the fact that the family theater was full.

As wrapped up in the career of *Agrippina* as Cardinal Grimani or Handel himself was Ernst Augustus of Hanover, brother of the Elector. Ernst Augustus, whom Handel is supposed to have met on his first visit to Venice, loved music, and he fell desperately in love with *Agrippina,* sitting in a loge to hear it night after night. It seems that he had earlier urged Handel to visit Hanover, even perhaps pitting the attractions of the Elector's musical court against the glowing account of a musician's future in London spread before the young Saxon by the Earl of Manchester, Queen Anne's Ambassador to Venice. Other Hanoverians, too, added their urgings. One of them was Baron Kielmansegge, later a busy figure at the English court, another the endlessly versatile Agostino Steffani, either or both of whom Handel may also have met on that first visit to Venice. Now he had seen Italy and conquered Venice. Perhaps he wanted to see his mother again after more than three years. At any rate, he accepted an invitation to visit Hanover, perhaps to settle there. With some idea also of a visit to London, he left Venice for the trip north.

When a young composer named Handel arrived at Hanover in 1710, the Elector Georg Ludwig, a great-grandson of James I of England, was fifty years old. He must have begun to ponder the question of whether or not the throne of England was ever to fall to him. It was not too far beyond his grasp to be a hopeless dream. Queen Anne, to whom, as Philip Chesney Yorke wrote, "marriage had brought only a mournful series of infant funerals," had lost her consort in 1708, and had announced that she would not remarry. She was in uncertain health, and would leave no direct heirs. Her brother, the Old Pretender, would not renounce his Catholicism, and therefore probably could not attain the throne by anything less than an unlikely revolution. Georg Ludwig's mother, a daughter of James I's daughter Elizabeth, was the nearest Protestant heir to the throne. But Sophia herself said that she was suffering from the incurable disease of being eighty years of age: in reality, Georg Ludwig himself was Anne's likely heir. But Anne was only forty-five. Despite her appalling roll of obstetrical mishaps and wavering health, it was not, the Elector of Hanover knew, unlikely that she would outlive him. Then the English throne would descend to his son Georg (already father to a three-year-old boy who would one day be Frederick, Prince of Wales), and he himself would be able to remain, as he wished, until death found him in Hanover. For Georg Ludwig both desired and did not desire to be crowned King of England.

The Elector was fond of music, as was his mother. Serving as his *Kapellmeister* was none other than Handel's acquaintance, Agostino Steffani, a man who successfully combined a first-rate career in music with ambassadorial positions and the robes and offices of an *abbé*. Sir John Hawkins, whose statements about Samuel Johnson have not withstood the tests of time, also knew Handel personally, and left accounts of talks with him. As Sir John was more musicologist than literary critic, it may well be that his musicological lore is more trustworthy, though the following suposedly direct quotation from an interview with Handel contains an obvious error of five years in Handel's age:

"When I first arrived at Hanover I was a young man, under twenty; I was acquainted with the merits of Steffani, and he had heard of me. I understood somewhat of music, and," putting forth both his broad hands, and extending his fingers, "could play pretty well on the organ. He received me with great kindness, and took an early

opportunity to introduce me to the Princess Sophia [8] and the elector's son, giving them to understand that I was what he pleased to
call a virtuoso in music; he obliged me with instructions for my conduct and behaviour during my residence at Hanover, and being
called forth from the city to attend to matters of a public concern,
left me in possession of that favour and patronage which he himself
had enjoyed for a series of years."

Handel had been in Hanover a short time when Steffani, perhaps eager to leave a somewhat cramped post, took a quarrel
with some of his choristers as reason for abandoning his *Kapellmeister*ship. He recommended the young Handel for the position. Such was Georg Ludwig's (or the Electress Sophia's) respect for Steffani's opinion, which may have been preceded or
seconded by words of praise from Ernst Augustus, that the untried young visitor was shortly in possession of a musical job that
guaranteed him about the equivalent of $1500 a year. The ap-
pointment was dated June 16, 1710. C. F. Abdy Williams pointed
out that the annual salary being earned at the same time by
Bach, Handel's exact contemporary, amounted to less than
eighty dollars.

Handel did not settle down to enjoy his perquisites. Probably
the Earl of Manchester's description of London returned to his
mind; perhaps the Earl had even promised to help him win pre-
ferment there. He obtained leave from his new master for a visit
to England, promising to return quickly. He was actually to be
away from Hanover almost exactly one year. According to some
early writers, Handel visited his mother at Halle before leaving
Germany. She was now nearly sixty years old, and her only companion in the half of *"zum gelben Hirschen"* that she still retained was her maiden sister, Anna. Her daughter Dorothea
Sophia had, on September 26, 1708, married Michael Dietrich

[8] Whether this refers to Georg Ludwig's mother, the Electress Sophia, or
to his daughter Sophia Dorothea, Crown Princess of Prussia, shortly to
become the mother of the future Frederick the Great, is unclear. It cannot have referred to the Elector's wife, another Sophia Dorothea, from
whom he had long been divorced, and who lived at Ahlden in an exile
amounting to imprisonment.

Michaelsen,[9] to whom, by the time of Handel's possible 1710 visit, she had already borne a daughter who would not outlive the year. Michaelsen, born in Hamburg in 1680, came of good family and was a man of official importance. Son of a high bailiff and royal councillor, he himself became a war councillor, serving as lord of the manor and justiciary at Eptingen. Frau Dorothea's younger daughter, Johanna Christina, had died in 1709 while her brother was in Italy. Financial cares, some at least purely subjective, combined with other, now undiscernible factors, had aged Handel's mother, but the frequently repeated statement that her eventual blindness had already become complete by 1710 is untrue: she had another twenty years of sight left her.

Handel is always described as bound to Frau Dorothea by bonds of strong affection, and the description is accurate if nicely interpreted. Every individual scrap of evidence on his character, at whatever period in his career, adds to the clear portrait of a very objective, extroverted, and self-sufficient man. He had a normal man's normal love and gratitude toward a sympathetic mother. But any attempt to paint him as linked to her by emotional cords stronger than such a statement implies must be based on romancing. More than once, he stayed away from her for many years at a time. In some of his few surviving letters he speaks of her as a man may speak of a fond stranger whom he once knew well. Certainly, nothing known of Frau Dorothea suggests a woman who could have been close mentally to her increasingly famous son, or could have understood well the nature of the activities that led him across what must have seemed to her a very wide portion of the world.

Handel's visit to Halle may or may not have taken place. He certainly stopped at Düsseldorf en route from Hanover to London. There Johann Wilhelm, Elector Palatine of the Rhine, welcomed him. The erudite and intelligent Elector was a close friend to Steffani, and so great an admirer of Corelli that he created him Marquis of Ladensburg. Also the Electress was a Medici, sister to both Gian Gaston and Grand Duke Ferdinand.

[9] Pronounced Micha-elsen.

In her, though surely without ever realizing it, Handel faced the last great member of the greatest family of the Italian Renaissance. The Electress Anna Maria Ludovica, outliving her brothers until 1743, was the last recorded direct descendant of that Giovanni di Bicci who had founded the major branch of the Medici in the fourteenth century. Dying at seventy-six, the childless and long-widowed Electress was to insure the continuing fame of Florence (and should have won the gratitude of a world that has mostly forgotten her) by bequeathing to the city her family had made a world center the whole unpriceable Medicean trove of art and history. She it was who completed the magnificent family tombs. Her own incomparable monument is nothing less than the contents of the Pitti Palace, the Uffizi, and the other Florentine repositories of art.

Perhaps, as Flower and others have suggested, Handel visited Düsseldorf by invitation. As news that he had been appointed to Steffani's former post in Hanover would certainly have reached the court there, it is very unlikely that such an invitation would have been for the purpose of offering him a musical position. More likely, and fitting well the characters of Johann Wilhelm and Anna Maria Ludovica, it resulted from otherwise unmotivated curiosity to meet a young musician of unbounded promise. Handel did not stay long. He either was very eager to reach London or had made some unrecorded promise — it could have been given the Earl of Manchester — to arrive there by a certain date. Having received a valuable token from the Elector Palatine, he again set out. Düsseldorf being where it is, his journey undoubtedly took him through the Low Countries, but his exact route is unknown. Nor is it now possible to set more exactly than autumn 1710 the date of the first occasion on which Georg Friedrich Händel (as he still called himself then) stepped onto the soil of England. Here was the island that his Electoral master at Hanover was to rule from the throne that Queen Anne now occupied, the land over which he himself was to lord it musically with the same mixture of Continental and, increasingly, English ways.

IV

HANDEL has more than once been named the murderer of native English music. This mistaken accusation has been formulated after looking correctly at the annals of English music and deducing the wrong conclusions from the obvious fact that Handel arrived in London during an interregnum, the comparatively empty space left by the deaths of Henry Purcell in 1695 and of John Blow — Purcell's teacher, predecessor, and successor — in 1708. Other appreciable native musicians, too, had died in the years just before Handel first visited London: Frances Piggott in 1704 and Jeremiah Clarke in 1707. In the very year of that visit (1710), the only native musicians of better than mediocre talent [1] who could have been active were two sons of that fanatic eccentric, Solomon Eccles [2] — John and Henry — the excellent singer William Turner, the organist John Weldon, William Croft (or Crofts), Henry Carey, and the Roseingraves, Daniel the father and his two sons Ralph and Thomas, the latter most talented of all and a friend in Italy of the Scarlattis. Carey, however, was only twenty years old in 1710, and his first im-

---

[1] Only jingoism or term-stretching could name great such men as Thomas Clayton, John Barrett, Charles King, and James Kent.

[2] Solomon Eccles (1618–83) became converted to Quakerism and made a bonfire on Tower Hill of his musical paraphernalia. Setting up as a cobbler, he demonstrated his dislike of churches by plying his trade in a pulpit two Sundays in succession. When the Great Plague swept London, Eccles ran about the streets calling on his fellow townsmen to repent their sins, first stripping himself to the waist and lighting a pot of coals to carry on his head. He wrote *A Musick Lector* (1667), a violent polemic against the art he had once practiced and taught. In later life, he accompanied George Fox and other Quakers to the West Indies and to the American Colonies.

portant public work was still five years in the future. That year, too, saw the births of William Boyce and Thomas Augustine Arne. But a correct reading of the annals will show that in the period just before 1710 music had fallen to an inert state in the native land of Dunstable, Bull, Byrd, Dowland, Gibbons, Morley, Tallis, Weelkes, and Purcell.

Into the vacuum created not only by the deaths of Purcell and Blow, but also by Purcell's failure, despite his genius, to establish successful and imitable forms of public music fitted to the times, foreign musicians had begun to flow before Handel's immigration. More of them were Germans than Italians, partly because groups of refugees from the wars and religious strife of the German states had sought and found a home in England. Of these German musicians, two were to play roles in Handel's life. One was Nicolo Francesco Haym (born in Rome of German parents), who, working first with Thomas Clayton and the French violinist Charles Dieupart, had been trying to build an operatic career in London from 1704 on. His adaptation of an opera called *Camilla* had achieved some success in 1706. Handel's stature eventually put him in the shade, but Haym held no grudge against his conquering countryman. On the contrary, he set to work and wrote many of the librettos Handel used.

The other German musician prominent in London at the time of Handel's first advent there was Johann Christoph Pepusch, today recalled principally as the inspired arranger of the music for John Gay's *The Beggar's Opera* and its sequel, *Polly*. When Handel's vast shadow began to fall across him, however, Pepusch was trying to cast one himself as the composer-arranger of serious operas, for which he lacked significant talent. He was driven more and more to find what satisfaction he could for his creative urge in the fabrication of masques and incidental music and in the writing of theoretical works, for which last he possessed both the requisite erudition and the proper style. He was seldom friendly to Handel, and *The Beggar's Opera* was to be conceived as simultaneously a blow in favor of opera in the audience's own language and a destructive satire on the exact sort of operatic

4 9

fare that Handel purveyed. That, however, did not come until
1728. In 1710, Pepusch had been in England for ten years; in
that year he became one of the founders of the Academy of
Antient Music, to which, forty-two years later, he was to bequeath most of his valuable musical library.

Handel did not, then, murder English music unaided. Indeed,
he took no part in murder at all. Abundantly supplying to a
melody-hungry city some of the greatest music of his — or any —
era, he dwarfed his English contemporaries, towered so high
above them that they remain visible only at spaced-out moments.
He would similarly have outtopped the native musicians of any
country (Bach remaining a little-known provincial) except perhaps Italy. And it would be a rash critic who would be willing
to support the thesis that a single one of the estimable, even
great, composers of eighteenth-century Italy united in himself
the power, grandeur, and fountaining creativity that marked
Handel at his best. England simply happened to be the country
on which that huge shadow fell longest and most completely.
It is certainly possible that, falling on musical organisms of low
vitality, that shadow stunted their growth. No proof can be
advanced for the claim that it killed them off incontinently.

Although he was a masterly instrumental composer and per-
former, Handel operated in the public eye principally in two
other roles — first that of opera composer and impresario, second that of creator and producer of mammoth oratorios. He
found at hand in England a living tradition of song. The English
were accustomed to singing together, and the infatuation that
Handel's many-voiced choruses evoked in them was natural. He
was followed, in a purely temporal sense at least, by many English composers and foreign composers living in (or popular in)
England who now seem to have been his imitators in choral
composition even when they were not. He was so surpassing a
master of grand choral effects that even the Haydn of *Die
Schöpfung* and *Die Jahreszeiten,* charming, persuasive, and masterly though he may be, appears dwarfed by his Himalayan
loftiness. The Mendelssohn of *St. Paul* and *Elijah* (not the best

Mendelssohn) could have been accepted in lieu of, or preferred to, the Handel of the oratorios only by a mass audience with decaying taste. The native British composers who put their small feet in Handel's old footprints,[3] though earnest and high-aiming workmen all, and not devoid of stately moments, are less than memorable.

And so Handel is accused of having murdered the tradition of English song and, by having substituted a foreign, presumably German Protestant, style for the natively sweet English style, of having made its resuscitation impossible. This is as silly as it would be to say that Chopin killed the great French keyboard tradition of Couperin and Rameau or, to change arts, that Henry James mortally interfered with the great tradition of the English novel or Picasso with that of French painting. Such men as Handel, Chopin, James, and Picasso, creating masterworks in a foreign land, have been able to subsume into themselves what is living and good around them, and then so to mix it in the alchemy of their own genius that they may appear to have created a scarcely peopled desert all about. They have grown so tall by their peculiar organic ability to thrive on foreign sustenance that they have outstripped all but the mightiest indigenous growths.

It is not the purpose of this biography to search out the myriad influences, borrowings, imitations, and outright thefts that Handel added to his innate native creativity in evolving his unique styles. But it is certain that English music, particularly English religious music and the music of Purcell, became increasingly large ingredients of that amalgam as his life in England lengthened. It is not necessary to point to the *Water Musick* for his relation to Purcell or to "Sweet bird" from *L'Allegro, Il Pen-*

---

[3] Among them may be named William Sterndale Bennett, with *The Woman of Samaria;* Sir John Stainer, with *The Daughter of Jairus* and *The Crucifixion;* Sir Edward Elgar, with *The Dream of Gerontius;* Sir Alexander Campbell Mackenzie, with *The Rose of Sharon* and *Bethlehem;* Sir Charles Hubert Hastings Parry, with (among others) *Job* and *King Saul,* and Sir Charles Villiers Stanford, with *The Three Holy Children* and *Eden.* Another, a more hopeful, manner is represented by the *Belshazzar's Feast* of William Walton.

seroso ed Il Moderato for his personal and Italianate adaptation of English madrigalesque vocal lines. Handel's music, which took on Italian coloring as soon as — at Hamburg — Italianate German music became easy in his ears, began to naturalize itself in England as soon as he settled there. He never wholly understood English prosody. But the inmost nature of English music became part of his own nature. Handel is as international as Mozart or Stravinsky. Germany gave him birth and sank certain predilections and means into his creative well. Italy gave him his most mature opera style. England is present in all the instrumental music he composed from 1710 on, and is the very spirit of the great Biblical and secular oratorios.

But the twenty-five-year-old musical employee of the Elector of Hanover who was presented to Queen Anne in 1710 or 1711 must have appeared to that thoroughly British last of the reigning Stuarts a very Teutonic (and perhaps therefore unpleasant) young man. If they held a conversation, it must have been in French: it is unlikely that Anne spoke either German or Italian, and Handel spoke English badly even after forty years in England. Somehow or other, however, the young German made his way to the very Englishman most likely to help him as he desired to be helped. This was Aaron Hill, traveler, dramatist, historian, patentee of a method of taking essential oil from beechwood for use in shipbuilding, and, at last, distiller. In 1710 the handsome and astonishing Hill was going through a lean period as manager of the Queen's Theatre in the Haymarket. When he heard of Handel's successes with Italian operas in Hamburg and Venice (it is likely that the Earl of Manchester's opinions had been noised about London), he at once asked the visiting German to bring forth a theater-filling miracle for the Queen's.

Italian opera was still something of a novelty in London. In December 1707, the *Camilla* arranged by Nicolo Francesco Haym was sung at Drury Lane Theatre partly in English, partly in Italian. The singers were (in Italian) Margarita de l'Épine, Valentino Urbani, and "the Baroness," and (in English) Mrs. Tofts, Mrs. Lindsey, Mrs. Turner, Richard Leveridge, and

Lewis Ramondon. *Camilla* was repeated by substantially the same company at the Queen's Theatre in January 1708, at which time a *pasticcio* called *Thomyris* was likewise sung in the two languages. After the arrival in London of the singer Nicolini (Niccolò Grimaldi), the company's repertoire was enlarged by Alessandro Scarlatti's *Pirro e Demetrio* and a *pasticcio* called *Clotilda*. Finally, in January 1710, an anonymous composer's *Almahide* was sung at the Queen's wholly in Italian[4] by a company that included Isabella Girardeau, Elisabetta Pilotti Schiavonetti, Cassani, and Boschi. Almost the same group, later in 1710, sang in Italian Francesco Mancini's *L'Idaspe fidele* and (perhaps in 1712) Marc' Antonio Bononcini's *Etearco*.

Aaron Hill supplied Handel with the outline of a libretto based on the tale of Rinaldo and Armida in Tasso's *Gerusalemme liberata*.[5] This outline was handed to an itinerant Italian hack named Giacomo Rossi — who seems previously to have written a stage play on the same subject — for expansion into an Italian libretto. While Rossi wrote *Rinaldo*, Handel began to compose it. Rossi later excused some of the libretto's obvious shortcomings by complaining that Handel composed too fast for him. What neither Rossi nor Hill may have realized was that Handel was only in part composing new music to their collaborative libretto: much of the music he married to it had served other texts and purposes — in *Armida, Il Trionfo del Tempo e del Disinganno, Aci, Galatea e Polifemo,* and *Agrippina,* in at least one case having been used more than once before.

Between Handel's arrival in London and the production of *Rinaldo,* several months elapsed, two weeks of which were filled

[4] An opera sometimes called *The Loves of Ergasto,* probably with music by Jakob Greber, was almost certainly sung all in Italian at her Majesty's Theatre, London, on April 20, 1705.
[5] This story served as the basis for the librettos of other operas: one by Philippe Quinault was used by, among others, Lully and Gluck. An Italian one was used by Rossini. There can be little doubt that it was somewhere in Wagner's mind, too, when he wrote the poem of *Parsifal*: Armida is clearly one ancestress of Kundry.

with the composition of the opera. In that interval, too, Handel encountered not only Queen Anne, Aaron Hill, and Giacomo Rossi, but two other individuals who, in differing ways, were to be important to his success and fame. One of them was reputedly the ugliest man in London, a native of Nuremberg named Johann Jakob Heidegger, known as "the Swiss Count." This promoter and good-hearted adventurer was to help Handel over more than one future hurdle. Before 1710 was out, he had taken his young countryman to Sir John Stanley's London home, where music was appreciated, and where a very small girl heard him play. Stanley's niece was the ten-year-old Mary Granville, who would take as her second husband Jonathan Swift's friend Dr. Patrick Delany, and would live to write six volumes of memoirs and letters that contain a wonderfully living picture of Handelian London.

Handel also may have met Thomas Britton in 1710 or 1711, and attended more than one of that famous small-coal merchant's musicals. These were held in a long, low-ceiled loft upstairs over his charcoal storehouse in Aylesbury Street, between Clerkenwell Green and St. John's Street. They are notable as having been probably the second series of true concerts as we understand them today — that is, of nontheatrical musical performances open to anyone.[6] Britton, who earned his livelihood by hawking charcoal through the streets of London, had taught himself music. He equipped his loft, for which, at first, he paid an annual rent of four pounds, and which had to be reached by narrow and perilous outside stairs, with a small five-stop organ, a Ruckers virginal, and other musicianly impedimenta. Through his concert series, initiated in 1678, he met and became friendly with many prominent people, learned men and purely social figures alike. At first he made no charge, but later, for at least some members of his audience, he added to the one penny he

[6] The first true concerts also took place in London; they were begun in 1672 in a house in Whitefriars by the leader of Charles II's band, the violinist John Banister. The public concert hall, then, came more than thirty years after the first public opera house.

had always taken for the refreshment of one cup of coffee, an annual door-fee of ten shillings. It may have been in Briton's loft,[7] where Handel is said to have played the organ, that the meeting of Handel and Dr. Pepusch occurred, for Pepusch enjoyed playing on Britton's virginal, called by some who heard it the finest on earth. There, too, he could have met William Babell, violinist and harpsichordist, who arranged and published harpsichord "lessons" on melodies from *Rinaldo*.

Handel's name was not wholly unknown to musical Londoners when, on February 24, 1711, the day after his twenty-sixth birthday, *Rinaldo* began its successful career at Aaron Hill's Queen's Theatre in the Haymarket. A few days later than that, he was the most famous composer in London. He began to be praised, attacked, published, and pirated. He began — surest portent of fame — to be stung by journalists and wits. Richard Steele flayed him in *The Tatler*, Joseph Addison in *The Spectator*. Both men had private axes to grind. Steele was lessee of Drury Lane Theatre and of a concert room in York Buildings, and he saw a threat to the size of his audiences in the popularity of Italian opera, now incarnated in the German newcomer. Addison had staged *Rosamond*, set to music that failed to please, the work of Thomas Clayton. He had visited Italy, and was acquainted with the siren charms of its opera. But he was convinced that those linked tunes to Italian words were the cause of the failure of *Rosamond* and other musical entertainments to English texts, and he pursued the Italian devil with barbed words in and out of season. Like his friend Steele, Addison saw Handel as the incarnation of doom to his own hopes and ideals in the musical theater.

But the upper-class public of London recognized the rich

---

[7] Britton's neighbor, Edward Ward, described the building as follows: "His Hut wherein he dwells, which has long been honored with such good Company, looks without Side as if some of his Ancestors had happened to be Executors to old snorling Diogenes, and that they had carefully transplanted the Athenian-Tub into Clerkenwell; for his house is not much higher than a Canary Pipe and the Window of his State Room but very little higher than the Bunghole of a Cask."

melodies and emotion-stirring harmonies and rhythms of
Rinaldo as the musical entertainment it wanted. It did not matter that scarcely a man or woman in the audiences could have
understood the words the singers were singing if they had been
printed in letters as high as a man. The music, the action, the
painstaking and elaborate staging, and the magical way in
which they were combined to tell the story were enough. *Rinaldo's* triumph was the first real operatic success in English history [8]: it became that simply because Handel was the greatest
composer who had ever composed an opera for London. He remains so to this day because no other composer of his genius
has, since 1711, been born in England or chosen to live there.

The only element of *Rinaldo's* impact on London audiences
of 1711 that we can understand today through actual experience
is the music — and not all of that can be reproduced as Handel
meant it or as Aaron Hill's gratefully large public heard it. We
can, that is, recapture the melodies, harmonies, and rhythms,
and most of the orchestration from those parts of the original
score which remain. Within these considerable limitations, then,
we can know Armida's *"Ah! crudel,"* Rinaldo's *"Cara sposa,"* Almirena's incomparable *"Lascia ch'io pianga,"* and — to cut short
a list that could be long — the "Battle Music" that Sir Thomas
Beecham used so adroitly in the score for a ballet called *The
Origin of Design.* But we cannot know *"Cara sposa"* as Handel
conceived it or as it was sung in 1711 by Nicolini. For Nicolini
was a *castrato.* As the problem of the *castrati* descends crushingly on the staging of a Handel opera, it demands discussion
here.[9]

The custom of castrating choirboys with notably beautiful
voices in order to prevent that deepening of the voice which is

[8] The opera was revived by Handel himself many times, and had not
exhausted its popularity in 1731. Nor was its success confined to London:
it was sung at Hamburg in 1715 and produced by Leonardo Leo, with
Nicolini's assistance, at Naples in 1718. In April 1711, too, it became the
first Italian opera sung in Dublin.
[9] The resurgence of the counter-tenor after World War II suggests a
(partial) solution preferable to that of transpositions.

a natural concomitant of male puberty seems to have originated in Rome very late in the sixteenth century or early in the seventeenth.[10] Women did not sing in churches, and choirmasters must have been driven to despair then — as they are now — by losing the loveliest of their boy's voices to the advent of manhood. For a time Spain produced, through a training and technique now not understood, a group of adult male sopranos and altos whose voices were kept up to childish pitch without castration. Although such falsettists or "*contraltini*" were employed in the Sistine Chapel, it was in that stronghold of Church music that, according to the best information available, *castrati*, both soprano and alto, first sang. In the beginning, these tuneful eunuchs were employed solely to carry the higher parts in polyphonal religious music. But their use in secular music followed close, and spread to opera shortly after its first outburst of popularity toward the middle of the seventeenth century.

Although *castrati* sang throughout Europe, they achieved their dizziest fame in Italy and England, in which latter country one known as Pergetti was flourishing in 1844. The quality of the *castrato* voice, which seemed natural despite its artificial provenance, would today no doubt partake of the nature of such an anomaly as a mature boy. For it was a boy's voice produced by a man's lungs, with the resonance of a man's body, and projected — by the greatest *castrati* — with the art and comprehension of a mature musical mind. A woman's voice, however fine, however much more beautiful from a purely sensuous point of view, is obviously something else. Nor would modern morality and humaneness permit castration for purely artistic reasons.

We may regret or congratulate ourselves that we shall never hear an adult male soprano or alto. What we must understand is that with this fact goes inseparably another: we shall never

[10] The earliest *castrato* (referred to also as *evirato* or simply *musico*) who can be named is "Padre" Rossini; he became a member of the Papal Choir in 1601. It was Clement VIII, Pope from 1592 to 1605, who declared *ex cathedra* that thenceforward the creation of *castrati* for use in church choirs was to be understood as *ad honorem Dei*.

hear a Handel opera — or, for that matter, almost any opera composed from about 1635 to about 1750 — with the sex of the singers straight, with the arias all sung as their composers intended,
or, in all likelihood, with the key relationships as originally plotted out. Whatever a listener's reactions to Gluck's *Orfeo ed
Euridice* may be, to take a familiar work that has suffered sea-
change because it was originally composed for a leading *castrato,* it must have been a more persuasive, a more beautiful
work when the role of Orfeo was sung by a man than it is today
when that role must be sung by a female in unconvincing disguise.

Rinaldo's wonderfully characteristic and touching aria *"Cara
sposa"* established Nicolini as the first of a line of castrated operatic idols in London.[11] He began as a soprano, but when his
high notes began to wear thin in his later years he took to singing
alto roles. Today *"Cara sposa"* would, in a production of *Rinaldo,*
have to be altered in one of two ways. It could be transposed to
a key in which a tenor, the modern ideal voice for an operatic
hero, could sing it: this would change either Handel's carefully
plotted key relationships or, if the transposition were an entire
octave, the scarcely less important pitch and tone-color relationships. Or the role could be sung by a female. But a woman, however well disguised, singing a tender love song about "her" wife
is far indeed from the realities Rossi, Hill, and Handel held in

[11] Nicolini was not the first *castrato* to win English hearers. In Purcell's time, for example, Giovanni Francesco Grossi, called Siface, had
been enormously popular in London, whither he had been summoned
by Mary of Modena. He had been caricatured. When he left England —
partly because his sort of entertainment had less place in the London of
William and Mary than in that of James II — Purcell signalized the event
with a brief harpsichord composition called *Sefauchi's Farewell.* That
was 1687; ten years later, Siface was murdered at Ferrara. Too, the very
Valentini who first sang Eustazio in *Rinaldo* had enjoyed some acclaim
earlier. In January 1710, he had been in that cast of *Almahide* which was
singing an opera wholly in Italian for the first time in London's history.
But it is true that Nicolini was the first of the line of operatic *castrati* that
at last included, among many others, Carestini, Caffarelli, and — most admired of them all — Senesino and the incomparable Farinelli.

mind while writing and composing. The insolubility of this dilemma is one of the causes, major in some instances, minor in others, for the complete disappearance of Handel's operas from the stage long before time has made them, from other points of view, unstageable except under special conditions.

Nicolini became a town rage through *Rinaldo*. But he was not the only singer in whom Handel touched fortune: the great Boschi lent his wildly admired bass to the role of Argante. Somewhat less applauded were Boschi's aging wife, Francesca Vanini, in the small contralto role of Goffredo, Cassani as the Magician, Valentini as Eustazio, Signora Pilotti Schiavonetti as Armida, Isabella Girardeau as Almirena, and two dancers — M. du Breil and Mlle la Fère, "especially brought directly from Brussels." [12] Given the melodies Handel had lavished on *Rinaldo*, however, Nicolini and Boschi were enough to insure it popular response. Aaron Hill, who said in a note that precedes *Rinaldo* in his *Dramatic Works* that one of his aims had been to give Italian opera stage productions worthy of its music and singers, deserved his rewards. The scenery and stage machines were complex and elaborate, and included fire-breathing dragons and a flight of live sparrows let loose in the theater to accompany an aria with words about singing birds. That the staging itself attracted considerable attention is proved by attacks on it that appeared in *The Spectator* and elsewhere. Addison and his friends could have saved breath and ink: Aaron Hill, Giacomo Rossi, George Frideric Handel, Nicolini, and Boschi — with Tasso dim in the background — had set a style that London was to cherish intermittently for decades.

Handel lingered in a London that lionized him while the tally of *Rinaldo*'s performances at Her Majesty's lengthened throughout the winter and spring of 1711. It became current that prominent persons had come to London from their country seats merely to hear *Rinaldo*. Its melodies were whistled in the streets. They were danced to. John Walsh published what amounted

[12] The dancers were not in the original cast, but were added to it after several performances had assured *Rinaldo*'s continuing popularity.

to a collection of song hits from the opera. He later stated that twenty guineas was the most he had ever paid Handel for the right to publish one of his operas; it is known that he earned about seventy times that amount from *Rinaldo* alone. When Handel learned of Walsh's success with *Rinaldo*, he said that Walsh should compose the next opera and let him publish it!

Rinaldo did not run continuously at Her Majesty's as *Agrippina* had run at Venice's San Giovanni Crisostomo. It alternated with other operas and *pasticci*, performances of which were announced as requested by "several ladies of quality" — such things as *Almahide*, Alessandro Scarlatti's *Pirro e Demetrio*, Conti's *Clotilda*, and Mancini's *L'Idaspe fidele*. When the approach of summer raised the temperature, *Clotilda* was in demand: it included a water scene that could be stretched out to include most of the evening. Yet *Rinaldo* remained the season's prime success. When Her Majesty's closed on June 2, 1711, Handel's first London opera had been sung to full houses fifteen times in fourteen weeks.

In view of Handel's subsequent choice of London as a permanent residence, it appears likely that he had little desire to abandon it in the summer of 1711. He had won remarkable success there. He was a lion. But he was also *Kapellmeister* to the Elector of Hanover, and he had promised to return to his duties in Germany. He was sometimes delinquent in the performance of such duties, but he never altogether failed to perform them, So he left London for Hanover after the opera season ended. En route to Hanover, he stopped again at Düsseldorf to wait upon his friends the Elector and Electress Palatine of the Rhine. He must have explained to Johann Wilhelm that he had remained away from Hanover longer than his Hanoverian master's displeasure might prove to have been wise. For Johann Wilhelm wrote letters to Georg Ludwig and the Dowager Electress Sophia, the first stating that he had kept Handel in order to show him some instruments and begging that the musician not be blamed, the second restating and rebegging in more urgent language.

Any fears that Handel may have harbored over his reception

at Hanover were groundless or were rendered unnecessary by the Elector Palatine's persuasive intervention. He shortly settled down there, a servant, however well treated, in the comparatively humdrum life revolving around the Electoral residence at Herrenhausen. He studied English. He kept in touch with London by letter. Writing in French to Andreas Roner, a fellow musician in the English capital, he said, toward the end of July, 1711:

Please convey my compliments to Mons. Hughes.[13] I shall take the liberty of writing to him at the first opportunity. If he will, in the meantime, honor me with his orders and include one of his charming poems in English, he will give me the greatest pleasure. Since I left you, I have made some progress in that language. . .

More immediately, Handel composed numerous songs and also chamber duets to be played with Princess Caroline of Anspach, the Elector's daughter-in-law, later known as Caroline, Princess of Wales, and still later as the unhappy consort of George II.

In the autumn of 1711, Handel's only surviving sister, Dorothea Sophia Michaelsen, gave birth to a daughter. She was given the names Johanna and Friederika, the first in honor of the Handel sister who had died, the second in honor of the Handel brother who had become famous. Under the circumstances, that brother could scarcely miss the baptism. Georg Ludwig granted his peripatetic *Kapellmeister* another leave. In November, Handel was at Halle. Once more he must have found rather somber the tiny household in *"zum gelben Hirschen,"* still made up only of Frau Dorothea and Fräulein Anna. What could he have told those aging provincial ladies of the great life of London, of operatic melodies that had set a city to talking and dancing, of the sweet taste of well-earned fame? What could they have understood?

Back to Hanover and Herrenhausen Handel shortly went. Back to composing chamber duets for Caroline of Anspach, oboe concertos, cantatas, when all his desire was to be composing op-

[13] John Hughes, poet and historian, 1677–1720.

eras for London. He held his ambitions in check through most of 1712, remaining in Hanover while the first great profits in the South Sea Company were reaped on paper, and Sidney, Earl of Godolphin, died, and London went about the various business of which he wanted to be a part. He kept up his correspondence with friends and acquaintances in England. He examined carefully *Il Pastor fido,* another hack libretto by Giacomo Rossi, and probably began to clothe it with music. This time he would not arrive in London emptyhanded.

In October 1712, Handel asked Georg Ludwig for, and received, permission to take leave for another visit to the scene of *Rinaldo's* success. When he landed in England in November, two years after his first arrival there, he honestly intended another short visit. Certainly Georg Ludwig expected his *Kapellmeister* to return to Hanover, for he appointed no one to take Handel's place as the leave lengthened. Neither Handel nor his Electoral master could have suspected the truth, which was that, except for brief visits to the Continent and to Ireland, George Frideric Handel had returned to London to remain there until his death more than forty-six years later. The greatest of England's adopted sons had come to take up his heritage.

Die
Durch Blut und Mord
Erlangete Liebe/
Oder:
NERO,
In einem
Sing=Spiel/
Auf dem
Hamburgischen Schau=Platz/
Vorgestellet.

ANNO 1705.

TITLE PAGE OF *NERO*

Handel's second opera, as published at Hamburg in 1705

GEORGE I

AARON HILL

V

URING much of the interval between Handel's first two arrivals in England, that country was suffused with the exciting, all-promising speculation that soon came to be known as the South Sea Bubble. The War of the Spanish Succession was dragging along, marked by the double-dealings, betrayals, purposeless nobility, incredible bravery, and shameless peculation that characterized wars then as now. In Parliament, and perhaps in the mind of Queen Anne, it may have occupied the position of greatest importance. But almost everyone else in England who had a supply of free funds was either hopefully following or hoping to follow the will-o'-the-wisp of self-multiplying wealth. There was some discussion, of course, of Her Majesty's ailments: her heirlessness and ill health brightened alternately the hopes of the Catholic Stuarts and those of the House of Hanover. Jacobites plotted or pretended to plot in favor of Anne's brother, whom Louis XIV called "James III." They felt intermittently that they had the support of Anne, who, though a Protestant, was known to harbor natural affection for her brother and dislike for her German cousins, the Electress Sophia and the Elector Georg Ludwig. It is a favorite idea of historians that if the Old Pretender had been pliant enough to renounce his Catholicism he would indeed have inherited the throne. But he was a sincere and fervent Catholic, and young enough (he had been born in 1688) to want the throne on his own terms or not at all.

Affairs at Her Majesty's Theatre in the Haymarket had not prospered while Handel was away. No entertainment offered there after the season of *Rinaldo*'s first success had been popular. Aaron Hill was no longer its manager. His place had been taken by Owen MacSwiney (or Swiney), who lacked Hill's brilliance and dash, substituting for them a cunning that frayed out into open dishonesty. This undependable man had been active, from 1706 on, in early attempts to acclimate Italian opera in London, and had turned his hand to producing librettos for the transitional, half-Italian, half-English works with adapted music [1] that had preceded the first all-Italian operas there. Now he was in financial difficulties, and welcomed the opportunity to put on an opera by the composer and librettist who had provided Hill with *Rinaldo*. Handel had scarcely settled down in London with an English friend — a Mr. Andrews — when *Il Pastor fido* was put into rehearsal for production at Her Majesty's. The end of the score is dated at London on October 24, 1712; the rehearsals started on November 4.

Nicolini, the chief singing attraction of *Rinaldo*, had left England for three years on the Continent. The chief male role (Mirtillo) in *Il Pastor fido* had to be assigned to a singer who had appeared in Handel's *Agrippina* in Venice, the locally untried and now second-rate counter-tenor called Cavaliere Valeriano Pellegrini. Valentini was on hand to perform a contralto role (Silvio). But the magnificence of Boschi was neglected or unavailable, and an English bass, Richard Leveridge,[2] served (Tiresio). Others in the cast included the future wife of Dr. Pepusch, Margherita de l'Épine (Eurilla), Pilotti Schiavonetti (Amarilli), and Mrs. Barbier (Dorinda). They were rehearsed for three weeks. Then *Il Pastor fido* was offered to the public on November 22, and it was found that Handel, in his haste, had failed to provide Rossi's inane libretto and the predominantly inferior cast with the one thing that could have guaran-

[1] MacSwiney was partly responsible for *Camilla* (1706 and 1707) and Haym's arrangement of Scarlatti's *Pirro e Demetrio*.

[2] This long-lived singer had first been heard, when little more than twenty, in the early 1690's; he was a composer of songs and theatrical music before Handel's advent in London — and was singing there as late as 1751. Several of his songs are still sung, notably *Black-Eyed Susan*, the text of which is by John Gay.

teed the opera a prolonged career — one of his high-spirited, well-made, and vigorous scores. *Il Pastor fido* was no second *Rinaldo*. The heart of the struggling MacSwiney must have become heavier. There is no evidence that Handel's did.

Addison, feeling himself assuaged for the success of *Rinaldo* by the public's tepid reaction to *Il Pastor fido*, and Steele, still harrying the German interloper, appear to have believed that Handel's first London success would now remain his last. But Nicolo Haym, who, with Pepusch, had bridled and guffawed when Handel first reached London, felt differently. Instead of standing aside to crow over Handel's defeat, Haym regarded *Il Pastor fido* accurately as the error, the temporary setback, that it was. He joined forces with its composer, supplying him with a libretto built around the Theseus-Medea myth. This, the only five-act libretto Handel ever set, is a veritable masterwork of dramaturgy for music if compared with Rossi's *Il Pastor fido*. Handel grasped it eagerly. It inflamed his musical imagination, as well it might after the pastoral banalities with which he had recently dealt, and he finished composing it on December 19, twenty-seven days after the *première* of *Il Pastor fido*.

The five short, brilliant, and exciting acts of *Teseo* were presented to London by MacSwiney in a costly production on January 10, 1713. The cast [3] was substantially that of *Il Pastor fido*, and therefore far from first-rate. But the dramatic vitality of nicely mated libretto and score swept singers and listeners alike. Medea and Agilea, in this opera, are individual women fired by passion for Theseus, also a credible human being. Agilea's tender, sensual aria *"Vieni, torna, idolo mio"* is one of Handel's most inflamed and seductive love songs. Medea is expressed most intensely through two wonderful *scene*, the first an incantation, the second her arrival at the decision that Theseus must die. There was no doubt of the success of *Teseo*: in a rhythm that

[3] Valeriano Pellegrini (Teseo), Valentini (Egeo), Mrs. Barbier (Arcane), Signora Pilotti Schiavonetti (Medea), Margherita de l'Épine (Agilea), and Signora Maria Gallia (Clizia).

was to become familiar in Handel's life, it obliterated at a stroke the miserable failure of *Il Pastor fido*. Its second performance guaranteed *Teseo* a run.

Then MacSwiney absconded with the box-office receipts of those first two capacity houses for *Teseo*. He had not paid for the elaborate stage machinery and costumes. He had not paid Handel or Haym or the singers, all of whom were faced with the choice of shutting down in admission of ruin or struggling somehow ahead. To their assistance came Handel's hideous friend Heidegger, the adventurous and proverbially ugly "Swiss Count." Heidegger took over the management of Her Majesty's, kept *Teseo* and those involved in it financially afloat, and operated through a paying season that lasted until May 30. The funds that had vanished with MacSwiney could not be made up, and Handel's portion of the later receipts was therefore small. On May 15, after the opera had run out most of the thirteen performances it had that year, a special one was given "for the benefit of Mr. Handel, with an entertainment for the harpsichord." As he was probably the greatest harpsichordist of the era, Domenico Scarlatti excepted, the "entertainment" attracted the public as much as did *Teseo* itself. This type of instrumental interlude became a more or less standard feature of Handel's career.

It was probably during the run of *Teseo* that Handel left the hospitality afforded him by the London house of Mr. Andrews of Barn Elms, Surrey, and took up residence at Burlington House in Piccadilly. Richard Boyle, Third Earl of Burlington, was only seventeen years old, but he was already a lavish patron of music, and he was convinced that Handel was a genius. In the then recently built Burlington House,[4] which he shared with his mother, the Earl staged musical performances, which Handel now directed, and played host to musicians and writers. Haym knew him: the libretto of *Teseo* was dedicated to him. Alexander Pope

[4] Most of the original Burlington House was destroyed by fire in 1854. The Royal Academy of modern fame, erected on its site, preserved intact only a small part of the original building.

and John Gay were among his wide acquaintance: Handel met
the two writers under the Burlington roof. The youthful, energetic, and enthusiastic Earl, by shedding the light of his protection and social prominence over his favorite composer, greatly
accelerated the unfolding of Handel's English career. He directly brought Handel into contact with men and ideas that
assisted his acclimatization and partial Anglicization.

The Elector of Hanover's truant *Kapellmeister* had again won
the favor of London. One of England's wealthiest and most
sympathetic noblemen was his host and patron. More exalted
favor still was being vouchsafed him. Learning that Queen
Anne's forty-eighth birthday would be celebrated on February
6, 1713, he decided to signalize the event by a special composition. The Peace of Utrecht, ending the War of the Spanish Succession, was being negotiated. Handel was no politician and
had no way of knowing that the Peace was to constitute an
agreement with England's enemies to betray her allies. He obtained from a now unknown writer the text of a *Birthday Ode*
for Queen Anne, a text opening with a chorus beginning "The
day that gave great Anna birth, who fix'd a lasting peace on
earth." He had also, on January 14, finished an English *Te Deum*
that he hoped to have used in the forthcoming official celebration of the Treaty — a curious work for a subject of the Elector
of Hanover, who must have looked at the Treaty of Utrecht with
extreme distaste. The right to provide official music of this sort
actually belonged to John Eccles, chief court musician and, as
required by statute, an Englishman. Only by winning the
Queen's personal favor and obtaining a royal command in contravention of the statute could Handel hope to hear his *Te Deum*
in St. Paul's Cathedral.

The Utrecht *Te Deum* was Handel's first important setting of
the English language, the *Birthday Ode* his second. Although
the language of his adopted country never became the language
of Handel's thoughts — which his note-scribbling and the reports of his friends prove to have been in German or Italian or
even French — his imperfect comprehension of its sound-values

6 7

is all that, here and there, mars his musical investiture of its meanings. His principal model for these first English works was Purcell. Handel probably heard performances of many of Purcell's similar compositions for official and religious ceremonies. The *Saint Cecilia Te Deum* of 1694, for example, was still sung annually in St. Paul's during Handel's first London years, as a benefit for the Sons of the Clergy. Nor is it only Handel's way of combining big instrumental effects with huge choral effects for the achievement of royal grandeur that stems from Purcell: his very harmonies, the melodies themselves of his solos, are "English" in profile and texture, blood-brothers to those in the ceremonial pieces of Purcell.

Although composed second, the *Birthday Ode* was sung first, on the Queen's birthday, February 6, 1713, probably at St. James's Palace. This slight composition, made up of brief choral passages, solos, and duets, thus had the honor to be first heard of a mighty line of English compositions that was to culminate in a brace of the greatest oratorios ever composed. The *Ode* clearly foreshadows, not the proportions, but the styles of *Israel in Egypt* and *Messiah*, the styles that Handel was to employ solely in non-Italian, non-operatic works. It suited the English as the style of Italian opera suited the Italians. It was derived from Purcell and other English composers. It was related to the genius of the English language as the more supple and sensuous style of Handel's finest operatic pages was related to the language of Italy. As first tentatively set forth in the *Birthday Ode*, it justly won him the royal favor he sought. Anne ordered him, rather than Eccles (an ode by whom had also been sung on that last but one of her birthdays), to prepare his *Te Deum* for use at the public thanksgiving that was to follow the proclamation in London of the treaty being signed at Utrecht. She requested that he add to it a *Jubilate*.

Abandoning England's faithful Catalan allies to the furious vengeance of Philip V of Spain, the negotiators, led by Bolingbroke, signed the Treaty of Utrecht on March 31, 1713. The dubious document was proclaimed in London on May 5, and the

thanksgiving was set for July 7 in St. Paul's. Queen Anne, rapidly
sinking toward the death that would overtake her little more
than one year later, was too ill to attend. But news of the beauty
of Handel's *Te Deum* and *Jubilate* reached her sickroom: she
ordered an annual stipend of £200 to be paid the composer.
Too, she later heard it in the Chapel Royal at St. James's. The
public's reaction to the music, to its rolling choruses and great
double fugues, to its magnificently singable rich counterpoint,
was overwhelmingly enthusiastic. For three decades, the
Utrecht Te Deum and *Jubilate* alternated with the *St. Cecilia
Te Deum* of Purcell as the work annually performed in St. Paul's
for the benefit of the Sons of the Clergy. It was finally displaced
in 1743 by a superior work, a masterpiece of Handel's greatest
period, the *Dettingen Te Deum*. Because of its power, massive
beauty, and historical interest, the *Utrecht Te Deum* and *Jubilate* should be revived today.

There is no reason for believing that Handel did not continue
to receive from Hanover his annual *Kapellmeister*'s salary,
equivalent to £300. This, with such earnings as those from the
Teseo benefit, had now been swollen by the English pension of
£200. Handel was very probably the best-paid composer in the
world, and he had no living expenses, being a guest-employee
at Burlington House. This may partially explain why no new
major composition of his was presented publicly between July
7, 1713 (*Utrecht Te Deum* and *Jubilate*), and May 25, 1715
(*Amadigi*). He enjoyed his life in the great Piccadilly mansion,
varying it with bouts of eating, drinking, and talking with fellow musicians at the Queen's Arms, a tavern favored by the
choristers of St. Paul's, which stood hard by. How long he would
have dared to remain truant from Hanover will never be known,
nor how long he would have been willing to ornament Burlington House (the Earl lived until 1753). Big international hap-
penings were preparing, and they were to make decisions for
him.

The question of the succession to the throne now had to be
decided. That Anne had not long to live became clear to every-

one at court or near it early in 1714. She had vacillated between a conviction that the Protestant succession must be assured through the Electress Sophia and the Elector Georg Ludwig and a natural, understandable preference for her own half-brother, the "Old Pretender," James Francis Edward Stuart. From 1705 on, she had been in politely friendly direct contact with Sophia and Georg Ludwig, and in 1706 she had created the latter's son Duke of Cambridge and honored him with the Garter. Addressing Parliament in 1708 with regard to the Pretender's ill-fated attempt to conquer Scotland, she had urged mercy toward the Scottish Jacobites, but had referred to her brother as "a popish pretender bred up in the principles of the most arbitrary government," not a portrait designed to endear him to her subjects. The infuriated Duchess of Marlborough said in 1713 that during all the years she had known "that thing" [the Queen!] she had "never heard her speak a favourable word of him."

On the other hand, Anne's indecision gave the many Jacobites near her very good reasons for hope. She had consistently refused to allow Georg Ludwig to be summoned to England. Although on April 27, 1714, she gave her solemn royal word to Sir William Dawes, Archbishop of York, that she was faithful to the Hanoverian succession, she became so angry after she herself had at last issued a writ summoning the Duke of Cambridge (the future George II) to England that she refused to receive Baron Schütz, the Hanoverian envoy to her court. When the Electress Sophia then memorialized her on the subject, urging the propriety of her grandson's visit to England, the dying Anne dispatched a reply so violent that it has been accused of causing Sophia's death, which occurred on June 8, 1714.[5] Perhaps, however, word reached Anne that her brother was attempting to plot with her Tory leaders, including both

[5] Sophia's death, though actually less dramatic, was picturesque. She was walking in the Herrenhausen gardens. It began to rain, and she hastened her steps. "You are walking too fast," an attendant told her. "I believe I am," the eighty-four-year-old Sophia replied, and dropped down unconscious. She died a few hours later.

Oxford and Bolingbroke. For she at last agreed to send Lord
Clarendon to Hanover to calm Georg Ludwig's fears. Clarendon
reached Hanover just when Anne's death settled the problem.

On July 27, Oxford, who had been losing power gradually,
resigned as lord treasurer as the direct result of quarreling
with Bolingbroke, who thus became the most important man
in England. As he was a Jacobite at heart and perhaps in action,
Bolingbroke would probably have proceeded to build up
strength for the struggle to enthrone "James III." But on the
very day of Oxford's resignation the Queen's council sat with
her, discussing this thorny matter of the succession until past
two o'clock in the morning of July 28. Going thence to her bed-
chamber, Anne became mortally ill. Mostly she stayed in a
coma. But the council, with the Whig leaders, Argyll and Som-
erset, waited upon her in one of her few moments of consciousness, and on July 30 saw her place the white staff of the lord
treasurer in the hands of the Whig Duke of Shrewsbury, saying,
"Use it for the good of my country." This symbolic gesture
expunged forever any chance the Old Pretender may have had.
"Good Queen Anne" had done her sworn duty.

On July 31, the council dispatched to Hanover a letter announcing the gravity of the Queen's condition and promising
to safeguard Georg Ludwig's succession to the throne. At 7:30
on the morning of Sunday, August 1, 1714, at six months less
than fifty years of age, Anne died. The age of the Stuarts and
the Commonwealth was over.

Georg Ludwig, Elector of Hanover, was, Marshal von der
Schulenburg wrote, "born with all the attributes of a country
gentleman, but he is devoid of those of a monarch." In Hanover, at Herrenhausen, this very German great-grandson of
James I could live without pomp the life of a very wealthy
country squire. In London, he knew, he would have to live the
public life of a monarch. Perhaps he would not have been too
saddened by news that James Stuart had, after all, been proclaimed King James III. He received word of his own succession to that strange, far-away throne without enthusiasm, and

took his own good time about proceeding to his new kingdom.
He did not land at Greenwich until September 18, or reach
St. James's until September 20. His coronation was solemnized
in Westminster Abbey on October 20.

The coronation of George I is a moment from which it would
be interesting to have at hand a letter or reliable report to
reveal the thoughts of George Frideric Handel. He was still
officially *Kapellmeister* to the Electoral Court at Hanover, from
which he had now been truant for two years, during which he
had established for himself a valuable position in England.
Now his master, the very Georg Ludwig whose displeasure he
might reasonably expect, had been crowned King at Westminster. Could Handel remain in England with any hope of pre-
ferment, or even of toleration, from the new reign? Could he
return to Hanover? He must have had most uncomfortable
thoughts. We cannot know what they were. We do know what
he did: he did nothing. He was comfortably established, and
he could afford to idle. He was not called to wait upon the
new King; he had not to supply official music. All of his production that dates from this interval with any certainty is a few
harpsichord pieces and a small opera, *Silla*.

Silla may never have been performed at all. Or, as Chrysander
guessed, it may have been staged privately at Burlington House.
Everything about it suggests that it was designed for amateurs.
Handel was absent from the London boards as far as any new
music went, though Heidegger revived *Rinaldo* so well that ten
performances of it were required during the 1714–15 season.
There was no royal boycott of Handel's music: a performance
of *Rinaldo* was attended by the Prince and Princess of Wales.
Nor was George I himself to be denied a pleasure so important
to him. He did not attend *Rinaldo* openly, but visited it in-
cognito and in disguise. This disguise was of little use, however,
for George seldom went anywhere without one or more of his
very Germanic mistresses and other female attendants. Everyone must have known, when several sedan-chairs brought a
portly gentleman and one or more German-gabbling ladies to

His Majesty's (as which, or as the King's, the Haymarket theater was now naturally called), that it was the King himself
with Madame Schulenburg, later Duchess of Kendal, or
Madame Kielmansegge, later Countess of Darlington. But the
half-preserved anonymity of these visits allowed the King to
hear Handel's music without officially forgiving him or even
recognizing his existence.

Heidegger finally attracted the too-long-silent Handel back
to the boards by writing (or perhaps arranging) a good libretto
for him. Anne's death and the peacefulness of the Hanoverian
succession had sent stocks up, and money had become freer in
the new Whig London than it had been in the Tory London of
the Queen's last years. The South Sea Company was prosper-
ing, one of a number of like ventures. It was a propitious time
to try fortune again with a new opera by the composer of
Rinaldo and *Teseo*, particularly as Nicolini had returned, drawn
Londonward by news, it may be, that large sums of money were
flowing there. So Heidegger offered Handel the libretto of
Amadigi, based on the old French romance *Amadis de Gaul*.
Handel set it through the winter of 1714–15. It required unusually complex stage machinery, which Heidegger, still man-
aging His Majesty's, undertook to provide. A clipping in Charles
Burney Jr's *Theatrical Register* indicates that on the day of
Amadigi's première, subscribers were advised as follows:

And whereas there is a great many scenes and machines to be
moved in this opera, which can not be done if persons should stand
on the stage, where they could not be without danger, it is therefore
hoped nobody, even the subscribers, will take it ill that they must
be deny'd entrance on the stage.

After a postponement from the originally announced *première* of May 21, 1715, *Amadigi* was first sung at His Majesty's on
May 25. The four principal roles were taken by Nicolini (Amadigi), Signora Diana Vico (Dardano), Signora Pilotti Schiavonetti (Melissa), and Mrs. Anastasia Robinson (Oriana) —
two sopranos and two contraltos. Mrs. Robinson, the future

beautiful and romantic Countess of Peterborough,[6] had made
her public debut little more than one year earlier, and still
retained her pleasing, if somewhat unsteady, soprano (after a
severe illness, she later become a contralto). Nicolini was at
his best; the other ladies were serviceable. The erotic, tragic fire
of Heidegger's libretto and Handel's score [7] were supported and
displayed by settings, costumes, and machines of a magnificence
that London had not seen. A fountain playing real water was
the center of one scene, and caused so great a sensation that the
inevitable parodies of *Amadigi,* by John Gay and others, made
great sport of it.

Amadigi was a hit. The management was forced to issue the
following announcement:

> Whereas by the frequent calling for the songs again, the operas
> have been too tedious; therefore the singers are forbidden to sing any
> song above once; and it is hoped nobody will call for 'em, or take it
> ill when not obeyed.

Having been presented late in the season, however, *Amadigi*
could not achieve a long original run. But George I went to
hear it, as he had heard the revived *Rinaldo,* with which it
alternated until the season closed on July 9. It was becoming
clear to the King, to Handel, and to men and women at court
that a reconciliation between George the King and George the
composer would increase everyone's happiness. And such a
reconciliation was brought about — or at least occurred. Although every writer who has ever dealt with Handel has attempted to discover how and when, no agreement has been
reached or seems likely to be reached unless through the discovery of now unimaginable documents. The two likeliest
stories, one of them among the most familiar of musical anecdotes, must therefore be told.

[6] The romance of Peterborough and Mrs. Robinson gave George Mere-
dith the subject of his novel *Lord Ormont and His Aminta.*
[7] Some sections of *Amadigi* were adapted from *Silla.*

The great violinist and masterly composer for strings, Francesco Geminiani, was two years Handel's junior. He passed many of his middle years in England and Ireland. Being invited to perform at court some of his recently composed concertos, he replied that he was notoriously difficult to accompany, and would consent to play only if he could be assisted by Handel. According to this tale, George I saw in this demand a graceful way of terminating the uncomfortable and now silly estrangement from his favorite musician, and agreed to let Geminiani have the accompanist of his choice. Handel thus made his first appearance at George's London court. The King was so delighted that he confirmed Handel's pension of £200 per year from Queen Anne, added a like pension from his own largesse, and fully readmitted the composer to his friendship. This story may well be true: Handel did continue to receive the first grant of £200, and was granted not only an additional £200 from George I, but a third like pension from the Princess of Wales when, about this time, he became her daughters' music master. His salary as *Kapellmeister* at Hanover ceased, but he certainly received royal stipends of not less than £600 per annum until his death.

If the story involving Geminiani were the only one accounting for Handel's reinstatement in George's favor, there would be very little reason to doubt it. But the other explanatory anecdote is widely believed. If true, this story of the *Water Musick* denies, not that Handel accompanied Geminiani at court, but that his doing so provided the occasion on which he was forgiven for his truancy. The story of the *Water Musick* was first published in Mainwaring. It is a good story (it has a plot), and it may be true. It runs as follows:

Johann Georg, Baron von Kielmansegge, Master of the Horse to the Elector of Hanover, whom Handel had encountered first at Venice, and who may have abetted Ernst Augustus' original suggestion that the young composer visit Hanover, was an important personage at the court of George I. His wife was the

King's illegitimate half-sister and favored companion.[8] This music-loving and indiscriminately friendly man was unhappy over the coolness existing between monarch and musician, and longed for an occasion or ruse by which he might assist in reconciling them. Then the King decided on a water party for August 22, 1715. It was to be a royal progress from Whitehall to Limehouse in decorated barges. It was Kielmansegge's opportunity. He won the Earl of Burlington's approval for his scheme: Handel was to compose special music for the occasion. And, Mainwaring says, Handel fell in with the harmless plot. The musicians played his music — the *Water Musick* — on a special barge, close enough to the one in which the King rode so that he could hear it all plainly. And the King too fell in with the scheme. He was so pleased by the sounds of Handel's wonderful music across the Thames waters that he asked who its composer might be. When he was informed that Handel was the man, he instantly relented toward him, sent for him, forgave him, congratulated him, and restored him to favor.

This story contains no intrinsically unlikely elements. Its only trouble is the existence of unimpeachable documents relating to a similar water party on July 17, 1717, accounts that describe the *Water Musick* and state that it was composed by Handel expressly for performance on that date. Handel was on good terms with George I before July 17, 1717, and if that day witnessed the *Water Musick*'s first performance, that piece cannot have had anything to do with reconciling them. Further, if all of the twenty-five sections that Handel published in 1740 as the *Water Musick* were composed expressly for the 1717 fete, we must decide either that the pieces composed in 1715 have been lost or that the undependable Mainwaring mixed up his dates

[8] Horace Walpole described this daughter of Clara Elisabeth, Countess von Platen, by George I's father as follows: "I remember as a boy being terrified at her enormous figure. Two fierce black eyes, large and rolling beneath two lofty arched eyebrows, two acres of cheeks spread with crimson, an ocean of neck that overflowed and was not distinguished from the lower part of her body, and no part restrained by stays — no wonder that a child dreaded such an ogress!"

and emphasis. The likeliest solution to this puzzle was originally suggested by R. A. Streatfeild, and has been accepted by Edward J. Dent and Eric Blom. It is that the 1740 publication is a collation of, or selection from, pieces composed in both 1715 and 1717. This leaves Mainwaring's tale possibly true (the water party of August 22, 1715 could even have been succeeded by Handel's actual appearance at court as Geminiani's accompanist). It leaves the veracity of the accounts of the 1717 fete unquestioned. Further, if the 1715 music-making on the Thames did happen, the King, ever a Handelian, would have been very likely to suggest another like it two years later.

The *Water Musick,* which modern concert-goers know only in bits and rearranged selections, is Handel's finest orchestral composition. It is superbly conceived for outdoor performance, and particularly for sounding over the wide, echoing spaces of a river. Dances, adagios, gigues, and minuets pour forth a wealth of melody, of vigorous, unmistakable Handelian harmony, and mobile, mercurial Handelian rhythm. Trumpets, bassoons, oboes, French horns,[9] flutes, and piccolos join the strings. This is not orchestral music in the modern sense, not orchestration as a musical means for its own sake: it is nicely judged placing of melodic, harmonic, and rhythmic materials with remarkable aptness for open-air performance. The hornpipes are as English as Purcell or Sir Arthur Sullivan. The issue of the *Daily Courant* for July 19, 1717, summons up for us the very atmosphere in which some or all of this music was first played for the delectation of Hanoverian George:

On Wednesday evening at about 8, the King took water at Whitehall in an open barge, wherein were also the dutchess of Newcastle, the Countess of Godolphin, Madam Kilmanseck, and the Earl of Orkney, and went up the river towards Chelsea. Many other barges with persons of quality attended, and so great a number of boats, that the whole river in a manner was covered; a city company's barge was employed for the musick, wherein were fifty instruments

[9] Unless Handel's 1740 publication represented revisions, the *Water Musick* of 1715/1717 contained his first use of the French horn.

of all sorts, who play'd all the way from Lambeth (while the barges drove with the tide without rowing as far as Chelsea [10]), the finest symphonies, composed express for this occasion by Mr. Hendel: which His Majesty liked so well, that he caused it to be played over three times in going and returning. At eleven, His Majesty went ashoar at Chelsea, where a supper was prepared, and then there was another very fine consort of musick which lasted till 2: after which His Majesty came again into his barge, and returned the same way, the musick continuing to play till he landed.

Amadigi di Gaula, the opera heard on May 25, 1715, was the sole Handel *première* of that year, though numerous operas by Handel and other composers were revived during that season. George I and the Prince and Princess of Wales were untiring operagoers. One of them may have requested the revival of operas that had been given before their arrival in England. Another explanation of Handel's apparent lack of activity, however, was the political situation, again threatening. Louis XIV had never altogether abandoned the unquestionably legitimate pretensions of James Stuart to the English throne. Nor had that foolish brother of Queen Anne ceased to style himself "James III, King of Great Britain and Ireland." Neither the death on September 1, 1715, of Louis XIV nor the fact that local Jacobite disturbances flaring up after George I's coronation had mostly died down — nothing, in fact, could quell the enthusiasm of the most inflamed Jacobites, many of them prominent Tories. They had decided on another attempt to conquer Scotland first and England second.

On August 2, 1715, John Erskine, Earl of Mar, having attended George I at St. James's the day before, set out for the north in the belief that he could rouse Scotland while Bolingbroke and other Jacobite Tories roused England. Learning of the French King's death, and knowing that it prejudiced their cause, Bolingbroke tried to halt Mar en route, but his message arrived too late: Mar had raised the Stuart banner at Braemar

[10] The supper was being given at Lord Ranelagh's Chelsea house by Lady Catherine Jones.

on September 6. The Highlanders took Inverness, Dundee, and Perth. Very quickly all of Great Britain north of the Tay was Jacobite in fact. Soon the Stuart armies, despite desertions by Highlanders refusing to cross into England, reached Preston on the Ribble. There, on November 13, the day that saw other Jacobite forces checked at Sheriffmuir in the north, they were forced to surrender. For the time being, the romantic and color-ful lost cause of the Old Pretender was lost indeed.

London enjoyed a pause of relief after months of uncertainty and worry. Then the Pretender himself landed at Peterhead, in Aberdeenshire, on December 22. He began to issue royal proclamations. The government in London, in which Sir Robert Walpole had begun to play a leading hand, jumped to the con-clusion that James Stuart would not have acted so rashly had he not been assured that help was coming from France despite the death of Louis XIV. The Duke of Argyll was therefore dis-patched with a good army to rout the Jacobites utterly before the French could arrive. As soon as Argyll's men threatened Perth, the Highlanders retreated to the north. At Montrose, the Pretender and the Earl of Mar, realizing that their game was up, abandoned their followers. On the day of their arrival in France, Argyll trounced at Aberdeen what remained of their army. It was February 8, 1716, and the muddleheaded, noble, silly uprising had been crushed completely.

The records of Handel's musical activity during the uprising are blank except for revivals of two or three of his operas. When George I left for Hanover on July 9, 1716, Handel ac-companied or followed him. He was to remain in Germany about six months. It was in all probability during that period that he composed, to a text by Barthold Heinrich Brockes, a Passion called *Der für die Sünden der Welt gemarterte und sterbende Jesus,* the personages of which are Jesus, Peter, John, James, Caiaphas, Pontius Pilate, Judas, Mary, and the Mag-dalenes. This feeble poetic retelling in German of Christ's Pas-sion had been set to music four years earlier by Handel's former employer, friend, and enemy, Reinhard Keiser. It was also set,

about the time Handel used it, by his early acquaintance, Georg
Philipp Telemann. A short while later, Mattheson, too, tried
his hand at it. Handel took his own setting of Brockes' text back
to England with him in 1717, had a fair copy made of it there,
and sent this to Hamburg, Brockes' home city. There it was first
sung, without Handel's presence, in the Lenten season of 1719.
Brockes, who seems to have been a foolish, pompous, and shady
little man, must have puffed up with pride when the four settings of his preposterous text — by Keiser, Telemann, Handel,
and Mattheson — were given under Mattheson's direction at
Hamburg Cathedral in the course of a single season.

Johann Sebastian Bach, whom Handel never met face to
face, made half of a complete copy of Handel's Passion, writing
on it *Oratorium Passionale: Poesia di Brocks et Musica di
Handel.* It consists of an overture (an allegro single fugue),
leading, by way of a typical operatic flute solo in recitative style,
to the customary arias, choruses, and accompanied recitatives.
The score, made up of more than fifty sections, includes instructions that one section of the chorale *"Schmücke dich, o liebe
Seele"* is to be sung by the entire congregation. The Passion is at
its best when it is most dramatic, most operatic; it clearly reveals Handel's consistent lack of subjective religious concentration in those passages which Bach would have made its chief
glories. Yet it is likely, in view of the partial copy in Bach's hand
and of some stylistic resemblances, that it was of so much interest to Bach that it influenced him in at least his *Johannes-
passion* (1724) and *Matthäuspassion* (1729). It was the last
complete composition that Handel composed to a text in the
language of his childhood.

While in Germany, Handel visited Halle, where the sixty-
five-year-old woman who had given him birth still lived. There,
too, he saw the widow of his first musical preceptor, Zachau,
who had died in 1712. Frau Zachau, suffering at the hands of
a scapegrace son, was in financial straits, and Handel, who always felt indebted to her husband and whose philanthropies
increased with his means, began the custom of giving her sums

of money. Besides Halle, he visited Anspach. He was music master to the small daughters of Caroline, Princess of Wales, who had come from Anspach, and it is possible that he went thither on an errand for her.

In Anspach, Handel encountered a friend of his Halle school-days, a musically inclined young wool merchant named Johann Christoph Schmidt. Schmidt's career is largely unknown. He turned up shortly after Handel's return to England in 1717, and passed the rest of his life as Handel's manager, treasurer, and general factotum. He became known as John Christopher Smith, which fact has confused biographers in a very curious way, leading them to the further confusion of their successors. For his son, born in 1712, was also John Christopher Smith, and also served Handel faithfully and long — until Handel's death. Smith the younger was the chief amanuensis of Handel's blindness, and himself became a composer with small successes of his own in opera (Italian and English), oratorio (English), and smaller forms. Father and son were intimates of Handel's lodgings for nearly forty-two years. The son was given musical instruction by Handel, Dr. Pepusch, and Thomas Roseingrave.

Besides visiting Hamburg in connection with his setting of Brockes' Passion text, Halle to see his mother, and Anspach probably for the Princess of Wales, Handel stopped in Dresden, maybe hoping to encounter singers who might be imported into England to the benefit of opera there. For while he lingered in Germany, plans were being made in London for revivals of *Rinaldo* and *Amadigi.* It was now two years since he had composed an opera; three more were to pass without a new one from his pen. His only music probably dating from 1717 is the *Concerto grosso* in F major (Opus 3, no. 4), which he composed to be played at a benefit for the members of the orchestra at His Majesty's Theatre.

Unless Handel's return to London preceded that of George I, he was not on hand at His Majesty's for one of Nicolini's greatest triumphs. For the King abandoned Hanover on January 5, 1717, and that was the very day of the revival of *Rinaldo,* a revival greeted with as much public enthusiasm as had welcomed its original production. Rinaldo's *"Cara sposa,"* Armida's *"Ah! crudel,"* and Almirena's surpassing *"Lascia ch'io pianga"* had not, in the hands of a roster of capable singers, lost their spell. *Rinaldo*, and to a smaller extent *Amadigi*, were, in truth, the only successful performances of opera at His Majesty's during the 1716–17 season. Otherwise the public, deprived of new music by Handel, tended to prefer the performances of a troupe of French dancers. The box office was poor for other revivals and novelties. When summer closed His Majesty's on June 29, 1717, there was little expectation that it would again open as an opera house. Opera in London was in one of its intermittent declines, this one destined to last almost three years: it was that long before another opera, Handel's *Radamisto*, was heard there.

Handel was thirty-two. He may have been weary of the trials, petty disturbances, and racking uncertainties of the opera house. A new work from his pen might recoup the fortunes of His Majesty's, but was unlikely to do much for him. Perhaps, like most composers, he longed intensely for financial security and the freedom to compose. Under the conditions then pertaining, he was unlikely to earn such security and freedom by supplying opera scores to managers. At any rate, he accepted, for the last time in his life, a position not unlike that he had held at Burlington House. Succeeding Dr. Pepusch, he became director of the music at Cannons, the palace of James Brydges, Earl of Carnarvon, near Edgware in Middlesex. He was to remain there for a peaceful interval of about two years that proved to be among the most productive and — for his ultimate future as a composer to English texts — fruitful of his life. Those two years at Cannons were the deceptive calm before a great series of storms.

VI

Acting as paymaster-general of the English armies during the War of the Spanish Succession, James Brydges had made himself vastly rich at the expense of Queen Anne's subjects. In 1714, on the death of his father, he had succeeded to the baronetcy of Chandos. Three days later, he had been created Viscount Wilton and Earl of Carnarvon. His final apotheosis was to come in 1719, when he was created Marquess of Carnarvon and Duke of Chandos. In 1712, while his father still lived, this magnificent peculator had embarked on his most costly daring. Making use of a piece of land that he had acquired through the first of his three marriages, he began the construction of a palace that was at last to cost him £230,000. It was designed in Italian style. He either loved music or esteemed its constant presence essential to proper ostentation: Cannons was to contain a fine Jordan organ, a salon especially designed for music, and living quarters for the members of his choir and orchestra. It also showed columns of marble and a staircase of the same stone. Frescoed ceilings were provided by Verrio and Laguerre, artists imported from France to paint them (the architects were headed by James Gibbs). As a final luxury, this grandiloquent man considered, but ultimately did not carry out, the plan of constructing a private road from his uncompleted mansion in Cavendish Square to Cannons, nearly ten miles away. He and guests he invited to Cannons frequently had good cause for regret that he had not built this road and stationed men to guard its length, for he was set upon more than once in the Edgware Road by desperadoes and footpads, and his guests came and went in reasonable trepidation.

8 3

In 1713, a section of Cannons became habitable. James Brydges moved in, at the same time outfitting from among the Chelsea Hospital pensioners eight stalwart veterans of Marlborough's army as Swiss Guards for the grounds and installing Dr. Pepusch as master of the music. Cannons became one of the renowned residences of England, threatening to outshine St. James's and its mere king. Nor did Brydges' lavish taste confine itself to a palace. Having added a private chapel to Cannons, he also had the near-by Parish Church of Whitchurch (or Little Stanmore) frescoed by the artists who had emblazoned the ceilings at Cannons, and then presented to it a Grinling Gibbons organ console and a silver communion service.

In all this marbled panoply, Brydges was only following a family tradition: one of his collateral ancestors, the Fifth Baron Chandos, had lived so lavishly as Lord Lieutenant of Gloucestershire that he came to be called "King of the Cotswolds." And Cannons itself was but a later, grander version of that Lord Lieutenant's Sudeley Castle. But the nominal visible signs of the greatness of the First Duke of Chandos were not to survive. After his death in 1744, his son and then his grandson succeeded him. After that his major titles became extinct: his great-granddaughter married the Richard Grenville who became the First Duke of Buckingham and Chandos, which title in turn became extinct in 1889. Worse, the First Duke of Chandos himself fell into financial trouble after losing £300,000 in the bursting of the South Sea Bubble. His son Henry, the Second Duke, is said to have had a taste for buying a groom's mistreated wife and marrying her, but he and his heirs lacked means of perpetuating the glories of Cannons. And so that storied house — Pope called it "Timon's Villa" in the fourth Epistle of his *Moral Essays* — was pulled down. Nothing remained of it but the renowned staircase of twenty-two-foot blocks of marble, which was installed in Chesterfield House (Mayfair).

Nothing whatever remained of the earthly splendors of James Brydges, First Duke of Chandos. For the Parish Church of Whitchurch, Middlesex, long referred to by chroniclers and its neighbors as the very chapel he had caused to be erected, is not that chapel — which, as has been said, was attached to Cannons, and which therefore disappeared when that structure and its contents were sold for £70,000. The Duke was buried in the Parish Church of Whitchurch, however, and it contains his tomb, on which his effigy is recumbent between those of two of his wives who predeceased him. The Parish Church, too, is sure of a continuing place in the annals of music. It is connected with a story as famous as that of the origin of the *Water Musick*, and even less certainly true.

In Whitchurch there stands a monument to "the Harmonious Blacksmith," William Powell, said to have been the parish clerk at the time when Handel was the organist of the Church. Now, Handel was never organist of the Church, and Powell, whoever he may have been, was certainly not "the Harmonious Blacksmith." There may have been a man known by that appellation, but he had no connection with the Church. If he existed, he was an apprentice blacksmith who happened to enjoy the delicious melody of the "Air and Variations" in the fifth Suite in Handel's first-published *Suites de Pièces* for harpsichord, music composed while Handel was attached to Cannons, and probably intended as practice material for one of the young daughters of the Princess of Wales. He whistled or sang the melody so much, it may be, that he came to be called "the Harmonious Blacksmith." Then, by one of those transferences that happen insensibly, his nickname became that of the "Air and Variations." That would not in itself be bad — the quality of music is not changed by giving it an inappropriate name, as Erik Satie proved, and *The Harmonious Blacksmith* is probably as good as another title.

Note, however, what became of this nickname. Shortly after 1820 (Handel having been dead more than sixty years), someone [1] published the "Air and Variations" as *The Harmonious*

---

[1] It may have been the merry blacksmith's apprentice himself. He was William Lintern, and his father, far from being a blacksmith too, was a bookseller. Bookselling and music publishing were not so far apart early

Blacksmith. The name stuck, and other editions soon multiplied the title. In 1835, an anonymous writer sent *The Times* a pretty and plausible explanation of it. Handel, this correspondent stated, had been caught in a thunderstorm, and had sought shelter in a Whitchurch smithy. There he was fascinated by the sounds issuing from the struck anvil, sounds to which the smith was singing a melody. When the thunderstorm passed, the composer kept in his mind that song to the ringing of metal on metal, and on it based the melody of the famous "Air and Variations." In 1836, an antiquarian named Richard Clark published an expanded version of this romantic tale in his *Reminiscences of Handel.* Clark was an amiable faker of learned lore: his *Account of the National Anthem* (1822) is a tissue of ingenious falsehoods about *God Save the King.* He had built the story of that inspiration during a thunderstorm into a net of plausible references — one cannot, in fact, resist venturing the unsupported guess that Clark himself had been *The Times'* anonymous correspondent of 1835.

In a forge near Whitchurch there had been found an anvil that, when struck, gave out first a B and then an E, important notes in the key of E, in which *The Harmonious Blacksmith* is composed. Clark made it the very anvil whose ringing Handel had heard during the thunderstorm. Then he proceeded to invent the story that William Powell — a man by that name may actually have been parish clerk of Whitchurch while Handel was at Cannons — had been the owner of the anvil and its harmonious striker on the day of Handel's visit to the smithy. Clark gave wrong dates for Powell's birth and death, and at last persuaded the citizens of Whitchurch to build a monu-

---

in the nineteenth century as they sound today, and William Chappell wrote (*Grove's Dictionary,* first edition) that in 1836 or 1837 one J. W. Winsor of Bath had known Lintern personally, and also knew him to have published the "Air and Variations" under the new title because he believed that the nickname, originally applied to himself, would help it to sell. No copy of Lintern's edition is known to exist; the earliest bearing the title is one published by the British Harmonic Institution in piano-duet form; it contains paper watermarked "1819."

ment to Powell at their own expense. This was a mere jerry-built structure of lumber: a stone monument was its natural successor a decade or so later. The original monument had an inscription stating that it had been erected through the efforts of Richard Clark and Henry Wylde, the latter then the youthful organist of Whitchurch. The stone version, of course, contained all the misinformation at once.

The later career of Clark's anvil is truly wonderful. W. S. Rockstro, in *The Life of George Frederick Handel* (1883), having quoted Clark's story at length, recounts the disposal of William Powell's effects as follows:

His stock-in-trade, including the traditional Anvil and Hammer, was bought by a wheelwright of Edgeware named Dormer. Dormer's son-in-law, George Hone (another Parish Clerk) inherited the tools, and bequeathed them to his son, whose widow sold them to George Jordan (another wheelwright), by whom the Anvil and Hammer were generously presented to the author of the "Reminiscences," together with a block of oak, cut from a tree in Cannons Park, and made to serve as a pedestal for the Anvil. In order to preserve these Reliques from future desecration, Richard Clark gave them to Master Henry Wylde, the "exceedingly promising young Organist" of Whitchurch, then thirteen years old, whose deep sense of the honour he enjoyed in playing upon Handel's Organ pointed him out as "the proper person to possess them." We next hear of the Anvil as the property of Mr. William Snoxell, of Charterhouse Square, whose collection was sold, by Messrs. Puttick and Simpson, on the 9th, 10th, 11th, and 12th of June, 1879, when the Anvil and Hammer — Lot 485 of the third day's sale — were "knocked down," for £14, to Mr. Maskelyne, of the Egyptian Hall, Piccadilly, who, in the August of the same year, contributed an account of them to "The Leisure Hour," and in whose possession they still remain.

In short, all this fabulous story would have an exact parallel if the tripping melody in the overture to Rossini's *Guillaume Tell* should be published separately as *Hi-Yo, Silver* because it was once attached to a wild-west radio program in which the leading character cried out those words, and then the horse called Silver should be transplanted back into Rossini's time and his faked skeleton sold to a collector because of its importance to Rossini, who had been inspired to his rhythmic jumpiness by Silver's gait. It is no more certain that Rossini never heard of Silver and never thought of that melody as wildly western than it is that Handel never conceived his E-major "Air and Variations" as anything but just that. This does not mean, of course, that we shall not go on referring to them as *The Harmonious Blacksmith*.[2] Nor does it mean that the melody was wholly original with Handel: melodies much like it existed in France and Sweden (*Notes and Queries*, Vol. I, 2nd series, p. 356) before the eighteenth century.

The *Suites de Pièces pour le Clavecin*[3] was the first purely instrumental music that Handel published. It was issued, probably by John Cluer, on November 14, 1720, its publication justified by the following note:

I have been obliged to publish some of the following lessons, because surrepticious and incorrect copies of them had got abroad. I have added several new ones to make the work more useful, which if it meets with a favourable reception, I will still proceed to publish more, reckoning it my duty, with my small talent, to serve a nation from which I have received so generous a protection.

G. F. Handel

[2] One other scrap of *Harmonious Blacksmith* lore is worth recording. The eminent Dr. William Crotch, so Richard Clark wrote, stated that "when he was at Cambridge, at Dr. Hague's, some years since, he saw a book with the same Melody, and which melody had the name of Wagenseil to it as Composer." On the basis of this secondhand reminiscence, Handel's melody has sometimes been attributed to Georg Christoph Wagenseil, who, having been born in 1715, was five years old when Handel published the *Suites de Pièces* containing the E-major "Air and Variations"! When adult, Wagenseil did compose variations on the melody — which he attributed to Handel.
[3] As Percy A. Scholes has pointed out, the fact that many of Handel's harpsichord works often move into remote keys indicates that Handel was composing for an instrument tuned in equal temperament. He never exploited the various keys as Bach did in *Das wohltemperirte Klavier*, but there is no doubt that he was fully acquainted with equally tempered tuning or that the harpsichord in his Brook Street house was so tuned.

Composed mostly at Cannons, the eight *Suites* were probably derived freely from lessons (the *Daily Courant* called them *Lessons for the Harpsichord*) concocted for the education of Princess Anne, eldest daughter of the Prince and Princess of Wales. When Handel's life became too crowded with other activities, he was to stop teaching royal pupils. The second publication of *Suites* did not occur until 1733. Meanwhile, the first set had spread throughout Europe, gaining a popularity impossible to understand unless the music has been heard on a harpsichord played by such a master of that instrument as Wanda Landowska, whose performance of five of the *Suites* has been perpetuated on gramophone records. Handel himself was a great harpsichordist, and probably regarded the written notes as little more than an outline of what was to be played. But that outline is often, in itself, a thing of surpassing loveliness when heard, not on the grand piano for which it was not conceived, but on the more discreet and personally expressive harpsichord.

The first set of harpsichord *Suites* was not the only music Handel composed (or arranged) during his residence at Cannons. To that period also belong the twelve Chandos Anthems, *Acis and Galatea, Haman and Mordecai, Radamisto,* and most of the *Concerti grossi,* Opus 3. If, as appears likely, he lived mostly at Cannons until he bought his own house in 1721, the period also included a long visit to Germany, a possible reunion with Domenico Scarlatti, the publication of the first *Suites de pièces pour le Clavecin,* the foundation of the Royal Academy of Music, and its first two seasons with Handel as director.

Handel's only surviving sibling — his sister Dorothea Sophia, who had married Michael Dietrich Michaelsen in 1708 — was in poor health much of the time. Of five children born to her between 1709 and 1716, only one lived to be more than not quite four years old. In order to provide her with the peace and restful atmosphere it was supposed that she required, her husband purchased in 1718 the estate of Stichelsdorf. But her condition was not to be bettered, and on August 8 of that year she died before her thirty-first birthday. At the funeral, which Handel could not, of course, attend (word could not have reached London, or he Germany, in time), the text of the pastor's sermon was "I know that my Redeemer liveth," a phrase that Handel himself was to mingle inextricably with music.

Meanwhile, in England, Handel was at work on the Chandos Anthems,[4] perhaps wondering about dividends due him on £500 worth of stock in the South Sea Company that he had bought before 1716, putting his harpsichord pieces in shape for their forthcoming publication by Cluer, and listening to the first plans considered by the founders of the South Sea Company's musical counterpart, the Royal Academy of Music. Following the pattern set by the new stockholding companies, of which the South Sea Company was merely the most notorious, the committee of twenty noblemen who formed the Royal Academy for the principal purpose of raising the quality of opera in London and the minor purpose of making money capitalized it at £10,000 (fifty shares valued at £200 each), of which George I subscribed £1,000. When the company was formed in February 1719, the Duke of Newcastle was appointed governor and Lord Bingley deputy governor. The other members included dukes, earls, generals, and gentlemen of prominence.[5] Heidegger was hired as manager. As the new operas envisaged would naturally require poets to supply their librettos, Nicolo Haym and Paolo Rolli were appointed. Three

[4] The Chandos Anthems are known by the opening phrases of their text: 1. "O be joyful in the Lord," 2. "In the Lord I put my trust," 3. "Have mercy upon me," 4. "O sing unto the Lord a new song," 5. "I will magnify Thee," 6. "As pants the hart," 7. "My song shall be alway," 8. "O come let us sing," 9. "O praise the Lord with one consent," 10. "The Lord is my light," and 11. "Let God arise." It is possible, though doubtful, that a twelfth, "O praise the Lord, ye angels of His," should be placed with them.

[5] Among them the Duke of Kent, Duke of Newcastle, Duke of Chandos, Duke of Portland, Earl of Rochester, Earl of Burlington, Lord Chetwynd, Lord Lansdowne, Viscount Limerick, General Wade, Sir John Jennings, Sir Matthew Decker, James Bruce, Brian Fairfax, Thomas Coke, William Pulteney, George Harrison, and Samuel Edwin.

musical directors, who were expected to compose and conduct, were named: Giovanni Battista Bononcini, Attilio Ariosti, and George Frideric Handel.

Handel must have decided to visit Halle immediately upon receiving word of his sister's death. The following letter to his bereaved brother-in-law shows, however, that events of importance prevented him from carrying out that intention. The letter, written in French and dated at London on February 20, 1719, is not the least interesting of the remarkably few personal letters from Handel that have survived:

Monsieur, mon trés Honoré Frere [it begins], Do not judge, I beseech you, my eagerness to see you by the delay in my departure. It is to my great regret that I find myself detained here by unavoidable affairs on which, I venture to say, my fortune depends, and which have stretched out longer than I had believed they would. If you knew the pain that I feel because of not having been able to put into action what I so ardently desire, you would have indulgence for me. But at last I hope to come from here in one month, and you may count on it that I shall brook no delay and shall travel without stopping. I beg you, my very dear brother, to assure Mama of this and of my obedience and, so as to lessen the anxiety and impatience I feel, to inform me once more how you, Mama, and your dear family are. You can well judge, my very dear brother, that I should be inconsolable if I did not hope to make amends quickly for this delay by staying as long as possible with you. I am astonished that the Magdeburg merchant has not paid the draft. I only ask you to take care of it, and it will be adjusted on my arrival. I have been advised that the pewter will soon be forwarded to you. I am ashamed of this tardiness, as well as of the fact that I have not been able sooner to carry out my promise. I beg you to excuse it and to believe that, despite all my efforts, it has been impossible to do otherwise. You yourself will understand this as soon as I have the honor of telling you about it by word of mouth. You must not doubt that I shall hasten my trip: I languish to see you more than you can believe. I thank you most humbly for the wishes you sent me on the occasion of New Year's. For my part, I desire that the Almighty may load you and your dear family with all sorts of prosperity and heal with his precious benedictions the sore wound he has seen fit to inflict on you, and which has hurt me equally. You may be assured that I shall always remember vividly the kindness you have shown to my late sister, and that my sentiments of gratitude will endure as long as my days. Have the goodness to present my compliments to Mr. Rotth [6] and to all my good friends. I embrace you and all your dear family, and remain, with lifelong affection [*passion inviolable toute ma vie*], Sir and most honored brother,

Your very humble and obedient servant
George Frideric Handel

The "unavoidable affairs" on which Handel ventured to say that his fortune depended were undoubtedly the preliminary arrangements for the first season of the Royal Academy of Music. Applebee's *Original Weekly Journal*, in its issue dated February 21, 1719, stated:

Mr. Hendel, a famous Master of Musick, is gone beyond the sea, by order of His Majesty, to collect a company of the choicest singers in Europe for the Opera in the Haymarket.

But Handel was still in London three days later than that, for a letter in French to Mattheson survives dated at London on February 24, 1719.[7] It is probable that Applebee's being a weekly journal, announced as having happened anything that was certain to happen before its next issue — and that Handel left London between February 24 and March 3.

Handel appears to have made Düsseldorf his first stop on the Continent. There he must have found few singers available and to his liking, for he engaged only the tenor Benedetto Baldassarri. Then he made a longish visit to Dresden, where Antonio Lotti had gathered together a splendid company of Italian singers to perform operas as part of the festivities surrounding

[6] Christian Roth, Handel's cousin, was successively deacon of the Halle Moritzkirche and religious councillor to the Duke of Saxe-Weissenfels. Like Handel, he had been born in 1685. He had married in 1712, and was to live until 1752.

[7] See Appendix A, which contains all the known surviving letters of Handel not quoted in the body of the text (page 309).

the marriage, in August, of the future Friedrich Augustus II, Elector of Saxony (Augustus III, King of Poland), to Maria Josepha, daughter of the Emperor Josef I. The bridegroom was the only legitimate son of Friedrich Augustus I, Elector of Saxony (Augustus II, King of Poland) — who had, it is said, as many illegitimate children as there are days in a year (one of them the redoubtable general known to history as Marshal Saxe) — and he cared all his life more for music and painting than he cared about the thrones of Saxony and Poland or any affairs of politics or state. The company Lotti had assembled for the gala Dresden season and the pleasure of this artistic prince was exactly the sort that Handel was shortly later to make familiar to London. He proceeded to raid it much as a Hollywood talent scout might today.

Handel hired a *castrato* soprano called Matteo Berselli, a Signora Maddalena Salvai, his old friend Giuseppe Boschi, and another Italian bass (of German descent) named Gaëtan Berenstadt. Most important of his Dresden finds, however, were Margherita Durastanti,[8] a soprano who, in the era when male sopranos and contraltos enacted female roles, was renowned for her impersonations of male characters, and a *castrato* mezzosoprano named Francesco Bernardi. Under his stage name of Senesino this unpleasant man was for a time to become a greater idol of the London public than even Siface and Nicolini had been. Despite his offensive manners and ungainly appearance, Senesino was to prove able to establish more firmly a successful good opera or to help save an unsuccessful bad one by the thrilling magnificence of his voice and singing style. The Royal Academy of Music was not, for its first seasons at least, to fail because of a scarcity of golden-throated birds of paradise.

Some time before returning to London, Handel visited Halle. His mother, now sixty-eight years old, and still living at *"zum gelben Hirschen,"* must have welcomed her only surviving child with eagerness and affection, but not without a sense of strain. She was a pious provincial lady of very limited horizons; he was

[8] She had sung in Handel's *Agrippina* in Venice in 1709–10.

a sophisticated man of importance in a far-off land. And it was
sixteen years since, a boy of eighteen, he had left home to return
only on brief, flying visits. In Halle, too, Handel probably saw
Michael Dietrich Michaelsen and his two surviving children by
Handel's late sister: a three-year-old boy named Emanuel Karl,
who died the following year, and the seven-year-old Johanna
Friederika who was to survive them all (including her husband,
Dr. Johann Ernst Flörke, who died in 1762 at Nürnberg, a
hostage of Halle), not dying until 1771.

One day in October or November 1719, George Frideric Handel bade farewell to the aging lady at *"zum gelben Hirschen"*
and set out for England, for London and the first season of the
Royal Academy of Music. Later that same day, a musician arrived in Halle from Leipzig, asking to see him. It was Johann
Sebastian Bach, who had walked from Leipzig [9] on hearing that
the famous Handel was visiting Halle, and who hoped to meet
so eminent a musician. It is a sorrow to musical historians that
the cantankerous musician-servant of Prince Leopold of Anhalt-
Cöthen — who was the most profound and accomplished subjective, introspective, and spiritual composer of the century —
did not meet and talk to the musical director of George I's Royal
Academy of Music — who was the grandest and most brilliant
objective, extroverted, and broadly human composer of the century. They were never to come face to face. Bach had the highest regard for Handel's music, but it is not certain that Handel
knew any compositions (or even the name) of Bach until much
later than 1719. Much ink has been spread about in attempts
to guess what they might have found to say to each other. The
safest guess, in view of the usual private conversations of composers, is that they would have discussed the technicalities of
composition, the ingratitude of princes or other patrons, and the
stupidities of the listening public. That they would have under-

[9] So the story is told. It is more likely that Bach walked from Cöthen,
where he was then living. However, the walk would be about the same
distance: Halle lies midway between Leipzig and Cöthen, a good twenty-
five mile walk from either.

stood or liked each other in any deep sense seems very unlikely. They lived universes apart: Bach was an indwelling and highly concentrated provincial, Handel a sophisticated cosmopolitan.

By November 1719, Handel was again in London. Soon after his return, he began to set Haym's libretto *Radamisto*, the re-telling of a story from Chapter 51 of Book XII of the *Annals* of Tacitus. But he had many duties and tasks, and *Radamisto* was not to be ready for the first night of the Academy season at His Majesty's. Handel had to take a leading part in the multifarious detailed arrangements, social preliminaries, and publicity-making activities that preceded the launching of an opera season in the eighteenth century, as they do today. He may also still have been living at Cannons, and an occasion demanded occasional music to please the man who had recently become Duke of Chandos, and who was not, for reasons of pique on his part or of slight on the part of others, a director of the Royal Academy.

John Gay's *Acis and Galatea*, set as a masque to be sung with scenery and costumes but without action, was performed at Cannons, in 1719 or 1720 before the opening of the Academy. In this masterly summing-up of the sort of pastoral masque that had been popular in Jacobean times, and had risen to great musical splendor in the hands of Purcell, Handel composed one of the most exquisite and nicely proportioned of his early English settings. The poetry of Gay is accomplished and pretty; the music Handel created for it throbs with sunlight, sweet passion, and terror. In later years, it was to be pirated and staged as "an English opera," and Handel himself was to create a third version of the story, combining much of the Italian *Aci, Galatea e Polifemo* of 1708 with the *Acis and Galatea* of 1719–20 and using a largely Italian text. Fortunately, the original English version has been preserved. Unfortunately, it has most often been presented as a cantata: it cries out for the scenery and costumes and prescribed postures that accompanied the Jacobean pastoral, serenata, or masque.

When it became certain that the Haym-Handel *Radamisto*

would not be ready for an early April opening of the Academy season at His Majesty's, the directors decided to present instead an opera by Giovanni Porta, a Venetian choirmaster who was in London as a household musician to the Duke of Wharton. Porta, who was to spend the last years of his life as court conductor at Munich, seems to have been an earnest composer of great energy and small talent. His *Numitore*, on April 2, 1720, made a disappointing opening night for the Royal Academy. After it had been sung five times, *Radamisto* made its bow on Thursday, April 27. It had been announced for the previous night, but had been postponed so that a company of French comedians could give a performance much desired by "several ladies of quality." [10]

The audience at His Majesty's included George I and "his ladies." By these words in her diary, Lady Cowper must have meant Baroness Kielmansegge (the King's half-sister, who was just possibly, as many have assumed, also his mistress) and his openly acknowledged mistress, Ermengarda Melusina von der Schulenburg, who by then had no fewer than three titles in the Irish peerage and three in the English, the most important of them Duchess of Kendal. The constant presence at the King's side of these notably Teutonic ladies contributed considerably to his unpopularity among his new subjects. Also in the audience at His Majesty's that April 27 was George Augustus, Prince of Wales, the future George II. Of the occasion Mainwaring wrote:

If the persons who are now living, and who were present at that performance, may be credited, the applause it received was almost as extravagant as his *Agrippina* had excited; the crowds and tumults of the house at Venice were hardly equal to those at London. In so

10 *Radamisto* indirectly caused Sir Isaac Newton's opinion of opera in general to survive. Meeting the aged scientist at the Ship Tavern, Temple Bar, William Stukeley observed to him that there was to be a rehearsal of *Radamisto* that night. Newton replied that "he never was at more than one opera. The first act he heard with pleasure, the second stretched his patience, at the third he ran away."

splendid and fashionable an assembly of ladies (to the excellence of
their taste we must impute it), there was no shadow of form or ceremony, scarce indeed any appearance of order or regularity, polite-
ness, or decency. Many, who had forced their way into the house
with an impetuosity but ill-suited to their rank and sex, actually
fainted through the heat and closeness of it. Several gentlemen were
turned back, who had offered forty shillings for a seat in the gallery,
after having despaired of getting any in the pit or boxes!

There was no doubt in the minds of the patrons of the Royal
Academy that Handel had supplied them with wonderful fare.
Radamisto was immediately an established success. This success was probably owing in equal parts to Haym's fine libretto,
Handel's splendid music, and the gorgeousness of the stage production. It was not owing to the singers; whose names, except
those of Margherita Durastanti (Radamisto) and Anastasia
Robinson (Zenobia), never figured among those of London's
reigning favorites. Polissena's wonderful aria *"Ombra cara"* obtained suffrage at once. Handel was to tell Sir John Hawkins
that he considered it and *"Cara sposa"* from *Rinaldo* — both
tributes by faithful spouses — the best arias he ever composed.
Of almost equal beauty is the aria with which Zenobia opens
the second act, *"Quando mai spietata sorte."* In *Radamisto*, for
the first time in a Handelian opera, if not in any opera, horns
were included in the orchestra. They add immeasurably to the
desired brilliance of the general effect.

Radamisto ran at His Majesty's until it was replaced on April
29 by Domenico Scarlatti's *Narciso*, conducted by the composer's pupil Thomas Roseingrave. For at least one performance
of *Narciso*, its composer himself may have been in the house, if
he did not conduct: he is said to have been visiting England
at the time. *Narciso*, however, was not popular, and achieved no
more than half a dozen nights. *Radamisto* was then remounted
for one showing, as was Porta's *Numitore*, with which last, on
Saturday, June 25, 1720, the first, hearteningly well attended
season of the Royal Academy of Music closed. There was no

doubt in anyone's mind that *Radamisto* had been the finest entertainment of the London year or that the season had been Handel's.

On December 15 of the same year, Handel published the score (as a collection of the chief numbers was then called) of *Radamisto* "at the warehouses of Richd Meares, at the Golden Viol in St. Paul's Churchyard, and Christopher Smith at ye Hand & Musick-book in Coventry Street." The latter was undoubtedly a shop Handel himself had set up to supply part of the living of the friend he had imported from Anspach. The composer supervised the edition and proofread the pages. Those who subscribed to the edition were presented gratis, early the following year, with eleven additional numbers from the revised version of *Radamisto* that was given at His Majesty's after the arrival from Germany of some of the principal singers Handel had hired there. This shows alterations in the vocal disposition: in the original, for example, the roles of Radamisto and Tiridate are, respectively, for soprano and for tenor, while in the additional songs they are for mezzo-soprano (Senesino) and bass (Boschi).

Radamisto contains, as Handel finally revised it, surprisingly little material borrowed from other works. There are relatively brief quotations from three of his own compositions: the Latin motet *Silete, venti,* the Brockes Passion, and *Rodrigo.* A particularly telling later addition to the score is *"O cedere o perir,"* sung by Polissena, Tiridate, Radamisto, and Zenobia. This is a dramatic quartet of great power, enough in itself to give the lie to those uninformed critics who have accused Handel of composing operas out of nothing but arias and, at the most, duets. In *Radamisto,* too, he makes forceful use of a chorus in a manner removed from the choral masses deployed in his later oratorios only as far as his sense of the styles required by Italian opera and English oratorio made essential.

Radamisto was to be revived often, and not only in London. In 1722, it was produced at Hamburg as *Zenobia,* the name of its heroine. This bilingual performance, in which the arias were left in Italian, the recitatives translated into German, was the opening gun in a campaign, in which Mattheson was involved, to form at Hamburg a company similar to London's Royal Academy of Music.

During the summer of 1720, Handel continued at least some of his duties at Cannons. There, on August 29, was staged a performance of what is likely to have been his *Haman and Mordecai*, a masque to a text Pope had based on Racine's *Esther*, and with music largely adapted from the Brockes Passion. As first presented, it differed little in character from *Acis and Galatea*. But it was to prove of far greater historical importance: as the result of a series of vicissitudes it underwent without his intervention, Handel was at last to remodel it as a full-fledged oratorio, greatly altering its musical texture and renaming it *Esther*. As that revised version of *Haman and Mordecai* preceded *Deborah*, it can justly be called the first of Handel's English oratorios.

The second season of the Royal Academy of Music was to open on November 19, 1720. Before that date, Handel had published the first volume of *Suites de Pièces pour le Clavecin*.[11] He had completed, at Cannons, most of the *Concerti grossi* for flutes, oboes, bassoons, and strings known as his Opus 3.[12] Only one new opera by Handel cheered London in 1720. But as that year drew to a close, he had begun to achieve greatly in all the forms of music at which he equaled or excelled the greatest of his contemporaries: Italian opera, music for the solo harpsichord, orchestral music, and English oratorio. He was thirty-five years old, and he was one of the most famous — as he proved himself one of the two most gifted — composers in the world.

[11] The first volume contains the following suites or lessons: 1. A major, 2. F major, 3. D minor, 4. E minor, 5. E major (of which *The Harmonious Blacksmith* is one movement), 6. F sharp minor, 7. G minor, 8. F minor.
[12] These so-called hautboy or oboe concertos are: 1. B flat major-G minor, 2. B flat major, 3. G major, 4. F major, 5. D minor, 6. D major-minor.

BOOK II

I

I N September 1720, South Sea Company shares nominally
valued at £100 stood at £1000. One month later they
had fallen to £300. This would have created a grave crisis
even if only private persons had been directly involved.
But His Majesty's Government was substantially in partnership
with the Company, and stood to be as shaken as its directors
by a catastrophe like the one threatening.

The national debt of England had increased from slightly
more than £660,000 in 1689 to nearly £50,000,000 in 1714.
Conservative economists were as Jeremiahlike then as they have
continued to be about the vastly larger national debts of modern eras. In 1711, the Earl of Oxford had acted to remedy the
existence of the floating portion of the debt, some £10,000,000
of scattered paper whose holders, had they demanded the payment to which they were legally entitled, could have made public the government's actual, but still secret, bankruptcy. By
allowing the formation of the South Sea Company, and by
granting it a monopoly of trade with the Spanish colonies in
America and with the Pacific islands, the government made its
stock so attractive that holders of government paper were
rendered willing to exchange it for the stock. The directors of
the Company thus took over nearly £10,000,000 of the debt.
They were promised interest of six per cent per annum, as well
as an annual payment of £8,000 for handling the transaction,
the government guaranteeing the payment of the annual interest by setting aside customs duties on tobacco, vinegar, wine,
and other commodities. This was, on paper and in the minds of
its promoters, a simple and wonderful scheme: no run on the
government's cash resources was possible, the Company would

make a profit on the Pacific and Spanish-American trade, and
the holders of the stock would therefore receive dividends. Handel himself owned £500 of stock in the Company (see Appendix A for letters concerning his dividends).

The first trouble into which the scheme ran was Spain's ob-
durate and annoying refusal to allow free trade with her parts
of America. The Spanish government permitted Britons to deal
in African slaves, to send one annual ship of less than five hundred tons, and to establish a few factories. Then, in 1718, war
broke out between Spain and England, and even those piddling
enterprises were cut short. By a good deal of scurrying and
doing things it was not supposed to do, the South Sea Company
kept afloat. Indeed, it burgeoned, and became in effect the Tory
rival to the predominantly Whig Bank of England.

Sir Robert Walpole in 1717 looked about him and discovered
that, with George I apparently enthroned for good, times were
relatively quiet. Private individuals and companies were borrowing money at four per cent while the government was continuing to pay as much as eight per cent on moneys it had
borrowed in less certain times. There was not much that Sir
Robert could do, but he did that little: he persuaded the Bank
of England to lend him £600,000 at the current interest rate
of four per cent. Then he invested that sum in stock paying
more than four per cent, and with the resulting profits began
to reduce the government's outstanding debt. Both the Bank of
England and the South Sea Company, further, agreed to reduce
the interest rate on sums previously lent to the government, and
together made it an additional loan of £5,000,000. With this
new money, Walpole was able to redeem from those holders
who had refused to accept lowered interest such paper as was
not specifically irredeemable. Shortly after these transactions,
he left the ministry.

In 1718, George I himself became Governor of the South Sea
Company.

Charles Spencer, Earl of Sunderland, the new First Lord of

the Treasury, lacked Walpole's grasp of finance. But he amiably attempted to carry Walpole's beginnings to their logical conclusion. His aim was Walpole's: to consolidate the national debt until the government had only one creditor. In 1719, the South Sea Company, hastening along the same line of thought, proposed to assume the liability of the £51,300,000 in paper, redeemable and irredeemable, then outstanding, and to receive in exchange new commercial concessions, including fishery rights. The Company was to pay the government £3,500,000. Instead of paying interest at the old rates, the government was to pay, on bonds it could redeem at will, five per cent until 1727, then four per cent. By this scheme the government would achieve Walpole's and Sunderland's purpose of reducing to one the number of its creditors. Simultaneously, it would lower the interest it must pay by as much as four per cent.

The South Sea Company's purpose in what, to the uninitiated, may look like a fantastically one-sided arrangement was to persuade the holders of government annuities to exchange them for South Sea Stock at a high premium. Its directors also estimated that, when all possible repayments had been made, it would still be receiving something like £1,500,000 per annum from the government. The profits of their Company — its prestige enormously enhanced by its close ties to the government — would, they felt certain, permit them to create a sinking fund out of which the remainder of the national debt could be paid off.

On January 22, 1720, a motion to put this scheme into effect was made in Commons. Several members immediately insisted that other companies be allowed to tender offers. John Aislabie, Chancellor of the Exchequer, protested that such a procedure would smack of auctioning off the nation, but a motion to entertain other offers was passed. The Bank of England bid £5,000,-000. The South Sea Company retorted with a winning bid of £7,567,000. The scheme was written into a bill passed in April. As W. E. H. Lecky wrote:

The South Sea project was too complicated to be generally understood. There was no efficient organ of financial criticism. The Government warmly supported the scheme. The large sum offered by
the company, which made success impossible, stimulated the imagi-
nations of the people, who fancied that a privilege so dearly purchased must be of inestimable value, and the complication of cre-
dulity and dishonesty, of ignorance and avarice, threw England into
what it is scarcely an exaggeration to term a positive frenzy.

The South Sea Company set about inducing holders of government annuities and bonds to exchange them for Company
shares. Another issue of shares was put on sale in order to obtain
cash with which to purchase annuities from those who would
not accept stock in exchange and also to pay the government its
£7,567,000. All the wiles of publicity and advertising then
known were lavished on the public of England in an effort to
build up a golden and roseate picture of the dividends soon to
be paid on South Sea Company shares. Holders of government
securities rushed to turn them in for stock; millions of pounds'
worth of stock were purchased for cash in a few weeks. The
shares, which had stood at £128½ at the beginning of 1720,
went to £330 in March. During the succeeding month, the directors were able to sell 2,250,000 shares at £300 each. May,
June, and July saw the market value per share at, respectively,
£550, £890, and £1000. Change Alley, where the dealers
kept offices, was inundated with money of which few had suspected the existence, money that materialized from hidden savings to be doubled, tripled, and quadrupled by magic (so it
seemed) in one day or one week. Men became dizzyingly rich.
Sir Robert Walpole, who had opposed the scheme with wisdom
and force, reaped huge profits by selling his stock at £1000 per
share.

As naturally as the success of an Italian opera by Handel
produced Italian operas by others, the South Sea Company's
fireworks produced pyrotechnic displays by other companies.
Of the more than one hundred such enterprises quickly
launched, one was for the cultivation of silkworms on mulberry

trees to be planted in Chelsea Park, one was for extracting silver from lead (then an impossibility), another for rendering salt water fresh, another for trading in human hair. The Prince of Wales became governor of a copper company, withdrawing from it with a profit of about £40,000 only after it was threatened with being declared illegal. One company was floated on an announcement that it was for "an undertaking of great advantage, but nobody to know what it is." This mystery enterprise was to have five thousand capital shares valued at £100 each. On the day its subscription lists were opened, its promoter took in eleven hundred deposits of £2 each and vanished with the £2200.

The South Sea Company's gigantic plan would have failed, if for no other reason, because the government's part of the bargain was far too favorable. However, its directors hastened the crash by taking out writs of *scire facias* against other companies. They succeeded in claiming as a monopoly the rich fields of speculation. They speeded the ruin of many who had invested in smaller companies, thus raising such fumes of distrust that their own shareholders began frantically to sell. So it came about that South Sea stock, standing at £1000 per share in September, fell to £300 in October, and to £135 in November. Shares in the Bank of England were affected, and fell in four months from £263 to £145. The result was a major panic that brought obloquy on the Company's directors, His Majesty's ministers, and the blameless George I himself. The throne was for a time endangered. The King wisely summoned Walpole, who quickly gathered into his hands so much power that he was able to stay at the helm for twenty-one years, the first man who may rightly be called Prime Minister of Great Britain.

Walpole's first proposal was that the Bank of England and the East India Company each take over £9,000,000 of South Sea Company stock. Parliament agreed to this, but developments had become too catastrophically swift to allow face-saving measures to succeed. In January 1721, Parliament passed a bill requiring the directors of the Company to declare the value of their private estates. In February, the secret committee of the Commons that had been examining the Company's affairs for two months reported. It had uncovered vast, proliferating corruption. The Company's books were composed in part of pure fiction. The support of some of His Majesty's important ministers had been purchased with gifts of stock on which they had realized huge profits. Those openly accused included Charles Stanhope, a treasury commissioner; the Earl of Sunderland; the James Craggses, father and son, respectively Postmaster General and Secretary of State, and the Chancellor of the Exchequer, John Aislabie. Aislabie was found guilty of "the most notorious, dangerous and infamous corruption," and was first denied his seat in Parliament and then imprisoned. The Craggses were both dead by March. Walpole intervened to help Stanhope and Sunderland, and was able to have them acquitted, Stanhope by the uncomfortable margin of three votes. The directors' estates, valued at £2,104,123, were confiscated. For their personal maintenance they were given back £354,600; the other £1,749,523 was used to relieve those who had suffered at their hands.

Parliament, under Walpole's able direction, began to clear away the wreckage. Some £11,000,000 that the directors of the South Sea Company had lent on the security of their own shares was remitted on payment of ten per cent (later five per cent) of the sums borrowed. The £7,567,000 the Company had promised to pay the government was canceled outright. Private individuals who had exchanged government bonds and annuities for South Sea stock were at last protected to the extent of about one half of what they had lost. For the time being, things became more quiet. A nation's dreams of wealth out of financial jugglery had been banished temporarily. By 1722, the throne of George I was safe and Sir Robert Walpole was, in effect, the ruler of England.[1]

[1] The South Sea Company, capitalized at almost £40,000,000, was permitted to continue in existence. Some of the schemes that it had advertised were put into effect. In 1750, for relinquishing certain monopolies granted it by the Spanish government, it received £100,000. As late as 1807 it

This blowing and bursting of the South Sea Bubble formed the noisy, nervous background for the second and third seasons of the Royal Academy of Music, itself a relatively harmless example of the mania for shareholding companies. Giovanni Battista Bononcini had arrived in London in the spring of 1720, and was being patronized lavishly by the Earl of Burlington and the family of the paralyzed, dying Duke of Marlborough. His attractive cello-playing was appreciated, but he did not immediately compose a new opera for the Academy, of which, with Handel and Ariosti, he was musical director. Not until 1720 was he ready with his *Astarto*, the text of which Paolo Rolli had adapted from one set by Tommaso Albinoni in Italy in 1708. *Astarto* ushered in the Academy's second season at His Majesty's on November 19, 1720. Senesino, with the single, later exception of Farinelli the most adored of *castrati*, made his London debut in it in a cast that also included Margherita Durastanti, Boschi, Berenstadt, Berselli, and Signora Salvai. It soon ran up ten performances, to which twice as many more were to be added in later seasons.

Astarto permitted the inception of the wholly ridiculous "war" between Handel and Bononcini, a war staged not by the principals themselves, but by members of their audiences, a war that involved politics, the private affairs of the Royal Family, fashion, literature, and the very foundations of the Royal Academy. Handel was favored by the Whigs, Bononcini by the Tories. Some latterday Handelians have enjoyed blasting Bononcini as a trifler, a self-inflated popinjay, the "ninny" of John Byrom's famous jingle.[2] And in truth the Italian seems to

---

still held other monopolies. Finally, in 1853, all existing South Sea stocks were either redeemed or converted into government securities.

[2] Some say, compar'd to Bononcini,
That Mynheer Handel's but a Ninny;
Others aver that he to Handel
Is scarcely fit to hold a Candle.
Strange all this difference should be
'Twixt Tweedle-dum and Tweedle-dee!

Years later, Charles Lamb was to echo Byrom:

have been crushingly vain, lazy, and foolish. But he was a composer of unusual talent, if not of genius, and a graceful melodist of lasting distinction. It was his serious misfortune that idle onlookers chose to pit him against Handel in much the manner that the talented Piccinni was to be set up as a straw man against Gluck in an even sillier and more famous "war." Bononcini was not "defeated" by Handel: when, years later, he abandoned the struggle to function as he wished in England, it was in part because of a plagiarism scandal in which laziness had involved him and partly because London's taste for Italian opera was swiftly diminishing, as Handel also discovered.

No Handel opera was heard at His Majesty's during the Royal Academy's second season until December 28, 1720, when *Radamisto* was revived, with Senesino and Durastanti in the roles Handel had rewritten for them. This ran intermittently until February 1, 1721, when *Arsace*, an opera mostly by Giuseppe Maria Orlandini took its place. Meanwhile, Paolo Rolli was preparing the text of a novelty that was, by accident or by design, to exacerbate the Handel-Bononcini factional strife. This libretto, called *Muzio Scævola*, was in three acts, each to be composed by a different composer, each to be complete with overture and terminal "chorus" as though a complete opera in itself. Bononcini and Handel were persuaded to set the second and third acts respectively; the first was set either by Attilio Ariosti or by Filippo Amadei (known as Mattei or "Signor Pippo"), a cellist in the orchestra at His Majesty's.[3]

Handel completed his act of *Muzio Scævola* on March 23, 1721. The hybrid work reached the stage of His Majesty's on April 15, the performance being interrupted at one point by an

Some cry up Haydn, some Mozart,
Just as the whim bites. For my part,
I do not care a farthing candle
For either of them, nor for Handel.

[3] Mainwaring, Burney, Hawkins, and Rockstro believed it to be by Ariosti. Mattheson and Chrysander, followed by Leichtentritt, Streatfeild, Flower, and most other modern writers, have agreed to attribute it to Mattei.

announcement of the birth of a third son to the Prince of Wales.[4]
The cast included the brightest names in the Academy's roster.
But *Muzio Scævola* did not live up to the excited anticipation
it had been used to arouse. It was succeeded on May 20 by
Ariosti's *Ciro*, with the eighth singing of which, on July 5, the
second season of the Academy closed.

Through musical, social, and court circles, argument blazed
over the comparative merits of Handel and Bononcini, of the
second and third acts of *Muzio Scævola*. Men and women who
disliked the German court, who hated George I, his women, and
all his entourage, began to include Handel in their dislike, and
to aggrandize Bononcini (along with the Prince of Wales) as
a stick with which to beat composer, monarch, mistresses, and
court. Supporters of the King tended to favor the German composer above the Italian. For a time Bononcini seemed to be
triumphing: he had most of the sharpest pamphleteers and wits
on his side, and his airy, tuneful fabrications were of more immediate appeal than the comparatively serious structures of
Handel, particularly during the worst of the South Sea panic.

Eventual victory, of course — if such it can be called — was
to be Handel's. He had now decided that London was his permanent home. In 1723 he purchased a house at 57 (later 25)
Brook Street, which was to be his residence until his death in
1759. There he was to compose not only the finest of his Italian
operas, but all of his great oratorios.

In 1721, Handel made a curious misstep, the sort of error
likely to be made by a composer who has not yet found the
musical form or manner that will release the best of his energies.
He composed an opera that can only be called an imitation of
Bononcini. It had a stilted and unhelpful text by Rolli called
Floridante. To this Handel applied thin and simple orchestration and charming, trivial songs of balladlike cast that might

---

[4] Someone pointed out to Geminiani that in Handel's overture to the third
act of *Muzio Scævola* — at a point in the answer to fugal subject — a
semitone was used in contravention of academic musical laws. "*E vero,*"
Geminiani replied, "*ma quel semitono vale un mondo.*" ("That is true, but
that semitone is worth a world.")

have come whole out of an opera by Bononcini at his best. It did not open the Academy's third season, which began on November 1, 1721, with *Arsace* and continued for almost seven weeks with Orlandini's opera, Handel's *Radamisto*, and Bononcini's *Astarto*. But it was the season's first novelty.[5] Bononcini's supporters cared for it only less than those who admired Handel. Although it was sung fifteen times, the anti-Handelians began to chirrup brightly. They were soon to have sound reasons for loud crowing.

Crispo, a delicious opera by Bononcini, was presented at His Majesty's in January 1722. At once the Academy's financial skies began to lighten. During the season of 1721–2, in fact, instead of assessing the stockholders five per cent several times (as had been done during the preceding seasons), the directors were able to pay them a dividend of seven per cent. So another Bononcini opera was put on to succeed *Crispo*. And this was *Griselda*, the Italian's masterpiece, rich in delightful melodies that could be hummed and sung, transcribed and danced to. The third season of the Academy, which closed on June 16, 1722, was clearly Bononcini's. Handel's enemies began to believe and say, his friends to fear, that Bononcini had ousted the German from the Academy and the affections of London. But Bononcini was fifty and at the summit of his powers; Handel was but thirty-seven, and still on a steep upward slope.

On June 16, 1722, the great Duke of Marlborough died at the age of seventy-two. There was a splendid funeral in Westminster Abbey. The funeral anthem was composed especially, not by Handel, but by Bononcini. The Duke left no sons: his daughter Henrietta, already Countess of Godolphin by marriage, succeeded to his title, becoming Duchess of Marlborough. She was a constant partisan of Bononcini, and settled an annuity of £500 on him, partly in the hope of weaning him altogether away from the Royal Academy, which she detested. This pre-

[5] When *Floridante* was first presented on December 9, 1721, the cast included Senesino, Anastasia Robinson (by this time changed by illness from soprano to contralto), Baldassarri, Signora Salvai, and Boschi.

ferment for Bononcini did not pass unnoticed by the public or, certainly, by Handel.

During the summer of 1722, Handel gave the earliest important demonstration of those capabilities in business which were at last to make him the first great operatic impresario. He understood that something more than a fine new opera was needed to re-establish his name with the patrons of His Majesty's. He could not depend even on the spectacular popularity of Senesino. He must introduce a new and unmistakable star, a star surrounded in advance by glamour and the clangor of elaborate publicity. He had heard good reports of a Parmesan soprano named Francesca Cuzzoni. She had, at the age of nineteen, made a brilliant Venetian debut in 1719, since when she had been singing to notable acclaim throughout Italy. So Handel dispatched Sandoni, a cembalist from the opera orchestra, to fetch her from Italy, authorizing him to guarantee her £2,000 a year if necessary. It was a daring, perhaps a desperate, gamble.

Probably recognizing the weakness of Paolo Rolli's librettos for *Muzio Scævola* and *Floridante*, Handel tried the Academy's other official poet, his old friend Haym, for his next text. That author of *Teseo* and *Radamisto* handed him a superior libretto called *Ottone*. Handel set it with care and with fountaining melodic, harmonic, and dramatic creativeness. He would open the Academy's fourth season with a splendid production of *Ottone* and thus re-establish his position. That was his plan. But Cuzzoni did not arrive on time. So the season opened on October 27, 1722, with a revival from an earlier season. November and most of December passed. And then Cuzzoni arrived. She was by this time Signora Sandoni, having married Handel's emissary before — or while — accompanying him to London. There is a persistent story, not unbelievable in view of what is known of her character, that she later tired of her humble husband and poisoned him in Venice. Sandoni, at any rate, disappeared from view, and his widow was banished from Venice forever.

When Handel first looked upon Francesca Cuzzoni, he must have felt his heart sink. He had already heard that the soprano

1 1 3

was spoiled, headstrong, and silly. Now he saw that she was inordinately ugly as well. "She was short," Horace Walpole later wrote of her, "and squat, with a cross face, but fine complexion; was not a good actress; dressed ill, and was silly and fantastical." She did not appear a *prima donna* likely to capture the fickle hearts of the gentlemen out front at His Majesty's. But Handel had staked heavily on her, and he intended to win. He addressed himself immediately to the task of subjecting her to his will, of making her perform his music as he wished.

"Oh, Madame," he is reported to have said to her in French, "I well know that you are a veritable female devil, but I myself, I shall have you know, am Beelzebub, chief of the devils." Then he told her to sing *"Falsa immagine,"* the luscious aria he had designed especially for her first appearance on the stage in *Ottone*. Cuzzoni sang it, but not as Handel had heard it in his imagination. So he told her how to sing it, and she refused. Handel was a big man, and Cuzzoni, though plump, was small. So he seized her around the waist and told her peremptorily that she would sing *"Falsa immagine"* exactly as he wished it sung, or he would drop her out of the window, toward which he began to move her. Cowed, if not terrified, Cuzzoni agreed. And then Handel must have felt true delight, for the reports of Cuzzoni's voice had not been exaggerated: it was one of the most beautiful he ever heard.

At last *Ottone* was scheduled for January 12, 1723. Handel was not going to stint on any detail: the cast was to have not only Cuzzoni, but Durastanti and Anastasia Robinson, as well as Senesino, Berenstadt, and Boschi. The evening came; Cuzzoni triumphed. *Ottone* triumphed; Handel the impresario triumphed with Handel the composer. Forgetting Bononcini, forgetting the others in the cast, the audience acclaimed and applauded "La Cuzzona." One fellow in the gallery is said to have interrupted one of her arias by calling out: "Damme, she has a nest of nightingales in her belly!" So great was the furor the news of her singing spread about London that places at the second night of *Ottone* (it ran for eleven consecutive opera nights in January and February) sold for as much as £5/5. Handel's gamble had swept the board.

Without Cuzzoni *Ottone* would have won less success. But it is certain that Handel, by the rich, unfailing beauty of the music in the score, had helped Cuzzoni as much as she him. Dr. Charles Burney thought *Ottone* the finest of Handel's operas, remarking that it would be difficult to point in it to one number, vocal or instrumental, that had not been a public favorite. All that Handel had failed to do in *Ottone* was to compose the sort of opera only he could compose: it is still, so to speak, a Bononcinian opera, light despite the presence of the profoundly moving *"Vieni, o figlio,"* the melancholy *"Affanni del pensier,"* [6] and one great dramatic *scena, "Tanti affanni." Ottone* brims with charming melody, has furthermore a myriad of swift touches of genius in orchestration, rhythm, and proportion. But whereas Handel's finest operas are both better than and different in kind from all other Italian operas of their time, *Ottone* is not. Did it come to us signed by Bononcini, we should merely — with small discomforts over its style — call it, rather than *Griselda,* his masterpiece.

About the time of Cuzzoni's first successes in London, John Gay said, in a letter to Swift:

As for the reigning amusement of the town, it is intirely music; real fiddles, bass viols and hautboys; not poetical harps, lyres and reeds. There's nobody allowed to say *I sing,* but an eunuch, or an Italian woman. Every body is grown now as great a judge of music, as they were, in your time of poetry; and folks, that could not distinguish one tune from another, now daily dispute about the different stiles of Handel, Bononcini and Attilio. . . . In London and Westminster, in all polite conversation, Senesino is daily voted to be the greatest man that ever lived.

[6] Mainwaring quotes "an eminent master . . . not on good terms with Handel" as saying of *"Affanni del pensier":* "That great bear was certainly inspired when he wrote that song." Many have guessed the "eminent master" to be Dr. Pepusch.

The shareholders in the Royal Academy of Music, rubbing their palms together in glee over Cuzzoni and the success of Handel's *Ottone*, must have thought that some of the wealth denied to the South Sea Company was to be theirs. On February 19, 1723, Oriosti's *Cajo Marzio Coriolano* (text by Haym), created another wild scene of public approval. And when, on March 26, Cuzzoni sang in her own benefit performance of *Ottone*, numerous gentlemen and ladies were willing to pay £50 — one fourth the price of a share in the Academy — for a seat. Four days after that, Bononcini's *Erminia* proved, if not equal to *Griselda* or Handel's *Ottone*, not a failure either. And Handel himself, on the crest of reborn powers, was working on still another new opera for the close of the season. It was set to another Haym text, *Flavio*. Furthermore, it was to be sung by Cuzzoni, Durastanti, Anastasia Robinson, Senesino, Boschi, Berenstadt, and a young Englishman named Gordon.

Young Gordon was allotted a single aria in *Flavio*, "*Fato tiranno.*" Rehearsing it one day with Handel at the harpsichord, Gordon complained that the accompaniment was being played wrong. Handel flew into one of his notable rages, which always sped him into invective in a mixture of German and English, with occasional French and Italian phrases tossed in. The disagreement surged up into a real quarrel. Gordon, beside himself with anger, shouted that if Handel persisted in playing the accompaniment that way he would jump up and down on the harpsichord, reducing it to bits. "Oh," Handel said, quieting down, "let me know when you will do that, and I will advertise it; for I am sure more people will come to see you jump than to hear you sing."

Flavio was disclosed at His Majesty's on May 14. It appears not to have matched *Ottone* in popularity. Still Bononcinian in character, it is not so seductive as its predecessor, though it has half a dozen beautiful arias, including "*Amor, nel mio penar*" and "*Parto si, ma non so poi.*" The most interesting novelty of the score is the finale, "*Doni pace ad ogni core,*" which, being a true quintet, may have adumbrated the act finales of Mozart, and was a new conception for Handel and his contemporaries. *Flavio* won eight performances before the fourth season of the Academy ended with it on June 15, 1723.[7]

[7] His Majesty's housed entertainments other than opera during this era. This explains why, for example, eight "consecutive" singings of an opera occurred over an entire month. These other entertainments were largely so-called masquerades run by Heidegger. They were occasions for somewhat unbuttoned revelry that often descended from the merely ribald through the obscene and rowdy to the violent. Sermons were preached against them, but they continued to prosper and to make Heidegger a handsome living.

II

INTERNATIONAL tours by an opera company were not unknown in the first quarter of the eighteenth century. The Royal Academy of Music looked like a success after four seasons, during at least one of which its directors had been able to pay a dividened to its shareholders. So Philippe II, Duc d'Orléans, invited the company to visit Paris. Orléans had only recently been forced to abandon absolute power over France, the majority of Louis XV having necessitated his relinquishing the regency. At the age of forty-eight, he needed ways to expend energy. Unfortunately, the proposed season of twelve performances to begin in July seems not to have materialized, though it was announced by at least two London weeklies and the *Mercure de France.* The Haymarket Theatre was redecorated, however, partly by use of a subsidy from the King. Heidegger wanted brighter surroundings for his "masquerades."

The fifth season of the Royal Academy began on November 27, 1723, with Bononcini's *Farnace,* found so little to the public's liking that after four performances it was replaced by a revival of Handel's *Ottone.* On the fourteenth day of the new year, after a few more attempts to establish *Farnace* had failed, a novelty was brought forth. This was Ariosti's *Vespasiano,* set to a Haym text. With Senesino and Anastasia Robinson, it achieved a run of nine successive nights. Burney, who thought that *Vespasiano* had "considerable merit," inserted into his *History* the notes Senesino sang to its aria "*Ah traditore spirar vorrei*" as "an exhibition of all the furbelows, flounces, and vocal fopperies of the times":

CARICATURE OF A SCENE FROM HANDEL'S *GIULIO CESARE*

[*with Senesino, Cuzzoni, and Berenstadt*]

CUZZONI AND FAUSTINA

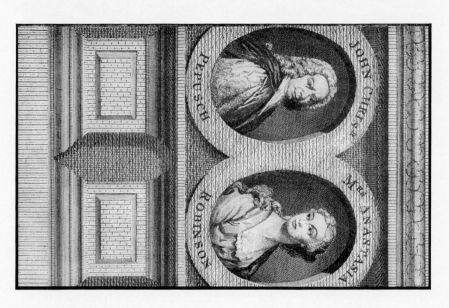

DR. PEPUSCH
AND ANASTASIA ROBINSON

Across the centuries this brings to us some conception of the supernal agility of one of the greatest among *castrati*. But *Vespasiano* did not replenish the Academy's coffers, ebbing from too many *Farnace*s and no novelty. A call of five per cent on the shareholders was again necessary. Indeed, the Academy's affairs were for a time at such a low point that doubt of its continuance, and even of the wisdom of offering Italian opera to London at all, seems to have been entertained.

Handel could save the day. To a better than average Haym text, he hurriedly composed *Giulio Cesare,* having it ready for a *première* by February 20,[1] 1724. It had a six-star cast: Cuzzoni, Durastanti, Anastasia Robinson, Senesino, Berenstadt, and Boschi. It conquered at once, reaching fourteen representations by April 11. It was to be revived often subsequently, even as late as 1787, when, according to Victor Schoelcher, "it was produced for the purpose of attracting to the theater poor George the Third, who was passionately fond of Handel's music." Even in a truncated modern concert version [2] with the roles of Tolomeo and Curio omitted, it proved a moving, incessantly interesting opera. Its chief glories are its wonderfully modeled accompanied recitatives — Cesare's *"Alma del gran Pompeo"* and *"Dall' ondoso periglio"* (in which the recitative intermittently broadens out into arioso) and Cleopatra's *"Voi, che mie fide ancelle"* —

[1] Edward J. Dent, for a reason I cannot determine, gives this date as February 14.
[2] Given at Town Hall, New York, on April 12, 1944, under the direction of Ernst Gebert.

and its intensely expressive instrumentation. Its use of four
horns, then unusual if not unique, is fully justified by the
abounding richness of the orchestral sound, integrated with the
entire vocal and dramatic texture. Had we but the singers today
(who could adequately sing *Cesare* in its original keys?), there
is no reason to foresee that a scrupulous revival of *Giulio Cesare*
would not succeed with the true musical public and at the same
time please general opera-going audiences at least as much as
Gluck's *Orfeo ed Euridice*.

After the April 11 performance of *Giulio Cesare*, Bononcini's
Calfurnia warranted a run of eleven nights, interrupted midway
by five performances of *Aquilio Consolo*, a *pasticcio* perhaps by
Ariosti. The closing night of the season, the June 13 presentation of *Aquilio*, marked Anastasia Robinson's last appearance
on the stage. Never a better than average singer, this English
girl had been completely overshadowed by Cuzzoni. In 1722,
also, her first husband having conveniently died, Anastasia had
secretly married her longtime admirer, Charles Mordaunt, Earl
of Peterborough and Monmouth, then about sixty-five. And
Senesino had publicly insulted her, snarling a coarse epithet.
This contretemps, riotously enjoyed by the public, had almost
caused the Earl, her husband, to give away the secret of their
marriage.

Infuriated by Senesino's action, Peterborough had rushed out
upon the stage, seized the terrified Senesino, and flogged him
with a cane in full view of a large number of onlookers.[3] Cuzzoni, Senesino, and a rich and titled husband combined, perhaps, to induce Anastasia to abandon the stage. She retired to

[3] Senesino was likewise made to appear ridiculous on another occasion.
Reminiscing in the *London Magazine* of February 1733, an anonymous
writer said: "When I was last at the opera of *Julius Caesar*, from which I
took the hint of writing this paper, a piece of the machinery tumbled
down from the roof of the theater upon the stage, just as Senesino had
chanted forth these words, 'Cesare no seppe mai, che sia timore' ['Caesar
does not know what fear is']. The poor hero was so frightened that he
trembled, lost his voice, and fell crying. Every tyrant or tyrannical minister
is just such a Caesar as Senesino."

live with her sisters in a cottage at Parson's Green, where she was generally regarded as Peterborough's mistress. However, when the Earl was nearing seventy-seven, he suddenly called his friends and relations together, announced that he and Anastasia had just been married for the second time, and publicly acknowledged her as Countess of Peterborough and Monmouth. A few months later, having taken her on a journey to Portugal, this once redoubtable quarreler (who nearly fifty years before had invited William of Orange to invade England) died. That was 1735: Anastasia survived him by twenty years, and then herself died, all but forgotten.

One of the few documented public appearances of Handel during this period of the Royal Academy's most intense activity occurred on August 24, 1724. On that day, seated at the recently enlarged organ of St. Paul's Cathedral, the only one in England equipped with pedals, he gave a concert for two daughters of the Prince of Wales, his pupils the Princesses Caroline and Anne. That would have been a recital to hear: he was the most accomplished organist in England, if indeed he had a superior in all of Europe. It is idle to speculate on what this enormously energetic man, who could compose an opera in a fortnight or twenty days, did to occupy his time during these seasons and interims of the Academy. He was no longer at Cannons, for he now lived in Brook Street. It has been suggested that he continued nonetheless to direct private music for the Duke of Chandos, as well as for his earlier patron, the Earl of Burlington, and for the Duke of Rutland. He did conduct some semi-amateur musicales in the so-called Queen's [Royal] Library in the Green Park, miscellaneous concerts in which members of the royal family took whatever parts their capabilities permitted, after the manner of Louis XIV and his gentlemen and ladies amusing themselves with Lully.

For some years more, Handel's prime energies were to be spent on the composition and staging of operas. After the fifth season of the Royal Academy, Bononcini was not re-engaged as a musical director, and the entire responsibility for the operas was divided between Handel and Ariosti. Handel's manner of shouldering his portion was to compose to a good text, in twenty days, the first opera of the sixth season, *Tamerlano*. There were new second principals in the company, also, and the cast that sang this new work at His Majesty's that October 31 of 1724 showed only Cuzzoni, Senesino, and Boschi of the familiar names. Replacing Anastasia Robinson was one Anna Dotti, while a tenor known as Borosini [4] made his London debut and the title role was sung by Andrea Pacini, an alto *castrato*.

One *Tamerlano* aria — a pastoral, *"Par che mi nasca"* — that was assigned to Anna Dotti is interesting because of a variant in its accompaniment. Although Handel's autograph score called for two cornets, one of the copies made for him by John Christopher Smith reads "clar. et clarin. 1° et 2°," obviously referring to clarinets, their only appearance in a Handel score. As this instrument had been altered from the ancient chalumeau by Johann Christoph Denner of Nuremberg some time between 1690 and 1700, this was one of its first uses in an operatic score (its first established appearance in any score — a Mass by J. A. J. Faber — dating from 1720).

So excellent a judge of musical effectiveness as W. S. Rockstro wrote early in the 1880's of the closing scene of *Tamerlano*, in which Tamerlano is moved to pity by the sight of Bajazete's daughter Asteria as she is caring for her father, who has just poisoned himself: "The tragic force of this powerful situation is irresistible. Its chief strength lies in the skill with which the Composer leads up to the touching climax: and so artistically is this accomplished, that it would be difficult to find a similar catastrophe more effectively treated, in any period of the history of Art." *Tamerlano*, nevertheless, was only a middling success, adding up nine performances through November. During that same month (November 17, 1724), the *Daily Courant* [5] ran

---

[4] The ribald comment of *Mist's Weekly Journal* on the arrival of this tenor was: "It is commonly reported this gentleman was never cut out for a singer."

[5] This, England's first daily newspaper, had been founded in 1702. By 1724, it had three daily and five weekly competitors.

three public notices to directors of the Royal Academy of Music. One informed them that, for the twelfth time, they were being called upon to pay a five per cent call on their shares. Another told them that a "general court" of existing directors would meet on Wednesday, December 2, for the purpose of choosing a new deputy governor and directors. The third reminded them that no member of the corporation would be allowed to vote in the selection of the new deputy governor if he had not paid all of the calls to which he had been liable.

After the eight November performances of *Tamerlano*, December was ushered in at His Majesty's with Ariosti's *Artaserse*, composed to a libretto by Apostolo Zeno of Venice and Vienna, a small fact that Haym failed to note, allowing the text to be printed as his own. Those who have examined Ariosti's *Artaserse* score with care have called it mediocre, but its run equaled that of *Tamerlano*. It, in turn, was succeeded by another run of *Giulio Cesare* during January and the first part of February. But on January 20, 1725, Handel had inscribed *"Fine dell' opera"* on still another new opera, one on which he set great store as a means of refurbishing the dimmed glory of the Academy. This was *Rodelinda*. Writing years later of its long-famous overture, Dr. Burney spoke of the minuet with which it closes, "which," he declared, "required no great science of sentiment to write, perform or hear." *Rodelinda* is, nonetheless, one of Handel's half-dozen finest operatic scores. In the hands of the cast that had sung *Tamerlano*, it opened on February 13 and ran for fourteen nights. Because of the presence of Borosini, Handel again ran counter to custom and public taste, assigning an important role to the tenor.

The sensation of *Rodelinda* was not Bertarido's magnificent accompanied recitative *"Pompe vane di morte"* or that character's almost equally expressive *"Dove sei,"* nor even Grimoaldo's *"Fatto inferno,"* which Streatfeild justly described as having "more than a suggestion of *Fidelio*," but one of Cuzzoni's costumes. She came forth in a brown silk dress trimmed with silver and cut to the very verge of indecency, "with the vulgarity and indecorum of which," Burney puffed, "all the old ladies were much scandalised," adding that "the young adopted it as a fashion, so universally, that it seemed a national uniform for youth and beauty." There was no doubt that *Rodelinda* was a smashing success, less doubt that Cuzzoni's brown and silver dress had helped to make it one. John Byrom, in his *Letter to R. L., Esq.*, indicated the opera's hold on the public:

> Dear Peter, if thou canst descend
> From *Rodelind* to hear a friend,
> And if those ravished ears of thine
> Can quit the shrill celestial whine
> Of gentle eunuchs, and sustain
> Thy native English without pain,
> I would, if 'tain't too great a burden
> Thy ravished ear intrude a word in.

Despite the impressive success of *Rodelinda* — which, to be sure, was followed in April and the first part of May by less well-patronized mountings of Ariosti's *Dario* and a tampered-with version of Leonardo Vinci's *Elpidia* — the Royal Academy still was not in the black when its sixth season ended on June 19. During 1725, there were two calls of five per cent on the stock-holding subscribers. One way to improve the appearance of the treasury was by retrenching. Bononcini had been dropped from the payroll; now Ariosti too was dropped. Another way was the one more familiarly tried in the later annals of opera: it was that of attempting to make a grand, resounding splurge. For some years, word had been drifting to London of the surpassing excellence of an Italian mezzo-soprano called Faustina Bordoni. Some attempts to import her had already, in fact, been made. Now the directors decided to bring her to the Royal Academy even though she demanded £2500 per year (Cuzzoni still received a paltry £2000!). Further, they would dare forked female lightning by commissioning Handel to prepare an opera with roles of equal importance for Cuzzoni and Faustina. If that did not start a war of wits and gentlemen to outshine the Handel-

Bononcini struggle, set the pamphleteers to working, and thus
fill His Majesty's, nothing would.

It was during 1725 that John Christopher Smith II, the thir-
teen-year-old son of Handel's friend and treasurer, had begun
to study music with Handel. The boy, maturing as something
of a composer himself, was to be a chief physical support and
aid of Handel's old age, to act as Handel's eyes and hands when
his own failed. The Smiths, father and son, seem to have lived
with Handel in Brook Street, and to have been recognized as full
members of his small household. The members of that menage
were unquestionably more immediately useful to Handel than
the ill-assorted crew in Gough Square, Fleet Street, was to be
to Samuel Johnson a few years later.

The sixth season of the Royal Academy of Music at His Majesty's, opening on November 30, 1725, had consisted of five
performances of a revival of Vinci's *Elpidia*, eight of Handel's
Rodelinda, six of a *pasticcio* called *Elisa*, and seven of Handel's
Ottone when, on February 28, 1726, the directors of the Academy announced another call of five per cent on the shareholders. This was payable by March 4. Eight days later, Handel's
Scipione, which he had finished on March 2, was offered at His
Majesty's.[6] It had a libretto adapted from a tried one by Apostolo Zeno. Between March 12 and April 30, during which period no other opera or *pasticcio* was sung, *Scipione* achieved
thirteen representations. The march played as the curtain was
raised became an enduring favorite with military bands. It may
have been composed earlier than the opera itself as a march for
the Grenadier Guards: certainly they adopted it as an official
march almost at once. It was also to be snapped up for use in
Polly,[7] sequel to *The Beggar's Opera*, where it was fitted to
words beginning "Brave boys, prepare."

[6] Its cast included such established favorites as Cuzzoni, Senesino, and
Boschi, as well as three newcomers, Antinori, Baldi, and Constantini, the
last a contralto.
[7] In which Handel's store was also raided for "Abroad after misses" and
"Cheer up, my lads," both based on minuets in the *Water Musick*.

Scipione was not the opera to brighten the Royal Academy's fading chances of permanence, particularly now that the King no longer showed much interest in the company's fortunes. But temporary salvation was at hand in the extraordinarily charming person of Faustina Bordoni, who arrived trailing the glamorous aura of her legendary successes in Venice (where she had been nicknamed *"La nuova Sirena"*) and, especially, Vienna. She was no mere singer, no better-looking counterpart of Francesca Cuzzoni, but a woman of commanding intelligence, proverbially sweet disposition, and compelling character. Born in 1693, she was to marry the eminent composer Johann Adolf Hasse in 1729 and to live with him, through wide vicissitudes of fortune and grief, for fifty-one years of happily shared life. Her contemporaries on the stage are now mostly the thinnest shadows, but something in the way that this gracious lady impressed the diarists and other writers of her day lent them the ability to touch their pictures of her with permanent life. It is a fact of which there can be no doubt: she was not adored only for the unquestioned perfection of her vocal art — she was loved for her self. Arriving for her Royal Academy engagement in 1726, Faustina was to make Cuzzoni seem the merest sweet-warbling viper, and to dazzle London for two brief seasons before leaving England forever.

So Handel's *Alessandro*, his twentieth opera (counting *Florindo* and *Daphne* as one), with a libretto by Paolo Rolli, opened on May 5, 1726, and ran until the season closed on June 7.[8] Rolli and Handel had balanced the roles sung by Cuzzoni and Faustina with minute care: each had the same number of solos, each had a duet with Senesino,[9] and they had an evenly bal-

---

[8] It would have been sung also on June 11 except that Senesino was unable, because of illness, to appear. Ticket money for that announced performance was refunded a few days later.

[9] A letter in *The World* for February 8, 1753 told that Senesino, leading his soldiers to the attack on Ossidraca in this opera, excitedly stuck his sword into one of the pasteboard stones of the town wall. Unable to pull the sword out, he was forced to enter the breached wall bearing the "stone" aloft on its point. The reminiscence was by Horace Walpole.

anced duet together. The opera was theirs: Senesino and Boschi, not to mention Luigi Antinori, the holder of the poor tenor role, and Anna Dotti, the contralto, were overlooked. For that night, perhaps for the first two or three nights, applause was divided evenly between the lumpish, stiff Cuzzoni with the wonderful high-soaring voice and the handsome Faustina of the rich mezzo.[10] Then the admirers of each, naturally detesting the rival of their particular heroine, introduced the custom of applauding wildly and hissing more wildly. The war of the Cuzzonites and the Faustinites [11] quickly became more important than the singers, the quality of their performances, or even the operas themselves. Cuzzoni had some hand in urging her cohorts to greater demonstrations, but Faustina contented herself with singing as only she could sing.

Senesino, in ill health, went off to Italy for a vacation, promising to return during the winter. Although he kept this promise, he did so too late to allow the autumn season of 1726–7 to open. An unknown company then revived in English an opera called *Camilla*, possibly Marc' Antonio Bononcini's opera of that name, which had been presented in Drury Lane in 1706 in an English translation by Owen MacSwiney. The prologue spoken before *Camilla* closed with these lines:

> Ye British fair, vouchsafe us your applause,
> And smile, propitious, on our English cause;
> While Senesino you expect in vain,
> And see your favours treated with disdain:
> While, 'twixt his rival queens, such mutual hate
> Threats hourly ruin to your tuneful state,
> Permit your country's voices to repair,
> In some degree, your disappointment there:

[10] Cuzzoni's range was from C to C *in alt;* Faustina's from B flat to G *in alt*, though she later extended it somewhat downward.
[11] Leading Cuzzonites were the Countess of Pembroke, Sir Wilfred Lawson, Sir William Gage, and Mr. Simon Smith; leading Faustinites, the Countess of Burlington, Lady De la Warr, Lady Cowper, and Sir Robert Walpole.

Here may that charming circle nightly shine;
'Tis time, when that deserts us, to resign.

This was the very choice of Cassandra: the Royal Academy of Music was rapidly sinking into bankruptcy. His Majesty's was in use, from November 1726 on, by a company of Italian comedians who proved close to the taste of George I. In December the Academy elected its governors and directors [12] for the following year and decided on an additional call of five per cent, which fell due on January 2, 1727. Cuzzoni and Faustina were at hand, but opera without Senesino or his counterpart was still unthinkable (good tenors were scarce then as now and not popular). There were, by the time of this crisis in the Academy's affairs, no annual subscribers, and its income therefore depended entirely on box-office receipts and calls on the shareholders, each of whom held a silver ticket (with a design engraved by Hogarth) that allowed him to enter the theater at will.

At last His Majesty's reopened. Senesino was again present either on that night, January 7, or on the second night, January 10. The opera was Ariosti's *Lucio Vero*, for which the audiences did not care, and which was therefore sung only seven times. On Tuesday, January 31, however, another Handel novelty, *Admeto*, temporarily averted disaster. The libretto, by an unknown poet after Euripides, deals with Alcestis, Antigone, Admetus, and Hercules, and is instinct with a demand for exactly the sort of dramatic music with which Handel clothed it. Its opening scene, with Admeto tormented by the Furies, is truly of intense power, and has justly been compared to the magnificent corresponding scene in Gluck's *Ifigénie en Tauride*. With Faustina, Cuzzoni, Senesino, Boschi, Baldi, Palmerini,

[12] Deputy governor: Duke of Richmond. Directors: Earl of Albemarle, Earl of Burlington, Hon. James Bruce, Hon. Patee Byng, Sir John Buckworth, Hon. James Brudenell, Marquess of Carnarvon, Earl of Chesterfield, Henry Davenant, Charles Edwin, Monsieur Fabrice, Sir John Eyles, Lord Viscount Limerick, Duke of Manchester, Earl of Mountrath, Sir Thomas Pendergrass, Sir John Rushout, James Sandys, Major General Wade, Sir William Yonge.

and Anna Dotti in its cast, it was a thumping success, running nineteen nights, on one of which it is possible (though not provable) that Voltaire was in the audience. Johann Joachim Quantz, the flautist who became the teacher and lifelong court musician of Frederick the Great, was visiting London during this run of *Admeto*. He found Cuzzoni an accomplished singer "rather cold in her action." His praise for Faustina was lavish: he described her as "born for singing and acting."

In February 1727, Handel, who had by then been a resident of London for fifteen years, wrote out the following petition:

To the Right Honourable The Lords Spiritual and Temporal in Parliament assembled.

The Humble Petition of George Frideric Handel sheweth that your Petitioner was born at Halle, in Saxony, out of His Majesty's Allegiance, but hath constantly professed the Protestant Religion,[13] and hath given Testimony of his Loyalty and Fidelity to His Majesty and the Good of this Kingdom.

Therefore the Petitioner humbly prays That he may be added to the Bill now pending entitled 'an Act for Naturalisating Louis Sechehaye.' And the petitioner will ever pray,

George Frideric Handel.

It has been suggested that Handel's tardy decision to become an English subject resulted from those attacks against him which stressed his being a German composer — this in a country where a German King and his German mistresses were constant objects of ridicule and revilement. A desire for preferments unavailable to him as a non-subject, and which came to him after the alteration in his status, probably was equally important in bringing him to this move. Nor does his having asked to become an English subject in 1727 in any way contradict his having written, seven years before, in a letter presenting a copy of *Radamisto* to George I,[14] that he was "Your Majesty's, Most

[13] Handel had been a familiar figure for some time at St. George's Parish Church in Hanover Square. He was, and remained, a Lutheran, but never is known to have suffered any disabilities from the laws regulating the activities of Nonconformists.

[14] See Appendix A (p. 310).

Devoted, Most Obedient, and most Faithful Subject and Servant." He was undoubtedly already a subject of George as Elector of Hanover.

On February 14, 1727, nine days before Handel's forty-second birthday, he went to the House of Lords, where the oath of allegiance was administered to him. Six days later, George I signed the necessary bill, and Handel thus became a naturalized British subject. Shortly thereafter, he was appointed Composer of Musick to the Chapel Royal. This was a largely honorary office that required of him only the occasional composition or performance of ceremonial music. The actual leadership of the King's musical establishments continued in the hands of William Croft and John Eccles.

On May 6, 1727, the last opera Bononcini was to compose for England was presented at His Majesty's by all the favorite singers. This *Astianatte*, to a Haym libretto, was to see the Handel-Bononcini and Cuzzoni-Faustina campaigns brought to their climaxes, and the former ended. It ran through nine performances, the last closing the season on June 6. But the successes of Handel's *Admeto* and Bononcini's *Astianatte* could not slow the horrid decline in the Academy's funds. The original subscription of £10,000 and the additional funds raised by calls and box-office receipts had been almost entirely used up: on May 10 there was a notice that five days later there would be a general court of subscribers for the purpose of discussing a new subscription. This meeting finally was held on May 22, but no new subscription was raised. There were to be the familiar five per cent calls in both October and December.

On the last day of the 1726-7 season, June 6, 1727, the singing of Bononcini's *Astianatte* was interrupted by a commotion among the ladies and gentlemen of the audience. Beginning on the opera's first night, when Princess Amelia's presence had failed to prevent riotous demonstrations for and against Cuzzoni and Faustina,[15] *Astianatte* had had a stormy career. On

[15] After this demonstration of May 6, 1727, the Countess of Pembroke felt called upon to ask the Mistress of the Robes to the Princess of Wales

the final night Princess Amelia's mother, the Princess of Wales herself, was in the house. Disregarding her presence, the Cuzzonites launched a pandemonium of hisses, boos, and roars when Faustina began to sing. A fight broke out. Personally involved at last, the two sopranos flew at one another's elaborate artificial coiffures and lustily joined in the fray. From the audience, gentlemen rushed up on the stage. Scenery was smashed. Not for many years had such disrespect been showed a member of the royal family for non-political reasons.

This bedlam of June 6 brought the slings and jests of the wits and near wits singing around the Royal Academy. Some wit wrote a ribald farce called *The Contretemps, or Rival Queans*, in which Handel (who has few lines to speak) advises that the ladies be left to fight it out. In *"The Devil to pay at St. James's: or a full and true account of a most horrid and bloody battle between* Madam Faustina *and* Madam Cuzzoni, *Also a hot skirmish between* Signor Boschi *and* Signor Palmerini. *Moreover, how* Senesino *has taken snuff, is going to leave the opera, and sing psalms at* Henley's *Oratory,"* a pamphlet usually attributed to Dr. Arbuthnot, the suggestion is made that the sopranos fight publicly. "I humbly propose that since these Ladies are not to be reconciled by any other gentle Means, 'tis best that they should fight it out at Figg's or Stoke's Amphitheatre [prize-fighting arenas]; that a subscription be opened for that purpose, and the best woman have the whole house." This suggestion may not have sounded completely absurd in a day when female prize-fighting was common. Handel, however, contented himself with calling the sopranos "hussies," reserving for Cuzzoni alone the appellation "she-devil," for the better-loved Faustina that of "Beelzebub's spoiled child." And

to assure her mistress that no disrespect to Princess Amelia had been meant. "I hope Her Royal Highness would not disapprove of any one preventing Cuzzoni's being hissed off the stage; but I am in great concern they did not suffer anything to have happened to her, rather than to have failed in the high respect every one ought to pay to a Princess of Her Royal Highness's family. . . ." (Letter to Mrs. Clayton, later Viscountess Sundon.)

133

he proceeded with plans for producing a new opera he had already composed with roles for both of them.

Eight days after the battle of the Royal Academy, word reached London that George I had died on the Continent in the palace of his brother the Duke of York, Handel's old friend Ernst Augustus. The King had left London only one week earlier, apparently in good health, but had been stricken with paralysis while in a coach en route from Delden (where he had left the Duchess of Kendal) to Osnabrück. Some said that it had long been prophesied that His Majesty would not outlive his poor divorced wife more than one year: she had died in November 1726. Others said that on her deathbed Sophia Dorothea had written him a letter of fiery excoriation, ending with a command to appear with her to be judged before the bar of Heaven within one year and one day. Still others said that the gourmand King had eaten too many melons for a man who had already suffered a slight apoplexy. He died at Osnabrück shortly after the midnight between June 10 and June 11, 1727, in his sixty-eighth year. On June 15, his forty-three-year-old son was proclaimed King George II.

If Handel had had reasons for fearing the succession of George I to Queen Anne, he had none for fearing that of George II to his father. The new monarch was his admiring friend, the father of his princess-pupils. Soon the King confirmed Handel in his annual stipends of £200 each from Anne and George I and a third £200 as teacher to the royal princesses. He was confirmed in the honorary title of Composer of Musick to the Chapel Royal, to which, he now being a British subject, was added that of Composer to the Court. As the latter, he was commissioned by George II to compose anthems for the coronation, set for Westminster Abbey on October 11, 1727.

The end of a thirteen-year reign and the dawn of another could not keep the mounting troubles of the Royal Academy of Music out of the press. On July 13, the *Daily Courant* contained the following notice:

John James Heidegger Esqr

HEIDEGGER

[from a painting by Vanloo]

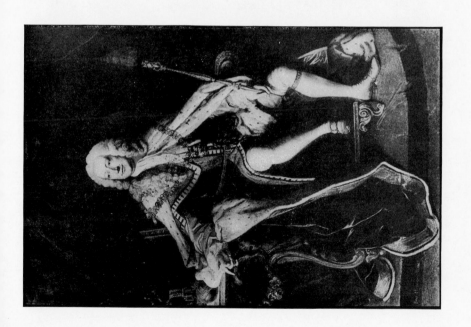

GEORGE II

[from a painting by Hudson]

DR ARNE.

THOMAS AUGUSTINE ARNE

Whereas several persons stand indebted to the Royal Academy for calls and otherwise, the court of directors do hereby order notice to be given, that they shall pay or cause to be paid, at the office in the Hay-market, or to the person attending them in that behalf, such sum or sums as they are owing, on or before Wednesday the 19th inst. otherwise they shall be obliged to cause process to be made at law against them, in order to recover the same.

And in October an extraordinary meeting of the general court of the Academy issued the nineteenth or twentieth call of five per cent on the shareholders.

A lofty ecclesiastic (perhaps two lofty ecclesiastics, the Archbishops of Canterbury and York), hearing that the King had ordered Handel to prepare anthems for the coronation, suggested to the composer that he would select from the Bible the texts to be set. And Handel is said to have replied, "I have read my Bible very well, and shall choose for myself." His choice fell upon I Kings, i. 38–40; Psalm 89, 14–15; Psalm 21, 1, and Psalm 45, 1. On these texts he built a four-part anthem of magnificent proportions entirely suited to its place as the support and display of solemn and bejeweled pageantry. Each of the sections — *Zadok the Priest, Let thy deeds be glorious* (also known as *Let thy hand be strengthened*), *The King shall rejoice,* and *My heart is inditing* — has come to be considered a whole in itself. *Zadok the Priest* has not failed to be part of every coronation service since 1727, overwhelmingly the most appropriate and dazzling music used.

Handel soon had to perform for George II more frivolous duties than that of supplying the Coronation Anthems. The King's forty-fourth birthday occurring on October 30, 1727, the Composer to the Court obliged with minuets for the Court Ball. These were published by Handel's old friend and enemy, the pirating Walsh. The Ball was held after the ninth, and final, season of the Royal Academy of Music had opened at His Majesty's Theatre with a revival, on October 3, of *Admeto.* The first new Handel opera of the season was heard on November 11, when his setting of a purposefully chosen patriotic libretto by Paolo Rolli, *Riccardo Primo, Rè d'Inghilterra*, again presented Cuzzoni and Faustina, as well as Senesino, Boschi, Baldi, and Palmerini, to the Academy's audience. Rolli received the title of Court Poet as payment for this historical rigmarole, but Handel's setting of it did nothing to extend the ebbing life of the Academy. Eleven performances of it succeeded one another in rather dismal fashion. Then, on December 26, Handel revived *Alessandro*, but we do not know what was played thereafter until February 17, 1728. Ominously on December 23, 1727, another call of five per cent was made on the shareholders: if it was the twentieth, such original members as remained would have doubled their investment without earning, so far as can be ascertained, more than one dividend of seven per cent. They had, of course, had free access to the operas of nine seasons.

The Academy was already dying when, on January 29, 1728, the proponents of musical entertainments in the English language gave the death-blow (a lingering wound) to Italian opera as a national institution. On that day, to a ribald and witty text by John Gay, the melange of folk-tunes and borrowings known as *The Beggar's Opera* was first presented at the theater in Lincoln's-Inn Fields. Proving himself a better critic than seer, Dr. Burney wrote of Dr. Pepusch, who helped Gay assemble this vulgate *pasticcio*, as follows:

> Soon after [1728], he was very judiciously chosen by Gay, to help him to select the tunes for the *Beggar's Opera*, for which he composed an original overture upon the subject of one of the tunes (I'm like a skiff), and furnished the wild, rude, and often vulgar melodies, with bases so excellent, that no sound contrapuntist will ever attempt to alter them.

The Beggar's Opera conquered London's usual theater-going public and won it new members. For performance after performance it poured money into the pockets of Gay, Pepusch, and John Rich, lessee of the Lincoln's-Inn Fields Theatre. "It made Gay rich and Rich gay." The first girl to play Polly

Peachum, its heroine, was Lavinia Fenton, and she became
Duchess of Bolton. More than half of its fortune depended on
Gay's racy and topical libretto, full of satire on Society and on
the government of Sir Robert Walpole. The rest of its fortune
was the anthology of folk-tunes and borrowings from other composers (Handel included) that Pepusch had married to it with
an appositeness that amounted to genius. It had simple, easily
comprehensible situations projected in simple, highly colored
language (the audience's own, not translationese), and it had
the slightly vulgar melodies Burney noted, tunes that could be
whistled and sung.

A list of the later revivals of *The Beggar's Opera* would certainly be as long as a list of its descendants, which began with
The Dragon of Wantley, Hurlothrumbo, and *Polly* (likewise by
Gay and Pepusch), and included the masterpieces of Gilbert
and Sullivan. As recently as 1920 the enduring vitality of the
first great English ballad opera was demonstrated. Then Sir
Nigel Playfair presented *The Beggar's Opera* in London in a
version re-orchestrated by Frederic Austin, and the all but bi-
centenarian work packed the Lyric Theatre (Hammersmith)
for two and one half years.

The Beggar's Opera possessed an abundance of the one quality that all but the best of Handel's (and Bononcini's and
Ariosti's) operas lacked: theatrical vitality for an English-speak-
ing audience. It ran for ninety nights, and should have taught
Handel the impresario a lesson; Handel the composer could
have learned nothing from it. Perhaps it did, eventually, teach
him a lesson, but it was one he learned with difficulty over the
thirteen succeeding years: that Italian opera could not for long
be made to pay in the London of George II. During those thirteen years Handel was to offer the London public more than
twenty operas, not one of them without surpassing beauties,
not one half so successful as *The Beggar's Opera.*

That a superb topical musical comedy (not too inaccurate a
description of *The Beggar's Opera*) should outdraw an opera
would not surprise the London or New York audiences of to-

day, used to seeing the most popular opera given a half-dozen performances in a season during which three or four musical comedies will run continuously and simultaneously. But in 1728 *The Beggar's Opera* was something new, and the partisans of musical entertainment in English (who foolishly therefore set themselves up as opponents of opera in Italian) — Gay, Jonathan Swift, and some anti-court sections of society among them — crowed prematurely over the demise of Handel and all his works.

Referring to Polly Peachum, Henry Carey, who was later to write the text for *The Dragon of Wantley*, sang:

> She has fired the town, has quite cut down
> The opera of *Rolli*;
> Go where you will, the subject still
> Is pretty, pretty Polly.
> There's Madam *Faustina*, Catso!
> And else Madame *Catsoni*;
> Likewise Signior Senesino,
> Are *tutti abbandoni*.

The Beggar's Opera had been crowding Rich's theater for nearly three weeks when, on February 17, 1728, George II, Queen Caroline, and their three elder daughters, Handelians all, went to His Majesty's for the *première* of the twenty-third opera of their court composer. *Siroe* was presented and even in part published as an original libretto by Haym; it was actually a slightly revised version of a libretto Metastasio had supplied to Leonardo Vinci in 1726. Nor was Handel's music to it all new: much of it he had borrowed in his usual manner from his own *Flavio* (1723). Although he might have been expected to put up against Gay and Pepusch one of his most careful and powerful operas, he did not. *Siroe*, though nowhere mere hack work, is notable for only one superb aria, Cosroe's larghetto "*Gelido in ogni vena.*" Not the matchless cast of Faustina, Cuzzoni, Baldi, Senesino, Palmerini, and Boschi could win it more than nineteen performances. And when, in later years, Handel came to revive many of the operas he had prepared for the patrons of the Royal Academy of Music, *Siroe* was never among them.

"Fine dell' opera, G. F. Handel, April 19th, 1728." So Handel wrote at the end of the last page of his setting of Haym's *Tolomeo, Rè d'Egitto*. And when *Siroe* had proved no box-office counterweight to the tripping, gay lasciviousness in Lincoln's-Inn Fields, he put *Tolomeo* on (April 30) at His Majesty's with substantially the cast of *Siroe*. It is better Handel, better music, better opera than *Siroe*. Cuzzoni must have sung wonders in *"Fonte amiche."* Senesino had a great scene ending with the profoundly stirring *"Innumano fratel"* and *"Stille amare."* Most taking of all was the echo song, *"Dite che fa"*: Cuzzoni sang it, Senesino repeating some of her phrases from behind the scenery. By all intrinsic merits, *Tolomeo* should have been a success. Instead, it ran up only seven performances. During that pitiful run, on May 16, the following ominous notice was printed:

That the general court of the Royal Academy of Music stands adjourned till eleven o'clock on Wednesday next, the 22d inst. in order to receive any further proposals that shall be offered for carrying on the operas.

The Royal Academy, launched with such brave hopes and plans eight years before, now was dying rapidly. Handel pulled *Tolomeo* off the boards and restaged *Admeto* on May 25. It played a second time three days later, a third four days after that. And with that June 1, 1728, performance of *Admeto* the final season of the Academy closed. For on the previous day, the notice had been:

The general court of the Royal Academy of Music stands adjourned till eleven o'clock on Wednesday the 5th of June next, in order to consider of proper measures for recovering the debts due to the Academy, and discharging what is due to performers, tradesmen, and others; and also to determine how the scenes, cloaths, &c. are to be disposed of, if the opera cannot be continued. N. B. All the subscribers are desired to be present, since the whole will be then decided by a majority of the votes.[16]

Exactly what happened at eleven o'clock on Wednesday, June 5, 1728, will probably never be known. No final decision to wind up the affairs of the Academy was taken, for as late as December 3 there was notice of a general court to be held three days later for the purpose of electing a deputy-governor and directors. That proposed December 16 court seems not to have met. Certainly the Royal Academy, nonetheless, finished expiring that June night when the revived *Admeto* reached its third singing. It was, in fact, quite totally dead.[17] And George Frideric Handel, in the forty-third year of his age, the composer of twenty-four operas, fourteen of them for the Royal Academy of Music, was a man without employment. He had, to be certain, his annual pensions of £600. But they depended on the continued benevolence of kings. Nor was Handel a man to muddle about a court, writing small music for piddling official ceremonies. He had tasted the life of the impresario in his dizzy seat. Opera, Italian opera, was in his blood. He could not, or would not, read the runes spelled out by the crowds still rushing to the theater in Lincoln's-Inn Fields. Opera, Italian opera, it must be. The problem, that summer of 1728, was to find more money (he had accumulated some), a partner, singers — for his warblers had dispersed when the Academy's doom became clear.[18] It would be done: nothing appeared beyond the powers of this huge source of energy once he had made up his mind.

[16] Calls of three per cent (twenty-first?) and two and one-half per cent (twenty-second?) had been levied against the shareholders on March 30 and April 24 respectively. Thus, the calls may have totaled 105½ per cent.
[17] The Royal Academy of Music, between April 2, 1720, and June 5, 1728, gave four hundred and eighty-seven performances of opera. Of these, two hundred and forty-five were of operas by Handel, one hundred and eight of operas by Bononcini, fifty-five of operas by Ariosti, and seventy-nine of operas by other composers.
[18] Burney stated that Venice, during the succeeding season, had Faustina, Senesino, and Baldi singing at one theater, Cuzzoni, Nicolini, Farinelli, and Boschi at another!

III

Y 1728 it was eighteen years since Handel had visited Italy, nine since he had left England or visited Halle, where his mother was now a woman of seventy-seven who could not logically be expected to survive much longer. He had paid at least passing attention to the need for a visit to *"zum gelben Hirschen"* on several occasions after his visit there in 1719. On June 22, 1725, for example, he had written as follows to Michael Dietrich Michaelsen, who, three and one half years after the death of Handel's sister, had married, as his second wife, Christiane Sophia Dreissig [1]:

Sir and most Honored Brother,

Again I find myself very guilty of not having satisfied for so long a time my duty toward you, the duty of letters. Nonetheless, I do not despair of obtaining your generous pardon when I assure you that this dereliction has not come from forgetfulness, and that my esteem and friendship for you are inviolable, as you have had proofs, my very Honored Brother, in the letters I have written to my Mother.

My silence, then, has been rather a result of a dread of overwhelming you with a correspondence that might bore you. But what makes me disregard these reflections in discommoding you with this present letter is that I do not wish to be so ungrateful as to pass by in silence, without remarking my very humble thanks, the kindnesses you have shown my Mother by your assistance and consolation in her advanced age. You are not unaware of how much I am touched by everything concerning her, and you can well estimate the obligations I feel toward you in this matter.

[1] Michaelsen was unfortunate with his wives: Christiane died on September 24, 1725. He was to marry a third time.

I should count myself happy, my very dear Brother, if I could engage you to give me from time to time the news you have; and you may be certain of the sincere part I take in this and of the faithful return you will always get from me. I had thought that I should be able to renew our friendship face to face, and that I should be journeying in your regions on the occasion when the King goes to Hanover. But my desires are again deprived of their fulfilment this time, and the condition of my affairs deprives me of this happiness. Nevertheless, I do not despair of there coming so happy a day. Meanwhile, it would console me greatly could I flatter myself that you would think well of me at times and honor me with your Friendship. For I shall never stop being, with inviolable passion and attachment,

Sir and most Honored Brother

Your very humble and most obedient Servant

George Frideric Handel

I pay my most humble respects to Madame your wife and I tenderly embrace my dear Niece and the rest of your dear family. My compliments, if you please, to all our friends [*Amis et Amies*].

The antique floweriness of Handel's French supplies no adequate reason for suspecting his sincerity. Although it is clear that he placed his career, his composing, the affairs of the great world through which he moved, above personal matters such as filial feelings or the emotions of his aging mother, he had truly had plenty of cause for not giving in to even a strong desire for travel. The Royal Academy of Music was the main cause; Bononcini, Senesino, above all Cuzzoni and Faustina, were supplementary causes. Nor, when the Academy had, practically speaking, ceased to exist, in June 1728, could he simply drop the complex threads of cause, effect, and hope that had been running through his hands and head, and rush off to the Continent.

That phenomenon of facial malformation, Handel's old friend Heidegger, was in 1728 lessee of the King's Theatre in the Haymarket. Heidegger had prospered far beyond the estate required of a "Swiss Count": his ridottos and loose-lived masquerades had drained streams of money into his coffers. He had

helped Handel earlier; he helped him now. The two entered
into a partnership for the further production of Italian opera.
Handel invested £10,000 of his savings — probably most of
what he had — in the new venture. Heidegger's financial risk
cannot be determined. Calling the venture the New Royal
Academy of Music, the two set it up after the machinery of its
predecessor, complete with governors, members, etc. In actu-
ality, however, Handel and Heidegger ran it. Its successes and
failures were to fatten and straiten them and their purses only.
It was the most ambitious speculative operative enterprise the
world had seen to that moment. For, though George II subscribed £1,000 a year to its support, it was as truly a private
enterprise as a modern Broadway theatrical production.

For nearly eight months, from June 1728 on, Handel seems
to have done very little but wait and plan. Then, on February
4, 1729, he set out from London on a Continental trip to recruit singers for the first season of the New Royal Academy.
"Yesterday morning," the *Daily Post* for January 29 had said,
"Mr. Handell, the famous Composer of Italian musick, took his
leave of Their Majesties, he being to set out this day for Italy."
But his trip was postponed one week.

By what route Handel traveled, in what order he visited the
centers of Italian music — these are facts difficult if not impossible to establish. He seems to have visited at least Milan, Florence, Rome, and Venice. In Rome, where opera (become the
national pastime of Italy, which it has since remained) was now
tolerated as long as all roles were sung by men, he encountered
at least two of the Arcadians who had patronized him as a
young man of twenty-three in 1708: Cardinal Pietro Ottobuoni
and Cardinal Colonna. A story has persisted that the latter
Prince of the Church endeavored to lure Handel into being
presented to the "Chevalier de St. George," otherwise James
Francis Edward Stuart. But Handel was too wily a Protestant
subject of His Majesty George II to accept a presentation to the
Old Pretender, and never came face to face with him. That
forlorn Prince was an ardent lover of music, and Cardinal

Colonna had held out the gift of a portrait of himself as an inducement to bring about the meeting. Handel wisely and firmly refused.

Although Handel is likely to have acquainted himself with operas and other music by Leonardo Vinci, Johann Adolf Hasse, Giovanni Battista Pergolesi, and Niccolo Antonio Porpora, all then popular the length of Italy, the most important discovery he made there was the extent and efficacy of the libretto-writing of the Abbé Pietro Trapassi, known as Metastasio. This son of a Roman greengrocer, born in 1698, had been adopted by a rich scholar, whose well-placed heir he thus became. By dint of exercising a true, if somewhat marmoreal, poetic talent, a knowledge of music, and an unabating productivity, Metastasio was well on his way, by the time of Handel's 1729 visit to Italy, to becoming librettist to the eighteenth century. Hasse was to be so won by Metastasio's classical charades that he set every one of them at least once, some of them twice, the *Artaserse* three times! Handel himself had already set Haym's adaptation of Metastasio's *Siroe*, and was still to set him un-adulterated. Almost every composer of opera for more than a century tried his hand at least once with a Metastasio libretto. The *Artaserse* was composed not fewer than forty times. The list of composers who set one or more of the Abbé's products is prodigious, and includes, besides Hasse and Handel, Traetta, Galuppi, Leonardo Leo, Porpora, Jommelli, Paisiello, Gluck, Piccinni, and Haydn. Mozart used, among others, *Il Rè Pastore* and *La Clemenza di Tito*, Meyerbeer the *Semiramide* in 1819, Giovanni Pacini the *Temistocle* as late as 1838. Metastasio lived to savor much of his own glory: he did not die until 1782, aged eighty-four.

Handel was in Italy on business more immediately pressing than that of acquainting himself with new composers, new operas, or even a remarkable librettist. His trip was for the purpose of hiring singers. He found Antonio Bernacchi, a male soprano who had failed to stir London audiences in 1716 and 1717, during which time he had sung the small role of Goffredo in Handel's *Rinaldo*. Bernacchi, however, had meanwhile been continuing the severe studies he had begun at the renowned Bologna school of singing founded by Francesco Pistocchi, and had trained a second-rate voice to be the vehicle of a first-rate vocal artistry. Handel hired him. He found Antonia Merighi, a personable contralto with marked ability as an actress; Annibale Pio Fabri, a tenor sometimes called Balino, and like Bernacchi a pupil of Pistocchi; Signora Fabri, schooled as a vocalizing male impersonator; the contralto Francesca Bertolli, and a secondary bass named Commano. Most important of all, in Venice he found a soprano with whom to attempt to replace Faustina and Cuzzoni: Anna Maria Strada del Pò, a woman almost as ill-favored as Heidegger himself. Sharp-tongued Londoners were affectionately to nickname her "the Pig," but the beauty of her voice and — despite her tantrums and exhibitionistic rantings — her loyalty were to be a longtime comfort to Handel.

From Venice, on March 11, 1729, Handel wrote to his former brother-in-law, whom it was now necessary to address as "Michael Dietrich Michaelsen, Councilor of War of His Prussian Majesty."

Sir and most Honored Brother
You will learn through the letter that I send to my Mother herewith that I have well obtained the honor of your letter of the 18th of the past month.

Permit me to thank you particularly for the lines you wrote, and to beseech you to continue sending me news from time to time while I find myself traveling in this country, for you cannot be ignorant of the interest and satisfaction with which it supplies me. You need only continue to address them to Mr. Joseph Smith, Banker at Venice (as I have mentioned to you earlier), who will forward them to me wherever I find myself in Italy.

You may well imagine, my very Honored Brother, the happiness I have derived from knowing that you find yourself with your Dear Family in perfect health, and with all my heart I wish you its continuation. The thought of embracing you soon gives me real joy. You will do me the justice of believing me. I assure you that this has been

one of the principal motives for which I undertook this Voyage with
greater pleasure. I hope that my desires may be realized during the
coming month of July. Meanwhile, I always wish you all prosperity,
and, presenting my Compliments to Madame Your Wife,[2] and embracing your Dear Family, I am, with inviolable passion, Sir and
most Honored Brother

Your

most humble and most obedient

Servant

George Frideric Handel

During the spring of 1729, however, Handel received word,
in all probability from Michaelsen, that the aged Frau Dorothea
had suffered a stroke. Her son abandoned Italy, and by June
was at Halle. Whether his aged spinster aunt, Anna Taust, still
shared *"zum gelben Hirschen"* or had died is not known. His
mother was sadly deteriorated: in her seventy-ninth year she
was quite blind and so crippled by paraylsis that she could move
only short distances, and them with extreme difficulty. Her son,
who must have understood that he would not see her alive again,
was unable to remain with her long: he had to return to London to prepare his season of Italian opera. Two or three weeks,
perhaps, he spent with this woman who had already survived
the death of her husband (who would have been one hundred
and seven, had he lived) by thirty-two years.

While Handel tarried briefly in Halle, an eighteen-year-old
boy arrived from Leipzig to invite him to visit the Thomascantor
there. It was Wilhelm Friedemann Bach, whose father had that
very year directed from the console of the Thomaskirche organ
the first singing of his *Matthäuspassion.* If Handel knew of Johann Sebastian Bach at all, which is not certain, it was as a
worthy church composer of a type familiar in every German
town, not much different from that Zachau who had given him
some early training. But his refusal of the invitation brought
by young Wilhelm Friedemann need not be taken to have indi-

---

[2] On September 18, 1726, Michaelsen had married Sophia Elisabeth
Dreissig, a sister of his second wife.

cated disdain, as some commentators have interpreted it. Handel would naturally remain with Frau Dorothea until he had to depart for London. The two greatest composers of their era were not to meet.

From Halle, Handel traveled by way of Hamburg, where he found, in Johann Gottfried Riemschneider, the principal deep male voice he had not been able to hire in Italy. Rushing on, he was in London by the end of June: the July 2 issue of the *Daily Courant* spoke of him as "just returned from Italy." He did not bother about finishing an opera with which to launch the first season of the New Royal Academy of Music until all other details of the venture were complete to his satisfaction. *Lotario*, composed to a libretto by Antonio Salvi and set for Venice by Orlandini as *Adelaide* earlier in 1729 was not completed until November 16. It was first presented sixteen days later, on December 2, 1729, at His Majesty's Theatre in the Haymarket. Neither *Lotario* nor the new company of singers captured London's fancy. The New Royal Academy was off to a bad start.

Of the new singers, the two first sopranos, female and *castrato*, were the cynosures. Of Bernacchi, past the zenith of his powers, Burney said that, in 1729, there was little left "except a refined taste and an artificial [i.e., artful] manner of singing, which only professors and a few of the most intelligent part of the audience could feel or comprehend." Anna Maria Strada del Pò was ugly and a poor actress. But she commanded a notable shake, and Handel had, in the very first aria she sang in *Lotario* ("*Quel cor che mi donasti*") supplied her with more than thirty opportunities to display it. None of the other singers in the company as first constituted, not Merighi, Fabri, Bertolli, or Riemschneider, was ever to win a following in London. But Strada del Pò, "the Pig," was at last, by her submissiveness to training at Handel's hands, her intelligence and persevering artistry, her loyalty to Handel when everyone and everything else wavered, to win herself a public. She was to be with Handel for nine years, or almost to the end of his career as an opera composer and impresario. But she failed to please during that December of 1729.[3]

The year 1730 opened in London with an unpleasant natural phenomenon, a New Year's Night fog thick enough to be remarked in letters and diaries. A number of stumbling, blinded pedestrians fell into Fleet Ditch. The porters of sedan chairs lost their way and pitched into ponds and canals. Even on the Thames, boatmen mistook their routes and ran each other down. The gloom of His Majesty's Theatre was scarcely thinner. Early in the month, Handel and Heidegger removed the lackadaisical *Lotario* from the boards after ten performances and revived *Giulio Cesare* for nine performances. Handel, meanwhile, worked toward completion his second original opera for the new company.

To a libretto by Silvio Stampiglia, originally supplied to a composer in Naples, Handel completed *Partenope* on February 6, 1730. In its pages, differing in many respects from his earlier operas, are to be found memories of the operas he had heard in Italy one year before, in particular the fashionable light works of Vinci and Hasse. Here was a bid for popularity and a fat box office. Nor is *Partenope*, however hastily composed, a skeletonic work like *Lotario*. Its brace of typically brilliant Handelian arias is matched by moving and attractive choruses. It contains a vocal trio and quartet and fine instrumental interludes in something as close as any composer of the era had come to what we now consider symphonic style. But London did not like *Partenope*, played first on February 24. It was no reply to the financial question the till asked of Handel and Heidegger. During its first run it achieved only seven performances, while in revivals later the same year and early in 1737 it won a few more before being left to posterity dead upon the pages of the manuscript.

George II honored the King's Theatre with his presence when Strada del Pò appeared in *Giulio Cesare*, chosen for her benefit performance on March 31, 1730. Four days later, having no

---

[3] It was during 1729 that the six concertos (*concerti grossi*) for oboes, bassoons, and strings known as Handel's Opus 3 were published.

new work of his own to throw to the audience tigers, Handel staged something called *Ormisda*, whether a *pasticcio* or an opera composed in 1722 by Antonio Caldara to an Apostolo Zeno libretto is not clear. This did better, particularly after, midway in its first run of thirteen performances, twelve new numbers were inserted into it, possibly new or refurbished arias from Handel's pen. Trying to woo the recalcitrant public that had once crowded to hear its favorite Handel operas, the composer revived *Tolomeo*, seven performances of which kept some coins clinking at the box office until the New Royal Academy's first season closed on June 13.

Of the company Handel had collected in Italy and Germany in 1729, Bernacchi had proved too poor an attraction to keep, and was sent back to Italy after the first season. The bass Riemschneider was little better, and he too was gone. Handel rightly considered Strada del Pò worth keeping while she improved, worth forcing on audiences until they accepted her. But he had realized in June 1730 that he must have new singers if Italian opera was to be given at all. On June 19/30, 1730, he wrote to Francis Colman, Envoy Extraordinary of His Britannic Majesty to H. R. H. the Duke of Tuscany, evidently a personal acquaintance, and later to provide Handel with the libretto of *Arianna in Creta* (probably a version of Pietro Pariati's *Arianna e Teseo*).

Sir,

Since I last had the honor to address you, means have been found for re-engaging Signora Merighi, and as hers is a contralto voice, it will be desirable that the woman to be engaged in Italy be a soprano. I am writing also to Mr. Swinny [4] to this effect, at the same time recommending that the woman whom he proposes to you play men's roles as well as women's. There is reason to believe that you have not again engaged a female contralto, but if you have, we must keep her.

---

[4] This was no other than Owen MacSwiney, who had run off with the box-office receipts of *Teseo* in 1713. While living in France or Italy, MacSwiney had somehow re-established his relationship with Handel, who clearly forgave him. In 1733, indeed, he was to prove most valuable to Handel in the matter of hiring a fine *castrato* named Carestini. Dying in 1754, MacSwiney willed a considerable estate to Peg Woffington.

I take the liberty to ask you again that there be no mention in the contracts of first, second, or third role, for that narrows our choice of drama and, furthermore, causes great inconvenience. We also hope to have, through your assistance, a man and a woman for the coming season, which will begin with the month of October of the current year and finish in the month of July, 1731, and we impatiently await your news so that we can inform the Court.

It only remains for me to reiterate my assurances of the special obligation I have to you because of your kindness toward me in this matter, I who have the honor to be, with respectful affection,

Sir,

Your

very humble and obedient servant

George Frideric Handel.

Colman replied in September with several suggestions and the news of one definite commitment. Of this last, as the following letter proves, Handel already knew when the Envoy's letter from Venice arrived.

London, $\frac{27}{16}$ October, 1730.

Sir,

I have just received the honor of your letter of the 22nd of last month N. S., from which I learn the reasons that determined your engaging Sr Sinesino at the sum of fourteen hundred guineas [£1,470], to which we acquiesce; and I give you my very humble thanks for the pains you have been good enough to take in this affair. The said Sr Sinesino arrived here twelve days ago and I have not failed, on the presentation of your letter, to pay him on account of his salary the hundred guineas [£105] that you promised him. With regard to Sig^{ra} Pisani,[5] we have not heard her, and as the season is well advanced and we shall shortly begin the operas, we shall get through this year without another woman from Italy, having already arranged the operas for the company we now have.

I am nonetheless much obliged to you for having thought of Sig^{ra} Madalena Pieri [6] in case we should absolutely need another

[5] Barbara Pisani never reached London.
[6] This was Maria Maddalena Pieri, who sang at various theaters and courts throughout Italy, but does not seem to have visited England.

1 5 0

woman who can act men's roles, but we shall content ourselves
with five personages, having found means now for supplying the
rest.

It is to your generous assistance that the Court and the Nobility
owe in part the satisfaction of now having a company to their taste,
and it now remains, therefore, only for me to mark my deep personal feelings of gratitude and to assure you of the very respectful
attention with which I have the honor to be, Sir,

Your

very humble and very obedient servant
George Frideric Handel.

It has been stated that Handel himself had tried to rehire
Senesino during his 1729 visit to Italy, but had found the pompous *castrato* intractable. If so, he now swallowed his pride and
took Senesino back on his own terms. As early as August 28,
1730, the *Daily Post* had reported that "Signor Senesino, the
famous Italian Singer, hath contracted to come over hither
against the Winter to perform under Mr. Heydegger in the
Italian Opera." On October 9, readers of the *Daily Journal*
learned that "Grand Preparations [were] making at the Opera-
House in the Hay-Market, by New Cloaths, Scenes, &c. And,
Senesino being arrived, they will begin to perform as soon as
the Court [which had been at Windsor] comes to Saint James's."

The musical public might logically have expected Handel
and Heidegger, with Senesino at hand, to open the second season of the New Royal Academy of Music with a carefully
wrought Handel novelty. Instead, the season was started, on
November 3, 1730, with Senesino in a revision of Handel's
Scipione of 1726; it ran through the rest of the year with restagings of the *Partenope* and *Ormisda* of the preceding season.
Senesino and Strada del Pò, who was now established as something of a favorite with sections of the nobility, seem to have
given *Partenope* a popular appeal it had at first lacked, for
Handel continued it for seven performances this time, the last
on January 9, 1731. Even then, instead of a new Handel opera,
the public was offered, for four performances begun on Janu-

1 5 1

ary 12, an opera or *pasticcio* called *Venceslao*,[7] with a libretto
by Apostolo Zeno and interpolated recitatives by Handel.

When, on February 2, 1731, the opera Handel had prepared
for the new season (he had completed it on January 16) was at
last vouchsafed the public, it proved a success of importance.
To Metastasio's *Alessandro nell' Indie* he had composed an
opera called *Poro*.[8] It won back much of Handel's lost public,
achieving sixteen uninterrupted performances that season and
several the next. Its first act closes with an extraordinarily powerful duet for Poro and Cleofide. Earlier in the story, the two
have discovered the tenderest love for each other; here they
fly into a jealous fury, repeating with superb dramatic effectiveness twisted snatches of their earlier love songs. For Poro,
too, Handel composed one of his grandest arias, *"Dov' e? Si
affretti."* Poro and Cleofide's final duet, *"Caro vieni,"* was
worked up into a finale any Mozartean must admire: it is sung
by the two alternately, then in real duet, and finally by the
chorus with them. It became a popular excerpt, as did *"Son
confusa pastorella,"* which soon became known in instrumental
transcription. But the most interesting section of *Poro* is Cleofide's remarkable aria *"Spirto amato."* In a manner very like that
of the renowned "When I am laid in earth" in Purcell's *Dido
and Aeneas*, its melody is built above a repeated short ground-
bass, in this instance of only one measure repeated fifteen
times.

In *Poro* Handel returned to the manner with which he had
first won the patrons of the original Royal Academy, disdaining
the more modern effects he had learned to imitate from Hasse,
Vinci, and possibly Pergolesi. The momentum its reception set
up was enough, when it was withdrawn after sixteen nights, to
guarantee success to two revivals: six performances of the

[7] This may have been music by the prolific associate *maestro di cappella*
of St. Mark's, Venice, Carlo Francesco Pollarolo, who produced a *Venceslao*
about 1703. Pollarolo composed more than seventy operas in the thirty-
five years from 1686 to 1721.
[8] It supplied roles to Senesino, Strada, Fabri, Commano, Merighi, and
Bertolli.

sempiternal *Rinaldo,* slightly revised, and eight of *Rodelinda.*
With the final *Rodelinda* on May 29, 1731, the second season
came to a happy end. During its course, furthermore, Antonio
Montagnana, a first-class bass, had been recruited to Handel's
fold, replacing Commano. Merighi had also made way for a
castrato called Campioli, Annibale Pio Fabri for one Pinacci.
There was every sign that the season might have been prolonged for uninterruptedly full houses, so brilliantly had Handel
for the moment given the lie to those who thought that Italian
opera was dead forever. But an unseasonable hot spell hit London, making the stuffy, unventilated theater quite unbearable.
Not even to hear Handel, Senesino, and Strada at their best
would Londoners bear the stifling atmosphere at His Majesty's.

Despite the heartening response of the New Royal Academy's
audiences to *Poro, Rinaldo,* and *Rodelinda,* it is doubtful that
Handel was in any state of mind to derive pleasure from success during the first half of 1731. On December 28, 1730, from
Halle, Michael Dietrich Michaelsen had written him that his
mother, Frau Dorothea Händel, had died at a few weeks less
than eighty years of age. The letter Handel dispatched in answer to this news has not survived. But Michaelsen sent him
further details about the funeral and other arrangements in a
letter dated January 6, 1731, and to this Handel's answer was:

$$\text{London the}\frac{23}{12}\text{February 1731.}$$

Sir and most Honored Brother.

I have duly received your honored letter of January 6, in which
I learn of the pains you have taken to consign my late Mother's
remains to earth in conformity with her last will. I am unable even
now to hold back the flow of my tears. But the All Highest has been
pleased to enable me to accept His holy will with Christian fortitude.
Your thoughtfulness I shall never forget until, after this present life
is over, we are reunited, which may the All Good grant us in His
mercy.

The innumerable obligations under which my honored brother
has placed me by the unflagging solicitude and care with which he

always watched over my late dear Mother must be acknowledged not through words alone, but through dutiful recognition.

I trust that my honored brother received my last letter, which was sent in answer to his own of December 28 O.S., and has found in it the enclosures for Herr Consistorial Rath Frank[9] and for Herr Deacon Taust,[10] my cousin. Also, I await his honored reply with impatience, expecting it to include notice of expenses incurred as well as the printed funeral oration and poetry. I am in his debt for the poem lately sent me, which I shall preserve as a treasured memento.

Finally, let me also condole most sincerely with my honored brother and his dear wife on the loss they have suffered through the death of their brother-in-law.[11] I am strengthened by the Christian calmness they display. May the All Highest grant all of us our worthy desires. To His Almighty keeping I commend my honored brother and all the members of his amiable family, and remain,

With sincere devotion,

My honored brother's

most humble and obedient servant

George Friedrich Händel.

There also survives another letter that Handel wrote Michaelsen on the same subject. Dated at London on August 10/July 30, 1731, it reads:

Sir and very Honored Brother

I learn from the letter you have done me the honor to write me on the 12th of July n. st. in answer to my preceding one, and from the specification you enclosed with it, what great pains you took on the occasion of the burial of my very dear Mother.

I am, furthermore, most obliged for the copies of the funeral ora-

[9] This was the Royal Prussian Ecclesiastical Councilor Johann Georg Francke, whose oration over the body of Handel's mother was printed in a twenty-six-page pamphlet.
[10] Johann Georg Taust was in all probability the son of a brother of Handel's mother. He served as deacon at a church in Halle from 1720 on.
[11] Probably a brother of the two Fräulein Dreissig, whom Michaelsen had married as his second and third wives.

tion that you have sent me, and to which you added the one made for (*pour feu*) my Dear Father; I await them from Mr Sbüelen.[12]

Later I shall know how to repay in part the obligations I have toward you. In the meantime, I beg you to pay my respects and compliments to Madame your dear Wife, to my Dear God-daughter, and to the rest of your dear Family, and to be persuaded yourself that I am, with inviolable affection,

Sir and most Honored Brother, Your

very humble and very obedient
Servant
George Frideric Handel[13]

Handel had legitimate causes for depression and inertia. His closest surviving relation now (unless one or more of the children of his father's first marriage survived) was his nineteen-year-old niece, Johanna Friederika, the only living child of his sister Dorothea Sophia by Michaelsen. If he had a grown man's normal attachment to the scenes and persons of his childhood and youth (it was certainly not more than normal), Handel must have felt himself alone in the world. He had the John Christopher Smiths, father and son. He had the cantankerous and eccentric Heidegger, his singers, his admiring but scarcely intimate friends among the noble and the mighty. But he was, and at the age of only forty-six, the sole survivor of a private

---

[12] Johann Wilhelm Sbülen (?–1738) was a Hamburg merchant, perhaps in the export-import trade.

[13] For a long time the manuscript of this letter existed only in mutilated form. The missing passages were (1) at the end of the second paragraph, from the semi-colon to "Mr Sbüelen," and (2) the last three lines, including the signature. Rockstro stated that the signature had been "cut away, for presentation to the 'Hendel Schütz.'" When, after considerable searching, I was ready to despair of learning the identity of the "Hendel Schütz," I came upon J. M. Coopersmith's "Four Unpublished Letters of Georg Friedrich Händel," in *A Birthday Offering to C[arl] E[ngel]* (New York, 1943). From Mr. Coopersmith's admirable notes I learned that the cuttings had been presented to Henriette Händel-Schütz, a singer who lived from 1772 to 1849. I am indebted to this article also for the letters of January 10, 1743, and March 15, 1748, as well as for the business letter of March 13, 1715.

world he had known well and that had passed away. London
heard and saw little of him from May 1731 to January 1732.

The New Royal Academy of Music, however, duly opened
its third season on November 13, 1731. Handel marked time
with revivals, through November, December, and the first half
of January, of *Tamerlano, Poro,* and *Admeto,* none of them
particularly well received. It seemed that the Midas-touch of
the preceding season had been charmed away from Heidegger
and himself. Again as in the doldrums of that other season, the
Handel novelty that was to bring it life was delayed until after
the beginning of the new year. This time it was *Ezio,* set to
what remained of a Metastasio libretto after someone had
hacked it to pieces. Given first on January 15, 1732, it had an
opening run of only five nights. But on every one of the five
except the first the King and members of his family were in the
Theater! Strada, Senesino, Bertolli and Pinacci were again in
the cast. The new voices were Montagnana, the bass of extraordinary range and power who was to charm London, in one
company and another, for years, and one Bagnolesi. For Montagnana, Handel had with the greatest care composed three
of his finest bass arias: *"Se un bell' ardire,"* [14] the forever fresh
"Nasce al bosco," and the full-dress trumpet-accompanied military proclamation, *"Già risuonar d'intorno."* From what is
known of the musical tastes of George II, it can be deduced
that it was the stirring martial music sung by Montagnana and
brilliantly accompanied by Handel's instrumentation that attracted him to His Majesty's Theatre for four consecutive performances of *Ezio.*

The score of *Ezio* cannot be exactly dated, for the final page
has unfortunately been lost. Also the manuscript is prefaced
by material intended by Handel for an opera that he never
completely composed. The first page of it has the superscrip-
tion *"Ouverture pour l'Opera Titus l'Empereur,"* and is followed
by a scene in which Titus is found in the throne room of his

[14] Long familiar as a recital number in a translated version that begins
"Droop not, young lover."

palace. Only after this scene does the opening march of *Ezio* itself appear. Nothing is known of Handel's intention to compose a *Tito*.

Handel was still having troubles, from time to time, with the same John Walsh who had published sections of *Rinaldo* more than twenty years before, during his first visit to London. Yet it was Walsh who had agreed to publish *Ezio*. He dallied, however, and it was pirated in part by Mr. and Mrs. Thomas Cobb. Mrs. Cobb was the remarried widow of the publisher John Cluer, who is sometimes credited with the invention of a method of engraving music on tin plates. The Cobbs carried on a business in Bow Churchyard. As the manuscript of *Ezio* survives only incomplete, it is fortunate that Walsh disregarded the pirated book of selections from it and published the opera. Only from his publication has it been possible, for example, to reconstruct with some accuracy that part of the opera which follows the stirring *"Già risuonar d'intorno"* and brings the whole to a close.

After the fifth singing of *Ezio*, the Handel-Heidegger management revived *Giulio Cesare* for four performances, from February 1 to 12. During this revival, on February 4, Handel completed the opera *Sosarme* to a Matteo Noris libretto originally called *Alfonso Primo*.[15] *Sosarme* was made ready for its *première* very speedily, and was given on February 15, the singers being those used in *Ezio*. It contains a notable passage for solo violin, inserted to display the accomplished artistry of Pietro Castrucci, a Corelli pupil who led the opera orchestra at His Majesty's. Eleven nights sufficed to exhaust the demand for *Sosarme*, which ran to March 21. The rest of the season, stretched out to June 20, was made up of five nights of Ariosti's *Coriolano*, four of Handel's *Flavio*, and four of a *Lucio Papiro, Dittatore*, probably by Caldara. June 24 witnessed the mounting of a pastoral entertainment composed by Bononcini and presented by command of Queen Caroline, who at the time

[15] He had actually composed two acts of it as *Fernando, rè di Castiglia,* and then altered the names of its characters throughout!

was acting as regent during the absence on the Continent of King George.

Ezio and *Sosarme* and the other entertainments sponsored by Heidegger and Handel at His Majesty's during the later half of the 1731–2 season had all but duplicated the success of *Poro, Rinaldo,* and *Rodelinda* during that of 1730–1. But the third season of the New Royal Academy was the more important: during its course several events occurred that were to initiate currents of thought and creativity that would swerve Handel from Italian opera altogether within ten years. They had, in reality, begun during the previous season, when, on March 26, 1731, John Rich had given a performance of Handel's *Acis and Galatea* at the Lincoln's-Inn Fields Theatre. What finally set Handel to thinking, however, was the private production of *Haman and Mordecai,* now called *The History of Hester* or simply *Esther,* that Bernard Gates gave on February 23, 1732, as a method of signalizing Handel's forty-seventh birthday. When this was repeated at the Crown and Anchor Tavern in Arundel Street, and again proved to the liking of a distinguished audience, Handel at last read the omens properly. He announced that he himself would stage *Esther* at His Majesty's Theatre under his own direction on May 2, 1732. This was the most important decision of his maturity, from a musical point of view the most important of his life.

BOOK III

I

J OHN RICH, lessee of the Lincoln's-Inn Fields Theatre, who
had directed the original production of *The Beggar's Opera*, and who, toward the end of 1732, was to open a new
theater in Covent Garden, was the first man to hit upon
the truth that one of Handel's serenatas, cantatas, or near-orato-
rios might be turned to profit.

On March 15, 1731, the following advertisement appeared in
the *Daily Journal*:

*At the Desire of several Persons of Quality. For the benefit of
Mr. Rochetti.* At the Theatre-Royal in Lincoln's Inn-Fields, on Friday,
being the 26th Day of March, will be presented, A Pastoral, call'd
ACIS *and* GALATEA. *Compos'd by Mr. Handel.* Acis by Mr. Rochetti;
Galatea, Mrs. Wright; Polypheme, Mr. Leveridge; and the other
Parts by Mr. Legar, Mr. Salway, Mrs. Carter, and Mr. Papillion.

On the day of the performance itself, it was further stated
that "Mr. Rochetti will sing the song, Son Confusa Pastorella,
being the Favorite Hornpipe in the Opera of *Porus*."

This performance of *Acis and Galatea* was not only given
without Handel's permission, but, as the presence of such an
extraneous role as "Coridon" and of the "other parts" proves,
in a version that must have been a *pasticcio* arranged by someone other than Handel. Clearly, it was presented as an English
opera, perhaps with the hope of winning for this garbled version of a serious work the sort of popularity *The Beggar's Opera*
had won for comedy sung in English. Unfortunately, we are
now unable to determine the reception awarded to this trial
flight, in all probability more consciously an attempt to inject
life into the moribund, corpselike frame of English opera than
the first public performance of oratorio in English.

It was Bernard Gates, Handel's exact contemporary, Master

of the Children of the Chapel Royal, who unwittingly started
into motion forces that were to lead Handel to the composition
and promotion of what became a British national institution, the
concert oratorio. Having obtained a copy of the *Haman and
Mordecai* that Handel had composed in 1720 for performance in
the Duke of Chandos' private chapel at Cannons (at which time
he himself had sung in it), Gates trained the Chapel Royal Children to sing it. Then he gave it, in two-act form, with action,
costumes, and scenery, and with an entirely English cast, at the
Crown and Anchor Tavern in the Strand on Handel's forty-
seventh birthday, February 23, 1732. Gates had persuaded the
poetaster Samuel Humphreys to make additions to the text, and
had renamed the work *Esther, an Oratorio.* Among the singers
were John Randall (Esther), in later years a professor of music
at Cambridge, and John Beard (Israelitish Priest), soon to become a tenor idolized by the London public. The semi-amateur
orchestra was that of the Philharmonic Society.

The performance of *Esther* on February 23 was so enthusi-
astically enjoyed that, almost certainly with Handel's permission, Gates arranged for two more singings of it, the second
under the auspices of the Academy of Antient Music,[1] again at
the Crown and Anchor Tavern in Arundel Street, Strand. The
Children of the Chapel Royal (with some Westminster Abbey
choristers helping out) again took part, but for the March 3rd
singing the Academy itself supplied the instrumentalists. As
only subscribers to the Academy and the Philharmonic Society
could gain admission to these two performances, they cannot
truly be called public. The amazing fact about their fine reception is that it still does not seem to have led Handel to the obvious conclusion that perhaps he could succeed better with
English oratorio than with Italian opera.

[1] The Academy had been started in 1710, and had long been in opposition to Handel as a representative of ultramodern trends in music. Its
name was literal: its chief purpose was the preservation through performance of the music of the past. Its willingness to perform *Esther* in 1732
may indicate that it had begun slowly to alter its attitude toward the
music of its own day.

On April 19, 1732, however, the following advertisement appeared in the *Daily Journal*:

Never Perform'd in Publick before, At the Great Room in Villars-street York Buildings, To-morrow being Thursday the 20th of this Instant April, will be perform'd, ESTHER an ORATORIO *or, Sacred Drama*. As it was compos'd originally for the most noble James Duke of Chandos, the Words by Mr. *Pope*, and the Musick by Mr. *Handel*. . . .

After the Crown and Anchor performances, Princess Anne had suggested one, with costumes, scenery, and action, at His Majesty's Theatre. Dr. Gibson, Bishop of London (and therefore in full authority over the Children of the Chapel Royal) was long said to have forbidden use of the Children even if they appeared holding texts in their hands. Then and now, the idea of acting out a Biblical drama upon the stage has shocked many worthy Englishmen. It is clear that this performance of *Esther* on April 20, 1732, has every right to be called the first public performance of oratorio in England, as well as the first public performance of an English oratorio anywhere.

The York Buildings *Esther* was to be sung without Handel's permission or tacit consent. He was properly irritated, and ire drove him to the step that his usually keen commercial mind should have found obvious earlier. He decided that he himself would present *Esther* publicly. It was not difficult to persuade George II to "command" such a performance. And so the April 19, 1732 issue of the *Daily Journal* also included the following notice:

By His MAJESTY's *Command*. At the King's Theatre in the Hay-Market, on Tuesday the 2d Day of May, will be perform'd, *The Sacred Story* of ESTHER: an *Oratorio* in *English*. Formerly compos'd by Mr. *Handel*, and now revis'd by him, with several Additions, and to be perform'd by a great Number of the best Voices and Instruments. N.B. There will be no Action on the Stage, but the House will be fitted up in a decent Manner, for the Audience. The Musick to be dispos'd after the Manner of the Coronation Service. . . .

For this performance, Handel increased the size of the orchestra far beyond anything he can have used at Cannons: bassoons, flutes, and oboes go in pairs; violins (at times *divisi in cinque*), violas, cellos, and basses are required in numbers to sound with the winds, harp, harpsichord, theorbo, and organ. Here, too, are the choruses in five and seven parts that were to allow the eventual development, after Handel's death, of performances of his oratorios into giant Barnumesque sideshows.

The singers of the Handel-Heidegger New Royal Academy of Music took the chief solo parts in *Esther*. What kind of English came from the mouths of Strada, Bertolli, Senesino, and Montagnana can be imagined by anyone who has heard the usual Italian-opera star sing English. But London took to *Esther* eagerly: after the performance on May 2, with the royal family present, it was necessary for the management to tell holders of tickets who had been unable to enter the theater that they could either have their money back or attend a subsequent performance. Five additional singings were required that month.

It was not to himself alone that Handel had now proved that his nonoperatic works could be sold to the large public. Thomas Arne, by trade a draper and upholsterer, had been running operatic and other performances in English at the Little (New) Theatre in the Haymarket, which had opened on December 29, 1720. Associated with Arne were John Christopher Smith the elder, a bassoonist named John Frederick Lampe,[2] and Henry Carey.[3] And Arne saw that there was money to be made from Handel's English works.

Speaking of Arne and his co-workers, the *Daily Post* of May 2,

[2] Lampe was a Saxon. His compositions included hymn tunes prepared for Charles Wesley, his personal friend, incidental music for plays, and songs. He married Isabella Young, sister to Cecilia Young (Mrs. Thomas Augustine Arne).

[3] Carey, the popular theatrical composer, has often been credited incorrectly with composing the tune used for *God Save the King* and *America*. He did write both the lyrics and the original music of *Sally in Our Alley*, now commonly sung to a folktune originally known as *What though I am a Country Lass*.

1732 (the first day of *Esther* at His Majesty's), carried the following notice:

We hear that the proprietors of the English Opera will very shortly perform a celebrated pastoral opera called *Acis and Galatea*, composed by Mr. Handel, with all the grand choruses and other decorations, as it was performed before his Grace the Duke of Chandos, at Cannons. It is now in rehearsal.

Four days later there was this frank advertisement:

At the new theater in the Haymarket, on Thursday next, 11th May, will be performed in English, a pastoral opera, called *Acis and Galatea*, with all the choruses, scenes, machines, and other decorations, as it was performed before his Grace the Duke of Chandos, at Cannons, being the first time it ever was performed in a theatrical way. The part of Acis by Mr. Mountier, being the first time of his appearance in character on any stage; Galatea, Miss Arne. Pits and boxes, 5s.

("It being impossible to get ready the decorations, scenes, and machines before that time," the performance was later postponed until May 17.) Mr. Mountier was a popular singer from Chichester; Miss Arne was Susanna Maria, then eighteen years old, later the famous wife of Theophilus Cibber. It also appears that Cecilia Young, the future wife of the elder Arne's more famous son, also sang in this *Acis and Galatea*, and that the role of Polyphemus was sung by Gustavus Waltz, Handel's one-time cook.

Handel was now fully roused, and no more likely to allow the Arnes to reap from *Acis and Galatea* (published complete by Walsh in 1731) profits justly his than he had been to let others profit from *Esther*. On June 5, the *Daily Journal* displayed his hand:

In the King's Theater in the Haymarket, the present Saturday, being the 10th of June, will be performed a serenata, called *Acis and Galatea*, formerly composed by Mr. Handel, and now revised by him, with several additions, and to be performed by a great number of the best voices and instruments. There will be no action on the stage, but the scene will represent, in a picturesque manner, a rural prospect, with rocks, groves, fountains, and grottoes, amongst which will be disposed a chorus of nymphs and shepherds; the habits, and every other decoration, suited to the subject. Also on the 13th, 17th, 20th. The libretto, printed for J. Watts [Walsh?], in three acts.

The first of these performances of *Acis and Galatea* was given ostensibly to supply the subscribers to the New Royal Academy of Music with the last of the fifty performances they had been promised during the season, of which they had been supplied with only forty-nine. It is to be noted that, unlike Arne, who referred to *Acis and Galatea* as "a pastoral opera," Handel continued to inscribe a heavy line between opera on one side and serenata, pastoral, and eventually oratorio on the other, inscribing that line so heavily, indeed, that it has persisted in England and the United States to this day. Only a handful of exceptional performances has ever crossed it.

The serenata presented at His Majesty's Theatre four times during June 1732 and four times during the following December was a collating of the Naples *Aci, Galatea e Polifemo* of 1708, the *Acis and Galatea* of 1720, and new music. To the original John Gay text, Handel now added lines by Pope beginning "Not showers to larks," by Hughes beginning "Would you gain the tender creature," and by Dryden beginning "Help, Galatea, help," these last translated from the thirteenth book of Ovid's *Metamorphoses*. Among the singers were again Strada (Galatea) and Senesino (Acis), who probably sang in Italian.

The season closed, not with a performance of the revamped and revitalized *Acis and Galatea*, but with a pastoral entertainment by Bononcini. It was as though the Italian had returned from semi-obscurity to prove that Handel was not alone in being able to fill the opera house without an opera. When Bononcini's pastoral was announced, the following curious public announcement was made by Strada's husband, Aurelio del Pò:

Whereas Signor Bononcini intends, after the serenata composed by Mr. Handel hath been performed, to have one of his own, and hath desired Signora Strada to sing in that entertainment: Aurelio del Po, husband of the said Signora Strada, thinks it incumbent upon him to acquaint the nobility and gentry, that he shall think himself happy in contributing to their satisfaction; but, with respect to this request, hopes he shall be permitted to decline complying with it for reasons best known to the said Aurelio del Po and his wife.

It is likely that Strada had refused the engagement out of fierce loyalty to Handel, to whose persistent training and support she owed the considerable success she had at last won.

It was during 1732 that the theater in Covent Garden was opened under John Rich's management. One of Rich's first projects was a revival of Ben Jonson's *The Alchymist*, for which play he asked Handel to supply dance music. Handel held no grudge against the man, and complied with a score fabricated mostly out of dance numbers from *Rodrigo*, the opera he had composed in Italy almost a quarter of a century before. At the same time, too, he was at work arranging his *Opera prima* (Opus 1), the series of "XV Solos for a German Flute, Hoboy or Violin with a Thorough Bass for the Harpsicord or Bass Violin," as well as the flute/oboe sonatas and fifteen trio sonatas (nine of them the present Opus 2). Opus 1 includes the six familiar so-called violin sonatas.

Handel had become set in the custom of opening the fall season with a revival, a *pasticcio*, or an opera by another composer. He saved his own novelty for after the beginning of the new year. So the fourth season of the New Royal Academy of Music, beginning on November 4, 1732, with a *Catone* that may have been Leonardo Leo's (originally given in Rome and Venice in 1728) or a *pasticcio* by Handel himself, was occupied until January 23, 1733, with six representations of that work, six of Handel's *Alessandro*, the forementioned four of *Acis and Galatea*, and four of Handel's *Tolomeo*. Of the company used during the previous season, Strada, Senesino, Bertolli, and Montagnana remained. Pinacci had left, and a soprano named Celeste Gismondi had been recruited.

Handel had completed the novelty for the fourth season on

November 20, 1732. It was a setting of *Orlando*, a libretto written in 1713 by Braccioli. This text had already been set by,
among several others, Giovanni Alberto Ristori and Antonio
Vivaldi. For this, the last opera in which he would have the services of the New Royal Academy company, Handel composed a
score so dramatically powerful and musically original that today
much of it would strike our ears with a strangeness other than
that of the antique. The opera's structure — the division of its
arias among the singers, the deploying of instrumental interludes and passages for chorus — is worth analysis. It is, furthermore, a fair example of the whole mature Handelian operatic
plan.[4]

Orlando is a typical opera of the period leading up to the so-
called reforms of Calzabigi and Gluck. It begins with an adaptation of the French overture as composed by Lully. It has no true
chorus. It consists of a string of discrete arias and recitatives,
having only an occasional duet or terzetto, very rarely a quartet
or quintet. The placing of the arias conforms to a scheme that
carefully preserves the prerogatives of *prima donna, primo
uomo, seconda donna, secondo uomo*, etc. Thus, Bertolli (Medoro) had only three arias or near-arias, the first of them the
ninth number in the first act; Gismondi (Dorinda) had four, beginning with the sixth in the first act; Montagnana (Zoroastro)
had five, including the opening number; Strada (Angelica) had
six, and though the first of these was the seventh number in
Act I, she also had the eighth. Finally, Senesino (Orlando),
brightest star of them all, had eight arias, beginning with the
second number of Act I and ending with that preceding the final
"chorus" quintet. There are two duets, in both of which Senesino
had one part, first with Gismondi and then with Strada. The
terzetto was allotted to Strada, Gismondi, and Bertolli, while
the concluding quintet was, of course, for all five singers. Slight
variations in this scheme of precedence were sometimes made
necessary by variations in operatic plots, by shadings of impor-

---

[4] For a brief analysis of *Orlando*, see Appendix B (p. 318).

tance among singers, and by the absence or presence of special concatenations of stars. But any major deviation from it was cause for alarm and for high, angry words.

Orlando was a success at His Majesty's in 1733. Having been first presented on January 27 (postponed from January 23 by illness among the performers), it attained eleven singings during its first run, the last on May 5. Walsh thought so highly of its sales possibilities that he had a ninety-page book of it engraved and for sale in seventeen days, a solo flute version later! But the anti-Handelian factions were beginning to be heard in greater volume, and there were signs of their crystalizing around the increasingly popular figure of Frederick, Prince of Wales. Whether Handel wanted another string to his bow if the demand for Italian opera should fail, or whether he was now bent upon exploiting the additional musical resources open to a composer of concert oratorio, he had been busy for some time completing the first English oratorio ever deliberately made for the purpose of presentation to a London audience. It was composed to Samuel Humphreys' adaptation of a French drama on the subject of Deborah. It was completed on February 21, 1733, and presented at the theater in the Haymarket twenty-four days later.

For the March 17 *première* of *Deborah,* which succeeded a revival of *Floridante,* the *Daily Journal* carried the following notice:

By His Majesty's command. *Deborah,* an oratorio or sacred drama, in English, composed by Mr. Handel. The house to be fitted up and illuminated in a new and particular manner; and to be performed by a great number of the best voices and instruments. Tickets, to be delivered at the office of the Opera-house on Friday and Saturday, 16th and 17th inst., one guinea each; gallery, half a guinea. N.B. — This is the last dramatick performance that will be exhibited at the King's Theater till after Easter.

As seats in the boxes and pit were customarily priced at 10/6, those in the gallery at 5/3, this meant that the rate had been doubled. The first performance was not included as part of the regular operatic subscription season, but was a personal benefit for Handel. The house was not full, and Handel found it necessary to lower the prices for subsequent performances of *Deborah*. The one on March 27 was attended by George II and some members of his family, not including Frederick, Prince of Wales. Subscribers were annoyed because it was repeated on nights when they were entitled to expect opera. Not Strada as Deborah could satisfy them. Gathering about the ample figure of Handel were stormclouds of rumor, pointed jokes, diatribes, and petty, waxing troubles. When the atmospheric condition became right, these clouds were capable of producing a first-rate storm. It waited, however briefly.

Deborah is strongest in its overture, its choruses, and its subtle, powerful characterization of old Abinoam, father of Barak. The overture is a microcosm of the epic drama of the whole oratorio, and quotes melodies from two of its choruses. The solo arias (like a few of the choruses) are adapted from such earlier works as the *Birthday Ode,* the Brockes Passion, and the Coronation Anthems; with few exceptions, they fail to measure up to the majestic, harmonically massive choruses. The whole is conceived on epic lines. Its drama is far indeed from that of opera, but a revival of *Deborah*'s considerable beauties would reveal it removed in quality rather than nature from *Israel in Egypt* and *Messiah*. In its most fervid pages it is touched with a grandeur that only Handel, in all the history of music, was able to achieve, a particular baroque grandeur of proportion and sublime majesty.[5]

---

[5] In his admirable *Mozart,* W. J. Turner has a footnote with which I disagree happily and violently. It ends with this sentence: "Handel had not got the universality of Mozart. Mozart might have composed the *Messiah* (only it would have been better) but Handel could never have composed *Don Giovanni*." I defer to no one in admiration for Mozart, but he was no more capable of composing *Messiah* than of composing Beethoven's Ninth Symphony, two works stamped line after line with the individual characters of their composers. Of course Handel "could never have composed *Don Giovanni*," which required not only another era but — again

Deborah was failing against the tides of animosity and partly political plotting being directed against Handel and his enterprise. He revived *Esther*, beginning on April 14, 1733, for several nights. He tried *Orlando*. He tried *Floridante*. Nothing helped. The New Royal Academy of Music was being swept against the rocks. Heidegger, on the verge of deserting the partnership, lent the theater to Bononcini for a performance of *Griselda*. By the time that this closed the season on June 9, the storm against Handel was in full cry.

Handel's partnership with Heidegger was to be broken up. He was to lose all his Italian singers except the faithful Strada. He was at last to lose His Majesty's Theatre. As at the climax of the Bononcini fray and the Cuzzoni-Faustina war, he was to suffer for political reasons as much as, if not more than, for purely musical or theatrical ones. His cause was to be identified in the minds of a large section of the public with the increasingly unpopular George II, whose prolonged stay in his Hanoverian dominions had caused many of his English subjects to come to the correct conclusion that he cared more for Hanover than for England. With less reason, Handel's cause was likewise to be identified with the advanced unpopularity of Sir Robert Walpole's government, which had been sponsoring unpopular taxes. His enemies were to find that attacking him was a method of indicating admiration for the Prince of Wales, who disliked his father, his mother, and his very Handelian sisters, and who yearned to cut a major figure in London life.

The most renowned of the public attacks on Handel was that printed in *The Craftsman* for April 7, 1733, as a letter from "P--lo R--li" (clearly Paolo Rolli, one of the two original poet-librettists of the Royal Academy, and author of several of

---

— the individual character of Mozart. Whatever might have been the result of Mozart's setting the text Handel used, it would not have been a "better" version of *Messiah* as we know it. It would, as the tasteless "additional accompaniments" to *Messiah* that Mozart prepared for Baron van Swieten prove, have been less baroque, more rococo, more Italianate and less English — in short, Mozartean rather than Handelian.

Handel's librettos). This was in all probability written by a
political journalist. Although in reality a charade — it is more
clearly an attack on Walpole than on Handel — this letter hurt
Handel's cause. It reveals clearly the tone that attacks on him
were being given.

Sir,

I am always rejoiced, when I see a *spirit* of Liberty exert itself
among any sect or denomination of my countrymen. I please myself
with the hopes that it will grow more diffusive, some time or other
become fashionable, and at last useful to the publick. As I know
your zeal for *Liberty*, I thought I could not address better than to
you the following exact account of the noble stand lately made by
the polite part of the world in defence of their *Liberties* and *Prop-
erties* against the open attacks and bold attempts of Mr. H - - - - l upon
both. I shall singly relate the fact and leave you, who are better able
than I am, to make what inferences or applications may be proper.

The rapid rise and progress of Mr. H - - - - l's power and fortune are
too well known for me now to relate. Let it suffice to say that he has
grown so insolent upon the sudden and undeserved increase of both,
that he thought nothing ought to oppose his imperious and extravagant will. He had for some time govern'd the *Opera* and modell'd
the *Orchestre* without the least controul. No *Voices*, no *Instruments*,
were admitted, but such as flatter'd his ears, though they shock'd
those of the audience. *Wretched scrapers* were put above the *best
Hands* in the *Orchestre*. No Musick but *his own* was to be allow'd,
though everybody was weary of it, and he had the impudence to
assert, *that there was no Composer in England but Himself.*

Even *Kings* and *Queens* were to be content with whatever low
characters he was pleased to assign them, as it was evident in the
case of Seignior *Montagnana,* who though a King, is always obliged
to act (except an angry, rumbling song or two) the most insignifi-
cant part of the whole Drama. This excess and abuse of power soon
disgusted the town; his Government grew odious, and his Opera
grew empty. However, this degree of unpopularity and general ha-
tred, instead of troubling him, only made him more furious and
desperate. He resolved to make one last effort to establish his power

and fortune by force, since he found it now impossible to hope for it from the goodwill of mankind. In order to this, he form'd a *Plan*, without consulting any of his *Friends*, (if he has any), and declared that at a proper season he would communicate it to the publick; assuring us at the same time that it would be very much for the advantage of the publick in general and of his *Operas* in particular. Some people suspect that he had settled it previously with Signora Strada del Pò, who is much in his favour; but all, that I can advise with certainty, is, that he had concerted it with a *Brother of his own,*[6] in whom he places a most undeserved confidence. In this Brother of his, *Heat* and *Dullness* are miraculously united. The *former* prompts him to anything new and violent; while the *latter* hinders him from seeing any of the inconveniences of it. As Mr. *H----l's Brother*, he thought it was necessary he should be a *Musician* too, but all he could arrive at, after a very laborious application for many years, was a moderate performance upon the Jew's Trump. He had, for some time, play'd a *Parte Buffa abroad*, and had entangled his *Brother* in several troublesome and dangerous engagements, in the commissions he had given him to contract with *Foreign Performers;* and from which (by the way) Mr. *H----l* did not disengage himself with much honour. Notwithstanding all these and many more objections, Mr. *H----l*, by and with the advice of his *Brother*, at last produces his Project; resolves to cram it down the throats of the Town; misuses great and *aweful Names*, as the patrons of it; and even does not scruple to insinuate that they are to be sharers of the profit. His *Scheme* set forth in substance, that the late decay of *Operas* was owing to their cheapness, and to the great *frauds* committed by *Door-Keepers;* that the *annual Subscribers* were a parcel of Rogues, and made an ill use of their Tickets, by often running two into the Gallery; that to obviate these abuses he had contrived a thing, that was better than *Opera*, call'd an *Oratorio;* to which none shall be admitted but by *printed Permits*, or Tickets of one Guinea each, which should be distributed out of *Warehouses of his own*, and by *Officers of his own naming;* which *Officers* would not so

---

[6] As Handel had no brother, this clearly refers to Horace (Horatio) Walpole, Baron Walpole of Wolterton (1678–1757), younger brother of Sir Robert, a diplomatic representative of England on the Continent.

reasonably be supposed to cheat in the collection of *Guineas,* as the *Door-Keepers* in the collection of half *Guineas;* and lastly, that as the very being of *Operas* depended upon *him singly,* it was just that the profit arising from hence should be for his *own benefit.* He added, that if any person should think himself aggrieved, and that the *Oratorio* was not worth the price of the *Permit,* he should be at liberty to appeal to *three judges of Musick,* who should be obliged, within the space of seven years at farthest, finally to determine the same; provided always that the said judges should be of his nomination, and known to like no other Musick but his.

The absurdity, extravagancy, and opposition of *this Scheme* disgusted the whole Town. Many of the most constant attenders of the Operas resolv'd absolutely to renounce them, rather than go to them under such extortion and vexation. They exclaim'd against the *insolent and rapacious Projector of this Plan.* The King's old and known servants of the two Theatres of *Drury-Lane* and *Covent-Garden* reap'd the benefit of this general discontent, and were resorted to in crowds, by way of opposition to the Oratorio. Even the fairest breasts were fired with indignation against this *new imposition.* Assemblies, Cards, Tea, Coffee, and all the other female batteries were vigorously employ'd to defeat the *Project* and destroy the *Projector.* These joint endeavours of all ranks and sexes succeeded so well, that the *Projector* had the mortification to see a very thin audience at his Oratorio; and of about two hundred and sixty odd, that it consisted of, it was notorious that not ten paid for their *Permits,* but, on the contrary, had them given them, and money into the bargain, for coming to keep him in countenance.[7]

This accident, they say, has thrown him into a deep *Melancholy,* interrupted sometimes by *raving Fits,* in which he fancies he sees ten thousand *Opera* Devils coming to tear him to pieces; then he breaks out into frantick incoherent speeches; muttering *sturdy Beggars, assassination!* etc. In these delirious moments, he discovers a particular aversion to the *City.* He calls them all a parcel of *Rogues,* and asserts that the *honestest Trader among them deserves to be hang'd.* It is much to be questioned whether he will recover; at

---

[7] Although it was true that parties and assemblies were scheduled deliberately to interfere with Handel's performances, this entire passage refers to a debate in Parliament.

FREDERICK, PRINCE OF WALES, AND HIS SISTERS

[after a painting by Nollekens]

"THE CHARMING BRUTE"

[caricature of Handel by Goupy]

least, if he does, it is not to be doubted but he will seek for a retreat in his *own Country* from the general resentment of the Town.

I am, Sir,

Your very humble Servant,

P - - lo R - - li.

P. S. Having seen a little epigram, lately handed about Town, which seems to allude to the same subject, I believe it will not be unwelcome to your readers.

EPIGRAM

Quoth W - - - - - e to H - - - l, shall We Two agree,
And *excise* the whole Nation?
H. Si, caro, si.
Of what use are *Sheep* if the *Shepherd* can't shear them
At the *Hay-Market* I, you at *Westminster*.
W. Hear him.
Call'd to order, their *Seconds* appear in their place;
One fam'd for his *Morals,* and one for his *Face*.[8]
If half they succeeded, in half they were crost:
The Excise was obtained, but poor Deborah lost.

This amusing farrago of complicated puns and *doubles entendres* was beyond question launched against Walpole primarily, Handel secondarily, by a partisan of the Prince of Wales, who at the moment disliked them both. Frederick was already hobnobbing with the opposition to Walpole, and now he undertook to attack Handel, whom he disliked principally because the composer was a favorite with his parents and his sisters. Around Frederick and those members of the nobility who sought his favor at the expense of the King's, a scheme accreted for the launching of an "Opera of the Nobility" that would overthrow Handel. Plans were matured during the spring of 1733. On June 15, a meeting was called, at Frederick's sugestion, at Hickford's Room, Panton Street, Haymarket. The young Duke of Marlborough, whose family had continuously supported Bononcini against Handel, was one of its energetic movers. The assembled

[8] The men referred to here seem to be Lord Hervey and Heidegger.

175

founders decided to engage as composer to their new company
the internationally famous Italian composer and singing teacher,
Niccolo Antonio Porpora. Further, they were to engage the best
Italian singers remaining to the moribund New Royal Academy
of Music. Before long, in fact, they had secured Senesino and
Montagnana, and had elicited from Cuzzoni a promise to return
to London. They would use the theater in Lincoln's-Inn Fields.
They had in plenty the necessity Handel and Heidegger were
more and more finding themselves without: money.

In the New Royal Academy of Music Handel had engaged
£10,000 of his personal funds, Heidegger probably at least that
much. By the end of the 1733 season (June 9), it is clear, nothing
remained of that approximately £20,000. Soon, in fact, Handel
was to find himself deprived not only of his best singers, but also
of his partner. For Heidegger too was about to abandon him.
Just at this time, Handel may have indulged himself in a care-
less insult that resulted in the town's having a cruel laugh at his
expense. While excitement rose over the advanced costs of
tickets for the *première* of *Deborah*, Handel is said to have invited to dine with him in Brook Street Joseph Goupy, drawing
master to the Prince of Wales, who had painted scenery for
Admeto and others of Handel's operas. He promised Goupy
nothing but the starkest dinner, saying that his fortunes, depleted by the failures at His Majesty's, allowed nothing richer.
The meal turned out no more warming than he had described
it in advance. At its close, Handel left the room, giving the excuse that he had just conceived a musical idea that he wanted
to commit to paper before it escaped him. Goupy, awaiting his
host's return, happened to glance into another room of the house.
And there sat Handel, downing a glass of Burgundy from one
bottle of an entire case. Outraged, Goupy — who is said to have
been a notable winebibber — rushed from the house.

It is certain that Goupy drew a bitter caricature of Handel, a
slashing attack that was quickly reproduced and widely spread.
It pictures the composer as a man so large as to be monstrous.
Seated at a small organ, he has a boar's snout. Upon his colossal

wig stands an owl representing solitude. The floor all about is a shambles in which may be seen empty barrels, a trumpet, a hunting horn, a bassoon, a kettle drum, a side drum, and a cello. Handel's reputation as glutton and bibber (this seems to have been well deserved) is played upon by scattered oyster shells, the head of a pig, the spigoted beer barrel on which he is seated, and the ham and edible fowl hanging on both sides of the organ. The boar-monster's right foot rests upon a scroll bearing the words "Pension. Benefit. Nobility. Friendship." At the top of the organ appears an inscription that seems intended to read "GH che Tocca" [George Handel who plays]. From behind the organ a dwarf with an animal-like face, said to represent Aesop, leans out to hold a mirror up to the boar-face. A donkey brays in the room, while outdoors beyond a ruined arch a park of artillery fires of its own accord, without human help — these details obviously intended to indicate the vast noise of the music being played.[9] Above the original picture is printed "The true representation and character, etc." Below it is this rhyme:

> Strange monsters have adorned the stage,
>   Not Afric's coast produces more;
> And yet no land, nor clime, nor age
>   Have equaled this harmonious boar.

Many years later, another version of Goupy's caricature had wide circulation as a print. Different in many details, this later version is called *The Charming Brute*. It contains a scroll inscribed "I AM MYSELF ALONE," and has the following rhyme:

> The Figure's odd — yet who wou'd think?
> Within this Tunn (of Meat & Drink)
> There dwells the Soul of soft Desires,
> And all that HARMONY inspires:

[9] Schoelcher says that a poet in one of Sheridan's first plays greeted Jupiter's announcement that he was sovereign of the skies by firing a pistol toward the wings and saying to the audience, "This hint, gentlemen, I took from Handel."

Can Contrast such as this be found?
Upon the Globe's extensive Round;
There can — yon Hogshead is his Seat,
His sole Devotion is — to EAT.

There is no doubt that the original version hit more marks. For
in addition to ridiculing Handel for gluttony, the only vice with
which it was possible certainly to charge him, it played on the
claim that his music was too noisy and accused him of ingratitude to the English nation for his pension, to the public that had
supported him, to the nobility that had patronized him, and to
his personal friends. It is not recorded that Handel's intimacy
with Goupy was ever re-established. But Paolo Rolli, whose
name could hardly without his knowledge and consent have
been used to close the attack in *The Craftsman,* was to live to
supply Handel with the libretto of his last opera, *Deidamia.*
Through all this turmoil, through the worse troubles that were
soon to emerge, the one participant in the affairs of the New
Royal Academy of Music who was to remain unwaveringly
faithful to Handel was Strada.

The stormy year 1733 saw the final removal from the English
scene of the greatest and most persistent rival Handel had
known, Bononcini. In an age when a composer's use or adaptation without acknowledgment of another composer's music was
common, the talented but silly Italian had stooped to deliberate
and outright plagiarism. In 1727 or 1728, Bononcini had handed
to Maurice Greene, for performance by the Academy of Antient
Musick, a madrigal entitled *La Vita Caduca.* In 1731, one of the
Academy's members received from Venice a collection of works
by Antonio Lotti. From it there was selected for performance a
madrigal beginning with the words *"In una siepe ombrosa."* This
turned out to be identical with Bononcini's *La Vita Caduca.*

Bononcini insisted that the composition was his own. Members of the Academy thereupon entered into official correspondence with Lotti, then organist of St. Mark's, Venice. From him
they received attested documents that proved the music to have
been composed and published by him a quarter of a century

earlier. Everyone involved, with the sole exception of Maurice Greene, became convinced of Bononcini's guilt. Worse, the Academy went on to issue a pamphlet entitled *Letters from the Academy of Antient Musick at London, to Sig^r Antonio Lotti of Venice, with his Answers and Testimonies.* About the time of the pamphlet's appearance, Bononcini tacitly admitted his guilt by fleeing England, never to return. Paris saw him briefly. He turned up in Vienna in 1748, an almost forgotten man of seventy-six. About two years later he died at Venice. He was a man of great talent and weak character who had allowed himself to be set up against a man of genius and strong character. And at last he had broken under the strain of so unequal a combat. It has, however, ill befitted Handel's apologists to minimize Bononcini the composer. Most of them have known little or none of his music, and the very man they have tried to aggrandize by excoriating Bononcini for his plagiarism from Lotti was himself probably without parallel in the history of music for the extent of his unacknowledged borrowings. If the custom of the time excuses Handel — and for the most part it does — then it all but excuses Bononcini too. The Italian's mistake was that he tried to pass off Lotti's madrigal as his own madrigal, that he failed to incorporate what he borrowed into a fabric of music he had himself composed or arranged. That is what Handel did, not once or twice only, but often. It is exactly what Marlowe and Shakespeare did with the dramatic ideas, situations, and characters of other writers.

As Tovey wrote with his witty insight: "Much light would be thrown on the subject if some one sufficiently ignorant of architecture were to make researches into Sir Christopher Wren's indebtedness to Italian architects!" It is certain that one way in which Handel (like Shakespeare and Goethe) showed his dramatic genius was his apt and often overwhelmingly telling use of borrowings both from others and from himself. There would be no moral dilemma involved for the modern critic if he had publicly acknowledged them — but to do so was not the ethical practice of musicians in an age of *pasticcio.*

II

IN 1733, Handel's unsought reputation as *the* Whig composer brought him an invitation to visit Oxford and present some of his music there. The University had been tinctured strongly with Jacobitism since the time of Cromwell. Now, however, some of its officers, led by William Holmes, recently appointed vice-chancellor, had become convinced that the descendants of George I were at St. James's to stay, and they were therefore intent upon establishing an entente with the Hanoverian dynasty. One of their avenues of *rapprochement* led to an invitation to the favorite composer of George I, George II, and Queen Caroline, not to mention the Princesses Anne, Emily, and Caroline. Handel was bidden to Oxford to be made a Doctor of Music and to present his compositions during the Public Act (later called the Commemoration).

Handel accepted the invitation to perform his music in Oxford, but for some reason refused the honorary degree. One story has it that when he learned that the document would cost him £100 in fees he flew into a notable rage. "I will not throw my money away for what the blockheads wish," he is reported as shouting. "I no want." There are other versions. The Abbé Prévost, in *Le Pour et le Contre,* for example, stated that Handel refused the honor out of modesty, an action nothing else he ever did suggests as likely. Chrysander and Dent agree in not believing this story. Eric Blom has suggested that Handel was asked to make a donation of £100 to a "charity or other worthy object" out of the profits of his visit to Oxford (said to have reached £4,000), in return for which generosity he would receive the doctorate "as a special acknowledgment." As Handel shortly later became a lavish donor to several charitable causes, his refusal of such an offer is an explanation that does not explain. The original story is wholly reasonable: Handel simply refused to purchase the degree whether with fees or with a donation.

Of the Italian singers from the New Royal Academy of Music company, only Strada remained to go to Oxford with Handel. And he had composed an important role in *Athalia,* the new oratorio he completed on June 7 for Oxford, with Montagnana in mind. Good basses were not plentiful. So out of his own past Handel summoned Gustavus Waltz, the German who had at one time been employed as his cook, that employment having probably been Handel's way of helping a fellow musician fallen temporarily on hard times. Waltz had sung the role of Polyphemus in the Arnes' performance of *Acis and Galatea* the previous year. If his former master had been angry at Waltz for that defection, he now forgave it by inviting the erstwhile cook to replace Montagnana at Oxford.

Handel's company reached the University town on Wednesday, July 4, 1733. At 5 P. M. the next day, Handel initiated his participation in the festivities with a performance of *Esther* in the new Sheldonian Theatre. This was repeated on the Saturday. On Sunday, July 8, the *Utrecht Te Deum* and *Jubilate* were sung in a church, the former in the morning, the latter in the evening. These, too, were repeated, on July 10. *Deborah* was given on the evening of the second Thursday, July 13, *Acis and Galatea* was presented on the morning of July 11 as a benefit for the musicians. But the center of the entire visit was occupied by two performances of *Athalia,* the first (postponed from July 9 because the presentation of degrees kept the Sheldonian too late) on July 10 before an audience of thirty-seven hundred persons who had paid five shillings a seat. Completed on June 7, *Athalia* was a setting of Samuel Humphreys' adapted translation of Racine's *Athalie.*

It is recorded that the Sheldonian Theatre was packed for all the performances Handel gave there. It was the July *Gentleman's Magazine* that reported *Athalia* as having been heard "with vast applause before an audience of 3700 persons." Nonetheless, the local Jacobites, anti-Hanoverians, and jingos were far from placated or won over. Thomas Hearne, a notable anti-quary who had been forced to resign as second librarian of the Bodleian Library because as a nonjuror he had declined to swear the oath of allegiance to George I, snarled at the whole entertainment in his diary. Part of Hearne's grievance was that Vice-Chancellor Holmes had given Handel the Sheldonian after refusing it to a company of players who, in order to attract some custom from Oxford, had set up in near-by Abbington. He wrote:

July 6th. The players being denied coming to Oxford by the Vice-Chancellor, and that very rightly, tho' they might as well have been here as Handell and his lowsy crew, a great number of foreign fid-dlers, they went to Abbington, and yesterday began to act there, at which were present many gownsmen from Oxford.

Hearne also objected strenuously to the admission price of five shillings, and commented thus on the printed libretto of *Athalia:* "N.B. — His book (not worth 1*d.*) he sells for 1*s.*"

The anonymous author of a pamphlet called *The Oxford Act, A. D. 1733* wrote as follows of the first performance of *Athalia:*

The company in the evening were entertained with a spick and span new oratorio called *Athalia.* One of the royal and ample had been saying, that truly it was his opinion that the theater was erected for other guise purposes, than to be prostituted to a company of squeek-ing, bawling, outlandish singsters, let the agreement be what it wou'd.

The controversy aroused achieved further prominence when a ballad opera was based on it. In this, *The Oxford Act: A New Ballad-Opera* (London, 1733), two undergraduates of Merton College have this to say:

Thoughtless — In the next place, there's the furniture of my room procured me some tickets to hear that bewitching music, that cursed Handel, with his confounded oratorio's; I wish him and his company had been yelling in the infernal shades below. *Haughty* — Our cases run in a parallel; nay, 'tis worse with me, for I question whether my gaping herd of creditors won't be for sequestering my fellowship or not. I don't see what occasion we had for this Act, unless it was to ruin us all. It would have been much more prudent, I think, had it pass'd in the negative; for I am sure it has done more harm than good amongst us; no one has gain'd anything by it but Mr. Handel and his crew.

The *Weekly Register* for July 14, 1733, however, records that the July 10 singing of *Athalia* was "perform'd with the utmost applause." It adds:

The Persons of Quality and Distinction who are come hither on this occasion make a very grand appearance, and are greater in number than ever was known heretofore: the little hutts of the neighbouring villages are mostly filled with the Gentlemen of Cambridge and Eton, there being no place empty in this or the Towns within five and six miles about us.

It was during this visit to Oxford that, according to Burney, Handel "opened the organ in such a manner as astonished every hearer. The late Mr. Michael Christian Festing, and Dr. Arne, who were present, both assured me, that neither themselves, nor any one else of their acquaintance, had ever before heard such extempore, or such premeditated playing, on that or any other instrument." Handel's virtuosity had not been dulled by the years.

At Oxford Handel had once again been an unintentional actor in a political drama. It was another part of the unending war that found Kings, Whigs, and Handelians on one side, Princes of Wales, Tories, Jacobites, and Bononcinians on the other. More consciously, however, Handel was engaged in an economic war of greater ultimate importance. He was struggling against discouragement, imminent bankruptcy, odds of every sort, to free himself from the ancient institution of patronage, to assert his right as a musician to be an earning member of society, a free man whose art could win financial support in the open market. This was a long, uneven struggle, with periods of apparent success, periods of complete defeat, periods of standing still. For Handel, it was to end in complete victory. It was a war that never touched Johann Sebastian Bach, and of which Haydn was to be only intermittently aware. Mozart was to fight it over again on the Continent, and Beethoven was to uplift it into a mighty human drama that has engaged the sympathies of his biographers and their readers ever since. But it was Handel in England who fought its first great skirmishes and won its first salient victories. He was at last to make himself a highly respected member of society, earn a fortune, and be buried in Westminster Abbey. No composer had ever before by his own efforts done anything exactly comparable to that.

Following his Oxford successes, Handel is supposed to have taken John Christopher Smith the elder with him on a trip to Italy in search of new singers for his operas. But this story is derived largely from a confused passage in Sir John Hawkins' *A general history of the science and practice of music* (London, 1776), and there is a strong probability that the trip never took place. The dates, first of all, are against it unless it was so short a trip as to have been recklessly extravagant. Handel was at Oxford as late as July 13, for *Deborah* was sung there under his direction the night before. He was in London in August, as is proved by a letter to Michael Dietrich Michaelsen.[1] He completed the opera *Arianna* at London on October 5, and opened the last season of his partnership with Heidegger at the King's Theatre on October 30. He could therefore not have been away from England longer than two months — in June, July, and August, or in August, September, and October. With traveling times what they were in 1733, this would have allowed him very scant time for a visit to Italy.

Part of the story of Handel's supposed visit to Italy in 1733 is that he heard two *castrati*, Giovanni Carestini and Carlo Broschi, called Farinelli, and selected the former because Farinelli's price was too high or because he actually preferred the less brilliant singer. But Handel knew of Carestini in the way

[1] See Appendix A (p. 311).

he had previously known of other singers successful in Italy: he had received word of the *castrato* in a letter from Owen Mac-Swiney, this time written to Francis Colman, who was to send Handel the text of *Arianna*. It is at least likely that Handel sent MacSwiney orders to hire Carestini, Scalzi, and the Negri sisters for him, and to rehire, after a decade's interlude, Margherita Durastanti. It is equally likely that the phenomenal Farinelli had already been caught by the Opera of the Nobility, and that his first appearance in London was postponed until October 1734 only because he was for the time being engaged at Dresden (not in Italy). Unless documentary evidence thus far lacking appears, Handel's traditional visit to Italy in the summer or early autumn of 1733 must remain shadowy and unlikely.

Sometime during 1733, two publications of nonvocal music by Handel were offered to the public. Walsh published what he called Opus 2, six sonatas for two violins (interchangeable with flutes or oboes) with harpsichord accompaniment. The sonatas seem to have been authorized by Handel. But Walsh had not altogether abandoned his pirating ways, for he also published, under the guise of "lessons for Princess Anne," which they may well have been, a second set of nine suites for harpsichord. Of these, the first, in B flat major, contains as its Prelude one of Handel's most beautiful keyboard works, and as the theme of its "Air and Variations" the basis of Brahms' magnificent *Variations and Fugue on a Theme by Handel*. The second "suite" is a lordly, surpassing Chaconne in G major.

Concerning this very period Burney wrote:

There were in England at this time several candidates for fame in theatrical and choral music. Arne, Lampe, [John Christopher] Smith, [William] Defesch, and Greene, tried their strength against Handel; but it was the contention of infants with a giant. Indeed, they composed for inferior performers as well as inferior hearers; but they appear to have been so sensible of their own want of resources, that the utmost they attempted seems to have been an humble and timid imitation of Handel's style of composition. Arne began to distinguish himself by new setting Addison's opera of

Rosamond [1733]; Lampe by *Amelia* [1732], an English drama written by Carey; and Smith by *Teraminta* [1732], another opera, written by the same author; these were all said, in the play-bills and advertisements, to be set in the *Italian manner*. Defesch set an oratorio, called *Judith* [1733], and Dr. Greene a *Te Deum*, and part of the *Song of Deborah* [1732]. These, though not very successful, contributed to diminish the public attention to Italian operas, and by that means injured Handel, without essentially serving themselves.

Musical London was, in the autumn of 1733, a terribly troubled place. As was his custom, Handel was not planning to present his seasonal novelty until January or his new singing star until things were well under way. He therefore opened His Majesty's on October 30,[2] with *Semiramide* (composer unknown, but with recitatives by Handel). After this had been sung four times, it was removed and replaced by a revival of *Ottone*: it was time to try the reaction of London to the new *castrato*, Carestini, a soprano become alto. After four singings, *Ottone* was replaced by *Cajo Fabricio* (also with recitatives by Handel), put on the boards on December 4. Carestini was, Burney reported, "tall, beautiful, and majestic," an actor of imagination and intelligence. In later years, Hasse said that whoever had not heard Carestini was unacquainted with a perfect style of singing. Handel had expected the *castrato* to be a high soprano, but does not appear to have been gravely disappointed on discovering that he was a very deep contralto. But the public did not take to him enough to win more than four performances for *Cajo Fabricio*. Senesino, a moving spirit in the gathering Opera of the Nobility, may, as has often been charged, have summoned his friends and supporters to do all possible damage to Handel's season. It had, in any case, begun badly.

[2] As this was George II's birthday, and as it is known that the court ball usually held on that day was abandoned, it seems likely that the date was set by Handel with the King's consent. The King and Queen and their daughters attended, and Frederick, Prince of Wales, had no choice on this occasion but to do likewise.

"Senesino's company," as it was often called, opened its season at the Lincoln's-Inn Fields Theatre on December 29, 1733, with Porpora conducting his own setting of Paolo Rolli's libretto *Arianna*. Rolli stated that he had written this *"per la nobiltà Britannica."* The opera had been rehearsed in a room at the Prince of Wales' house in the Royal Gardens in Pall Mall, before a large concourse of the *nobiltà*. It may have been a good opera. Good or bad, it was supported in a spirit of faction, and achieved twenty performances in less than six months. Cuzzoni had not yet arrived; Farinelli could not appear for another year. So the Porpora-Nobility company must have been made up chiefly of Senesino, Bertolli, Montagnana, and Segatti. Porpora's *Arianna*, having won ten performances before Cuzzoni's appearance, was revived after her arrival (which occurred in March or April 1734) for ten more. In this season, Lincoln's-Inn Fields heard four singings of Porpora's *Ferdinando*, five of Bononcini's *Astarto*, four of a *pasticcio* called *Belmira*, and six of Porpora's *Enea nel Lazio*, for a season's grand total of thirty-nine operatic performances. During the same period, the Handel-Heidegger company mounted about the same number, plus several oratorios.

After the beginning of 1734, Handel marked time with eight singings of Leonardo Vinci's(?) opera *Arbace*, with recitatives by himself. But his setting of *Arianna in Creta*, completed on October 5, 1733 was at last given its *première* on January 26.[3] It won considerable success. The minuet, played during the opening scene, in which Minos accepts tribute from Athenian youths and maidens, achieved a truly astonishing popularity. It was published in transcription for violin and harpsichord. It became a song, "How is it possible?" For decades it was heard in England. Goldsmith made reference to it in *She Stoops to Conquer*, Sheridan in *The Critic*. And the opera itself was well enough liked to be sung seventeen times between January 26

[3] With a cast that included Carestini, Scalzi, Gustavus Waltz, Strada, Durastanti, and Maria Caterina Negri.

and April 20; it was revived for five or six more performances the following autumn.

On February 12, 1734, was published a pamphlet called *Harmony in an Uproar; a letter to Frederick Handel, Esq., Master of the Opera-house in the Haymarket, from Hurlothrumbo Johnson, Esq., Composer Extraordinary to all the Theaters in Great Britain, excepting that of the Haymarket, in which the rights and merits of both O----s are properly considered.* This satire has been generally supposed to be the work of Dr. Arbuthnot, well known as a Handelian, though some biographers of Arbuthnot have denied him the authorship.[4] In it, Handel is represented as being on trial. The judge's charge reads, in part, as follows:

Court — Frederic Handel, hold up your hand. Know, you are brought to answer to the several following High Crimes and Misdemeanors committed upon the Wills and Understandings, and against the Peace of our Sovereign Lord the Mobility of Great Britain, particularly this Metropolis. *Imprimis*, you are charg'd with having bewitch'd us for the space of twenty Years past, nor do we know where your Inchantments will end, if a timely stop is not put to them, they threatening us with an entire Destruction of Liberty and an absolute Tyranny in your Person over the whole Territories of the Haymarket. *Secondly*, you have most insolently dar'd to give us good Musick and sound Harmony when we wanted and desir'd bad, to the great Encouragement of your Operas and the ruin of our good Allies and Confederates the Professors of bad Musick. *Thirdly*, you have most feloniously and arrogantly assum'd to yourself an uncontroul'd Property of pleasing us, whether we would or no, and have often been so bold as to charm us, when we were positively resolv'd to be out of Humour.

---

[4] There seems to be no reason to deny its authorship to the Samuel Johnson (1691–1733) who had published *Hurlothrumbo*, a musical satire. Johnson, a dancing master from Manchester, was a keen critic of theatricals. When *Hurlothrumbo*, produced at the Lincoln's-Inn Fields Theatre in April 1729, had proved a considerable success, John Byrom had written an epilogue for it. This epilogue contains the following lines:

> *Handel* himself shall yield to *Hurlothrumbo*,
> And *Bononcini* too shall cry — *Succumbo*.

The Prisoner's plea is: *"Guilty of the whole Charge."*

There is much more to *Harmony in an Uproar,* most of it a satire on convoluted legal language. The most interesting section after the charge is a nonsensical fanfaronade in which the Court attempts to prove that the Prisoner cannot be a good musician because he has no degree, is not a doctor. "Why, Dr. Pushpin and Dr. Blue [clearly Pepusch and Greene] laugh at you, and scorn to keep you Company; and they have vow'd to me that it is scarcely possible to imagine how much better they composed after the Commencement Gown was thrown over their Shoulders than before. . . ." This passage surely suggests that Handel's inability to refer to himself as "Dr." Handel must, at one time or another, have been held against him.

During the period when *Harmony in an Uproar* was causing winds of discussion and laughter to sweep the coffeehouses of London, Handel was called upon to make a musical acknowledgment of royal festivities. George II's eldest daughter, Handel's pupil and loyal admirer the Princess Anne, was betrothed to William IV, the deformed Prince of Orange and future Hereditary Stadholder of the Netherlands. London had not yet heard *Athalia,* but a solemn oratorio was scarcely appropriate to a supposedly happy occasion. So Handel adapted much of its music to an Italian serenata libretto dealing with the celebration, by Apollo and the Muses, of the marriage of Thetis and Peleus on Mount Parnassus. On March 13, 1734, the day before the royal wedding, this *Parnasso in Festa* replaced *Arianna* on the boards of the King's Theatre. The first performance was attended by the prospective bride and groom, the King, the Queen, the Prince of Wales, and other members of the royal family.[5] Four repetitions of the serenata, in which Carestini and Strada sang leading roles, were called for. Then the remainder of Handel's final season at the King's Theatre in the

---

[5] On March 14, 1734, at the actual wedding of the Princess Royal to the Prince of Orange, a choir with full orchestral support sang an anthem, "This is the day," arranged by Handel from sections of the Chandos Anthems, *Parnasso in Festa,* and *Athalia.* It contained no new music.

Haymarket was made up of performances and revivals of *Arbace, Deborah* (three times, two by command of George II),
Arianna, Sosarme, Acis and Galatea, and a revised version of *Il
Pastor Fido,* the last being sung fifteen times from May 18 to
the actual end of the season on July 15.

Discussing the marriage of the Princess Royal to the Prince
of Orange, Lord Hervey expands on the subject of the ill feeling
between Anne and her brother Frederick. He says that the
Prince of Wales objected to his sister's marrying before himself.
He goes on:

Another judicious subject of his enmity was her supporting Handel, a German musician and composer (who had been her singing
master, and was now undertaker of one of the operas), against several of the nobility who had a pique to Handel, and had set up another person to ruin him; or, to speak more properly, and exactly, the
Prince, in the beginning of his enmity to his sister, set himself at the
head of the other opera to irritate her, whose pride and passions were
as strong as her brother's (though his understanding was so much
weaker), and could brook contradiction, where she dared to resent
it, as little as her father.

What I have related may seem a trifle, but though the cause was
indeed such, the effects of it were no trifles. The King and Queen
were as much in earnest upon this subject as their son and daughter,
though they had the prudence to disguise it, or to endeavour to disguise it, a little more. They were both Handelists, and sat freezing
constantly at his empty Haymarket Opera, whilst the Prince with all
the chief of the nobility went as constantly to that of Lincoln's Inn
Fields. The affair grew as serious as that of the Greens and Blues
under Justinian at Constantinople. An anti-Handelist was looked
upon as an anti-courtier, and voting against the Court in Parliament
was hardly a less remissible or more venial sin than speaking against
Handel or going to the Lincoln's Inn Fields Opera. The Princess
Royal said she expected in a little while to see half the House of Lords
playing in the orchestra in their robes and coronets; and the King
(though he declared he took no other part in this affair than sub-
scribing £1,000 a year to Handel) often added at the same time
that he did not think setting oneself at the head of a faction of fid-

dlers a very honourable occupation for people of quality; or the ruin
of one poor fellow so generous or so good-natured a scheme as to
do much honour to the undertakers, whether they succeeded or not;
but the better they succeeded in it, the more he thought they would
have reason to be ashamed of it. The Princess Royal quarrelled with
the Lord Chamberlain for affecting his usual neutrality on this occasion, and spoke of Lord Delaware, who was one of the chief managers against Handel, with as much spleen as if he had been at the
head of the Dutch faction who opposed the making her husband
Stadtholder.

When Handel gave up the lease on the King's Theatre, his
former friend and partner Heidegger placed it at the disposal
of the now rapidly expanding Opera of the Nobility. To the
cronies of Senesino and Frederick, Prince of Wales, it must have
looked as though Handel was conquered as both opera composer and impresario. But the German, as they liked to insist
that he remained, had still considerable fight left in him before
he would concede the war. He had forgiven John Rich completely for his part in weaning away part of the opera public
by producing *The Beggar's Opera*. As early as 1732, indeed, he
had composed (or arranged) the music for Rich's production
of *The Alchymist*. Partly because of the fortune Rich had made
through *The Beggar's Opera*, he had been able to become pro-
prietor of the nearly completed theater in Covent Garden. Handel joined forces with him, the arrangement being for alternating performances of English plays and Italian opera. Most of
Handel's singers remained with him.

The theater in Covent Garden would obviously not be ready
for use in time for Handel to score one point against the Sene-
sino-Porpora company by opening his season earlier than theirs.
So, on August 12, 1734, he began to set the opera that became
Ariodante, using Antonio Salvi's *Ginevra, Principessa di Scozia*,
a story of pseudo-Scottish history derived from Ariosto's *Orlando
Furioso* and originally made into an opera in 1708 by Jacopo
Antonio Perti. He completed it, one of his so-called "dance-
operas" (like *Alcina*, it provides special music for dancing), on
October 24.

Handel opened his Covent Garden season on November 9, 1734, with a revival of *Il Pastor Fido,* preceded by a *prologo* — in reality a ballet-opera or French ballet with songs — called *Terpsicore.*[6] This was composed by Handel especially to display the graces of a French dancer billed as "Madlle. Sallé." This *danseuse* had already won considerable public attention in several masques or pantomimic ballets that Rich had staged at Lincoln's-Inn Fields. It is evident that Rich counted heavily on her for attracting audiences, for when the double bill of *Terpsicore* and *Il Pastor Fido* was withdrawn from the boards in Covent Garden, it was replaced on December 18 by a *pasticcio* entitled *Oreste,* arranged by Handel, with a new overture, from his own earlier works, and containing important passages for dancing that were unquestionably designed for Mlle Sallé. Also, both of the new operas Handel presented during the spring of 1735 were unusually rich in dance movements composed with her in mind. Mlle Sallé, who left England at the end of this season, was well appreciated in Paris also. There, in August 1735, she danced in the *première* of Rameau's *Les Indes galantes.*

Porpora had entered the seasonal fray on October 29, 1734, at the King's Theatre in the Haymarket, with an *Artaserse* composed largely by Johann Adolf Hasse (who had married Faustina Bordoni in 1730), partly by Riccardo Broschi, brother to the company's resplendent *castrato* star, Farinelli. The Nobility company put forward this season casts that included Cuzzoni, Bertolli, Segatti, Senesino, and Montagnana, in addition to Farinelli, whose performance in *Artaserse* was so admired that the opera achieved eleven singings during this season alone, a total of forty during his three years in England. This opera

---

[6] That *Terpsicore* was not, as several writers have asserted, first presented at Lincoln's-Inn Fields seems to be proved by the following announcement in the *Theatrical Register:* "November 9, 1734. Theater Royal, Covent Garden. By his majesty's command, on Saturday next, will be performed Pastor Fido, an opera with several additions, intermixed with choruses; which will be preceded by a new dramatick entertainment in musick, called Terpsicore."

contained the two arias, "*Pallido e il sole*" and "*Per questo dolce amplesso,*" that, according to a time-honored story, Farinelli in later years was to sing to Philip V of Spain every night for a decade, that mad and melancholy king having discovered that only the *castrato*'s rendition of them could soothe his troubled spirit and quiet him to sleep. When the first London run of *Artaserse* was over, it was succeeded, on December 10, by an "*Otho.*" As it is unlikely that the Opera of the Nobility would have staged Handel's *Ottone* (sometimes called *Otho*), this was probably the *Ottone in Villa* that Vivaldi had composed for Venice in 1729. The Porpora company ran out the season with five performances of it.

Despite Mlle Sallé, Handel and Rich were having hard sledding against the Farinelli wind. On this account, for reasons of economy, perhaps, and because Porpora had cornered the Italian market, Handel began to use English singers in prominent roles. Notable among those who first sang for him in the season of 1734-5 were the tenor John Beard, later greatly admired, and Cecilia Young (Arne).

The *Daily Post* of November 4, 1734, stated that Handel had taken the score of a new opera, intended for presentation as his January novelty, to the King, who had been so favorably impressed by it as at once to subscribe £1,000 to the Covent Garden season. If this report was correct, then Handel must somehow have performed some of it, there being no reason to believe that George II could read any music so complex as an opera score. While the Haymarket house resounded twice weekly to applause for Farinelli in *Artaserse,* this novelty was presented at Covent Garden on January 8, 1735,[7] and ran intermittently for ten performances to March 3. It was *Ariodante,* set by Handel to a libretto by Antonio Salvi, who had based it on an episode in the sixth book of Ariosto's *Orlando Furioso.* The story, containing a curious prefiguration of the Lohengrin-Elsa relationship as conceived by Wagner, is in general plot outline

[7] It was first sung by a cast including Cecilia Young, Strada, Negri, Carestini, Beard, and Waltz.

something like *Much Ado About Nothing*. To clothe it in appropriate music, Handel had not resorted to his big dramatic style. Instead, he had made it all tenderness and grace and sensuous passion. It is an entire delight throughout. The dance music at the end of each act, the lulling pastoral symphony, the vignette (almost a small tone poem) that depicts the rising of the moon as the second act opens, all these display Handel the orchestral composer at his best. They are, perhaps, superior to the vocal sections of the score.

Ariodante did well for Handel and Rich. But the rage for Farinelli mounted ever higher, attracting large sections of what might have been Handel's audiences to the musically inferior operas at the King's Theatre. When, on February 1, 1735, Porpora offered the first performance of his setting of a Paoli Rolli libretto called *Polifemo*, George II, Queen Caroline, and several members of their family were present to applaud Farinelli, Senesino, and Montagnana. *Polifemo* equaled or surpassed the first run of *Artaserse*. Only when Porpora rashly tried to challenge Handel in the matter of oratorio did he find himself bested in the bitter contest for public favor. His *Davide e Bersabea,* put on during Lent, got no more than seven hearings, while Handel was able to present six performances of *Esther,* three of *Deborah,* and five of *Athalia.* During the lenten season of oratorios, Handel continued his custom of himself performing organ concertos between the parts or sections of each work, perhaps begun at the first London performance of *Athalia.* But when the Haymarket company went back to opera, with Sandoni's *Issipile* and Porpora's *Ifigenia in Aulide,* more performances of the Hasse-Broschi *Artaserse,* and a final singing of *Polifemo* on June 7 by command of the Queen, the King's Theatre was full while Handel played his operas to houses that were often half empty.

The second Handel novelty of the 1734-5 Covent Garden season was, like the first, composed to a libretto based on Ariosto. *Alcina,* however, is more fierily dramatic: Antonio Marchi's retelling of the Alcina-Ruggiero-Bradamante story from the

sixth and seventh books of *Orlando Furioso* harks back to
the strong librettos Handel had found for *Amadigi* and *Rinaldo*.
The enchantress Alcina herself belongs to the line of impressive
operatic characters that includes Handel's own Armida (in
Rinaldo), Melissa (in *Amadigi*), Gluck's Armide, and Wagner's
Kundry. Her victims gave Handel cause to include a true chorus
in this opera, which also has a magnificent trio for the three
chief characters. The first scene, in the palace of Alcina, inter-
mingles choral passages and dances in a powerfully suggestive
pattern that Gluck was to adopt. Most famous of the single
arias in *Alcina* is Ruggiero's "*Verdi prati*," originally sung by
Carestini. It is reported that when the *castrato* first looked at
it, he found it not to his liking and returned it to Handel with
word that it was not good enough for him to sing. Handel
rushed to Carestini's quarters and burst into the room shouting.
"You dog!" he is quoted as bellowing. "Don't I know better
as yourself what is good for you to sing? If you will not sing all
the songs what I give you, I will not pay you one stiver!" Carestini bowed his head against this storm and agreed to sing "*Verdi
prati.*"

George II and Queen Caroline did not lessen their support of
the Handel-Rich company because of their willingness to honor
the Opera of the Nobility with their presences in despite of their
unabating quarrel with the Prince of Wales. Burney stated that
Alcina [8] was sung intermittently eighteen times from April 16,
1735, to the July 2 end of the season "always by command of
their Majesties, till the King went to Hanover, and then by
command of her Majesty only." Mlle Sallé also made her last
London appearance in this run of *Alcina*, during which, Prévost
records, she was actually hissed. The house was not always full,
and the financial tallies appeared ominous. Handel had been
ailing for some time, and toward the end of the season his

[8] With Strada, Cecilia Young, Carestini, Savage, and Beard. It is a remarkable fact that when Burney was writing his *History* fifty-three years
after the *première* of *Alcina*, three of its original singers — Cecilia Young,
Beard, and Savage — were still living.

condition became at first aggravated and finally grave. He was only fifty years old, but he had been driving himself and his large body hard for more than thirty years, and it is little wonder that his mind often became clouded with melancholy, his physical functions clogged with sloth. A final blow fell as soon as the season ended: Carestini, probably smarting under Handel's dictatorial ways, left the company, left England never to return, and began his greatly successful quarter-century career on the Continent.

Handel was too ill and temporarily too discouraged to plan for an autumn season of opera. Rest and some sort of anodyne for his aching body and whirling brain were required. But he hung about London through the summer, as is proved by the survival of two letters dated from there in July. The first was written in reply to a communication from Mattheson, his Hamburg crony of thirty years before, who was preparing his *Grundlage einer Ehrenpforte,* and had evidently addressed his onetime friend for autobiographical data:

At London. This $\frac{29}{18}$ July 1735.

Monsieur Mattheson, secretary of
the British Embassy at Hamburg.
Sir,

It is some time since I received one of your obliging letters; but I have just now received your latest, with your work [*Die wohlklingende Fingersprache*].

I thank you, Sir, and assure you that I have all esteem for your merit; I only wish that my circumstances were more favorable toward my giving you the signs of my inclination to serve you. Your work is worthy of the attention of connoisseurs, and as for me, I render you justice.

For the rest, it is impossible for me to collect together some epoch (of my life), for a continuous application to the service of this court and nobility keeps me from every other affair. I am with most perfect consideration, Sir,

Your very humble and obedient servant
G. F. Handel.

This letter indicates that Handel's feelings toward the friend and enemy of his young manhood were now formal, not to say distant. Offended by the stiffness of this letter and by its refusal of the assistance he had sought, Mattheson is reported to have said that Handel's coolness arose from a false belief that some sort of present was expected of him in return for the book sent him.

The other Handel letter surviving from the July of 1735 is more interesting. It was written to Charles Jennens, Junior, who was later to have a hand in the preparation of four of Handel's texts: *Saul; L'Allegro, Il Pensero ed Il Moderato; Messiah,* and *Belshazzar.* Jennens was a colorful person. He showed such a taste for luxurious living at his country home (Gopsall, Leicestershire) that he was called Solyman the Magnificent. He also kept a city house in Great Ormond Street, Bloomsbury. One tale about him said that when he drove the short distance from it to the office of his printer in Red Lion Passage he used four horses and was attended by four lackeys, of whom one had the task of sweeping discarded oyster shells and other rubbish from the places where Jennens had to walk. Born in 1698, Jennens lived long enough to publish an edition of Shakespeare that brought him into violent controversy with no less redoubtable quarrelers than George Steevens and Samuel Johnson. Handel had evidently known him for some time, as this letter proves:

London July 28, 1735

Sʳ

I received your very agreeable Letter with the inclosed Oratorio. I am just going to Tunbridge, yet what I could read of it in haste gave me a great deal of Satisfaction. I shall have more leisure time there to read it with all the Attention it deserves. There is no certainty of any Scheme for next Season, but it is probable that something or other may be done, of which I shall take the Liberty to give you notice, being extreamly obliged to you for the generous Concern you show upon this account. The opera of Alcina is a writing out and shall be send according to your Direktion, it is allways a great Pleas-

ure to me if I have an Opportunity to show the sincere Respect with
which I have the Honour to be

Sir

Your

Most obedient humble

Servant

George Frideric Handel.

It is impossible to determine exactly what text Jennens had
sent Handel. In all likelihood it was either one that Handel decided not to use or that of *Saul,* which he was to set exactly
three years later. The reference to *Alcina* has been misinter-
preted, despite the date of the letter, to mean that Handel was
composing it when he addressed Jennens. This is, of course,
impossible, *Alcina* having been staged more than three months
earlier. The reference probably indicates that the wealthy Jennens had enjoyed the opera so much that he had asked Handel
to have a complete copy of it autographed for him.

"There is no certainty of any Scheme for next Season," Handel had told Jennens. This undoubtedly referred to his own lack
of plans, but it may also have referred to a similar lack on the
part of the Opera of the Nobility. Some of the supporters of the
Prince of Wales were finding the opera enterprise less amusing
than they had in advance supposed it would prove. Farinelli
had brought them full houses, but he had failed, together with
Porpora, Senesino, Montagnana, and the others, to drive George
Frideric Handel from the London scene. In London that summer of 1735 rumors were heard that autumn might disclose no
opera at all either at His Majesty's in the Haymarket or at the
Theatre Royal in Covent Garden.

So Handel went off to Tunbridge Wells and took a several
weeks' cure of the waters there. Carestini had left him, but he
had no time, no energy, no funds for a trip to the Continent tc
find new *castrati* or other warbling vanities. The success of his
most recent lenten oratorios showed him the way to recoup his
losses. By the time autumn and winter had rolled around and

the Opera of the Nobility had managed to reopen, he had made up his mind. He had obtained from his friend Newburgh Hamilton a text arranged for Thomas Clayton in 1711 from Dryden's *Alexander's Feast; or, The Power of Music/ An Ode in Honor of Saint Cecilia's Day*. He would return to Covent Garden with a setting of that. Although he does not seem to have been active in public in the early part of the 1735–6 season, he did not embark on the setting of Hamilton's text until after Christmas. Then, working for only twenty days, he completed *Alexander's Feast* on January 17, 1736. It is one of his greatest compositions, and was to afford him part of the heartening success of his old age.

At His Majesty's Theatre in the Haymarket, the Porpora season had been launched on October 28, 1735, with a revival, performed eight times, of the director's *Polifemo*. The year ran out with seventeen singings of *Adriano*, an opera by Francesco Maria Veracini, a Florentine who had composed it especially for this visit to London. Nothing held the boards for very long: *Adriano* ran intermittently from November 25 to early January, when the formerly popular *Artaserse* proved good for only four performances and was followed by a *pasticcio* called *Mitridate*. Again four singings were enough, and Veracini's *Adriano* was returned for seven between February 7 and March 2.

During that second run of *Adriano* Handel reopened Covent Garden to an audience in excess of 1300 persons with the *première* of *Alexander's Feast*. The date was February 19, 1736, and the cast had the still-faithful Strada, Cecilia Young, a bass named Erard, and — in his first important role — John Beard. This tenor, still no more than eighteen or nineteen years old, was to help Handel's ode as much as it helped him. From its *première* really dated his phenomenally long and bright career, during which he married John Rich's daughter and became manager of Covent Garden. Of that February 19 performance of *Alexander's Feast*, the *Daily Post* said:

There never was, upon the like occasion, so numerous and splendid an audience at any theater in London, there being at least thirteen hundred persons present; and it is judged that the receipts of the house could not amount to less than £450. It met with general applause, though attended with the inconvenience of having the performers placed at too great a distance from the audience, which we hear will be rectified at the next time of performance.

Although many members of the audience at Covent Garden at once recognized the greatness of *Alexander's Feast*, it did not at first achieve more than four or five performances, about one each week to past the middle of March. Then Handel put up *Acis and Galatea* and, during Lent, *Esther* with the customary organ concertos between acts. The rapid falling away of his fortunes was not being slowed quickly enough by the performing of oratorios. He was losing his public. Turning from side to side in desperation, he next decided to import another *castrato* from Italy and stake more of his vanishing funds on Italian opera. He could not read the signs all about him, signs that should have told him of a public weary of serious music for the time unless it was presented with something to waken interest anew. A London paper of April 13, 1736, said: "We hear that Signor Conti [Gioacchino Conti, called Gizziello or Egizziello after his teacher, Domenico Gizzi], who is esteemed the best Singer in Italy, being sent for by Mr. Handell, is expected here in a few days."

Affairs were also deteriorating at His Majesty's. The management there tried a *pasticcio* called *Orfeo* with music by no less a group than Hasse, Vinci, Francesco Araja, and Porpora, and managed to squeeze out thirteen presentations of it during three weeks beginning on March 2. Then, on March 27, the eternal *Artaserse* was remounted for Farinelli's benefit performance. When this was repeated on March 30, the playbill carried the following notice: "Whereas the repetition of songs adds considerably to the length of the opera, and has often been complained of, it is hoped no person will take it ill, if the singers do not comply with *encores* for the future." The clamor that, despite some waning of the Farinelli furor, the vocal mastery of the master *castrato* always roused may just possibly have affected the nerves of the other singers, always sensitive to such noise. After a third *Artaserse*, the run of *Orfeo* was resumed without interruption (except for one singing of F. Campi's *Honorius* on April 13) from early in April until May 1.

Frederick, Prince of Wales, was engaged to marry the seventeen-year-old Princess Augusta of Saxe-Gotha. The nuptials of the heir apparent, scheduled for April 27, 1736, called for significant musical festivities. Handel's first contribution was the Wedding Anthem, "Sing unto God," sung at the actual ceremony in the Chapel Royal. Porpora, not being a court offcial, could do no better as his first part in the celebrations than schedule a special singing of *Orfeo* for Thursday, April 29, two days after the wedding. This performance was attended by George II, Queen Caroline, and the Prince and Princess of Wales, and was repeated two days later. Then, on May 4, Porpora overreached himself, staging his own setting of a Paolo Rolli oratorio text called *La Festa d'Imeneo*, with Farinelli in the chief role. This had no action, and was sung before one set painted by Kent. It did not catch on, and was withdrawn after four singings. Porpora's company then filled out what was left of its thin season with a few performances of *Adriano*, one of *Artaserse*, and four of *Orfeo*, the last closing the house on June 22.

The arrival from Italy of Gizziello, a very high soprano, at last permitted Handel to reinstate Italian opera at Covent Garden, where none had been heard since July 2, 1735. On May 5, 1736, he revived his *Ariodante* for two showings before presenting, on May 12, his chief contribution to the continuing wedding festivities. Although often classified as an opera, this *Atalanta* is actually, as Hugo Leichtentritt has said, an Arcadian pastoral play. On the day after its *première* the *Daily Post* said:

Last night was performed at the theatre-royal Covent-Garden, for the first time, the opera of Atalanta, composed by Mr. Handel on the joyous occasion of the nuptiels of their Royal Highnesses the Prince and Princess of Wales [who had selected this very evening to attend, in Drury Lane, a tragedy and a farce — *Cato* and *Taste à la mode*]. In which was a new set of scenes painted in honour of the happy union, which took up the full length of the stage: the fore-part of the scene represented an avenue to the Temple of Hymen, adorned with statues of Heathen Deities. Next was a triumphal arch, on the summit of which were the arms of their Royal Highnesses. Under the arch was the figure of Fame on a cloud, sounding the praises of this happy pair. The names Fredericus and Augusta ap-peared above in transparent characters. The opera concluded with a grand chorus, during which, several beautiful illuminations were displayed. There were present, their Majesties, the Duke,[9] and the four Princesses,[10] accompanied with a very splendid audience, and the whole was received with universal acclamations.

Atalanta[11] completed the season at Covent Garden; though George II left for Hanover on May 22 to be gone almost eight months, at least two later performances were by royal com-mand: that of June 2 by command of the Queen, the Duke of Cumberland, and the Princesses, that of June 9 by command of the Queen alone. With the latter performance Handel ended the Covent Garden season. The name, if not the substance, of *Atalanta* was long to outlast the 1735–6 season. Gizziello was the first important high soprano *castrato* Handel had had to compose for, Senesino, Carestini, and Nicolini all having been mezzo-sopranos or contraltos. And for Gizziello's first song in *Atalanta* he had written to the phrases beginning "*Care selve*" one of his most beautiful and enduringly popular arias. Today "*Care selve*" is all of *Atalanta* that even the most persistent lis-tener can know unless he consults a score.

[9] William, Duke of Cumberland, Frederick's younger brother.
[10] Anne, Princess of Orange; Amelia (or Emily); Caroline; Mary, later married to Frederick II, Landgrave of Hesse-Cassel, and Louisa, later mar-ried to Frederick V, King of Denmark, were Frederick's sisters. It is likely that, as the Princess of Orange had gone to the Netherlands, the last four were present at the performance mentioned, though Mary would have been only thirteen years old, Louisa but twelve.
[11] With Strada, Maria Negri, Gizziello, Beard, Waltz, and a bass named Thomas Reinhold.

What a man of unusual sensibility noticed most when he went to *Atalanta* is well demonstrated by a passage from a letter that Thomas Gray wrote to Horace Walpole on June 11, 1736:

. . . the first is a common Scene of a wood, & does not change at all, till the end of the last Act, when there appears the temple of Hymen, with illuminations; there is a row of blue fires burning in order along the ascent to the temple; a fountain of fire spouts up out of the ground to the ceiling, & two more cross each other obliquely from the sides of the stage; on the top is a wheel, that whirls about, & throws out a shower of gold-colour, silver, & blue fiery rain . . .

Frederick, Prince of Wales, continued on the worst possible terms with his parents. Also, he had either begun to tire of the attention demanded of him by the Opera of the Nobility or had come to the late realization (he was an intelligent man, a man of some taste) that Handel had more force and originality than Porpora and Hasse. In any case, the Prince had expressed pleasure over the Wedding Anthem with which Handel had provided him and his bride, and even greater pleasure over the honor paid him and the Princess by *Atalanta*. He suddenly withdrew his support from the group at His Majesty's Theatre in the Haymarket and began ostentatiously to patronize Covent Garden and Handel. This was too much for George II to bear, and he in turn shortly canceled his annual subscription of £1000 to Handel's company. The two companies, in effect, simply exchanged their dwindling audiences and uncertain royal patronage.

The effort of the 1735–6 season had again told on Handel's unstable health, drained his temporarily ebbing vitality. He does not seem to have returned to Tunbridge during the summer or autumn of 1736, but neither did he do much of anything else. It was as though he had disappeared, as though his large, familiar figure had been obliterated from Brook Street and the other parts of London in which he had been best known. There were rumors that he was dying, even a few that he was dead. The gossips had not counted on that unshakable basic strength, inherited from Georg and Dorothea Händel, which was still equal to carrying him through twenty-three years, a majority of them abundantly fruitful.

Both operatic enterprises now sent emissaries to the Continent to recruit singers for a resumption of their ridiculous struggle in the autumn of 1736. Porpora obtained Antonia Merighi, Margarita Chimenti, and Elisabetta du Parc, called La Francesina; Handel's new recruit was Domenico Annibali, a *castrato* referred to in the newspapers before his arrival as "Signor Domenichino, one of the best singers in Italy." In August, Handel in his quiet retirement began to compose *Giustino* to a text by Count Nicolo Beregani. He completed this opera in eight weeks. Meanwhile, on September 15, he began to compose, to a text some describe as written by Heidegger, another opera for the new season, *Arminio*. He completed the composition of this in four weeks on October 14. This was the invisible sick man whom idlers in the taverns of London were discussing as though he were dead. It was Porpora, in truth, who had given up the battle, probably discouraged by the open defection of the Prince of Wales. His place as composer in chief to the Opera of the Nobility was given to Giovanni Battista Pescetti, who was imported from Venice.

Sometime during August 1736, Handel had received from Michael Dietrich Michaelsen at Halle word that his niece, that Johanna Friederika Michaelsen whose christening he had attended on November 23, 1710, was betrothed to Johann Ernst Flörcke, a professor at the University of Jena. And in the latest of Handel's surviving letters to her father he wrote:

at London the $\frac{28}{17}$ of August 1736

Sir and most Honored Brother

As there remains no person closer to me than my Dear Niece, whom I have always perfectly loved, You could not enlighten me with more agreeable news than that She is going to marry a Person of a Character and a merit so distinguished. Your decision alone would suffice to place her on the peak of her happiness, and I therefore take

it as a sign of Your Amiability that you should ask for my approbation. The good Education for which She is indebted to You will
assure not only her felicity, but will also return to Your Consolation,
toward which you need have no doubt that I shall contribute all that
is in my power.

I have taken the Liberty of sending to Monsieur Her Husband a
Wedding present of a Delharmes gold watch with a Gold Chain and
two seals, one of Amethyst and the other of Onyx. Permit that on this
same occasion I send as a small Wedding Present to my dear Niece
the Wife a Diamond Ring with one Stone only that weighs seven
grains and a half and a little more, of the first Water and all Perfection. I shall address both of them to Monsieur Sbülen at Hamburg,
who will hold them for You. Obligations toward You Monsieur and
Madame Your Wife, whom I ask you to assure of my Regard, are a
separate matter, of which I shall attempt to acquit myself on the
first occasion. Permit me to assure you that there cannot be more
sincerity and unvarying emotion than I have the honor to hold
toward you Sir and most Honored Brother

Your

very humble and very obedient
George Frideric Handel.

At Covent Garden, on November 6, 1736, the season was
opened by Handel with a performance of *Alcina*. After repeating this twice, he restaged *Atalanta* in honor of the Princess of
Wales' birthday, running off set pieces of fireworks on the stage
at the end of the performance. Although their rival had thus
managed to be first on the seasonal scene, those who now ran
the Opera of the Nobility opened the doors of the King's Theatre in the Haymarket on November 23 with Hasse's *Siroe*.
Of this staging Burney remarked: "This is the first time that I
ever perceived the composer of an opera named in the advertisements and bills of the day." It was thought wise to mention
Hasse's name not only because his music was well liked, but
also because the public had come to assume that operas at the
Haymarket were by Porpora, those at Covent Garden by Handel. Hasse, also, was unquestionably sharing the musical direction of the Opera of the Nobility with Pescetti. Nevertheless, it

may safely be assumed that from the larger public's point of view the chief attraction of *Siroe* was not Hasse's thoroughly delightful music, but the inhumanly agile singing of Farinelli.

Handel filled most of December with performances of a revival of *Poro*, in which Annibali was featured. The Haymarket company, now definitely on thin days, found it necessary to add to *Siroe* the attractions of an intermezzo called *Il Giocatore*. To this double bill, on New Year's Day of 1737, went Queen Caroline, the Prince and Princess of Wales, the Duke, and the Princesses. George II was not present because he was unable to reach London until the middle of January, unfavorable winds having detained him for more than five weeks at Helvoetsluis. When the combined *Siroe* and *Il Giocatore* no longer sufficed to attract even meager audiences to the King's Theatre, they were replaced by a *Merope*, composer unknown. This filled in for about three weeks in January, after which nothing better could be found as an excuse for keeping the house open than the very *Siroe* of which the public had already showed itself weary.

Part of the falling away of the opera audiences had resulted from greatly increased popularity for spoken drama. Henry Fielding, in March 1736, was managing the "Great Mogul's Company of English Comedians," which played at His Majesty's Theatre alternately with Porpora's troupe. One of Fielding's own plays, *Pasquin, a Dramatick Satire on the Times*, quite simply captured the town.[12] It was a play in which keenly pointed burlesque of manners alternated with palpable hits at Sir Robert Walpole and the other ministers. Fielding followed this excellently received play with George Lillo's *Fatal Curiosity* and his own outspoken and more violently anti-Walpole *Historical Register for the Year 1736*. Although the violence of

[12] In a letter to Swift, Mrs. Delany wrote: "When I went out of Town last autumn the reigning madness was Farinelli [whose popularity had waned meanwhile to the point at which he could not secure an audience for Porpora's *La Festa d'Imeneo*]; I find it now turned on *Pasquin*, a dramatic satire on the times. It has had almost as long a run as the *Beggar's Opera*, but in my opinion not with equal merit, though it has humour."

QUEEN CAROLINE AND THE DUKE OF CUMBERLAND

GENERAL VIEW OF VAUXHALL GARDENS

this satire drove the Walpole government into concocting the Licensing Act of 1737, under which no play could be produced without a license from the Lord Chamberlain, and thus in effect ended Fielding's career as dramatist and manager, his place was soon filled by others. The spoken drama continued to flourish at the expense of opera as the public's favorite entertainment.

Handel still did not understand the public. After one performance of *Poro,* on January 12 he brought out *Arminio,* the first completed of his two new operas, and the season's first novelty.[13] *Arminio* was a hollow failure, not attracting enough people to be run for more than six nights. Financial ruin was rushing upon Handel. Swiftly he revived *Partenope.* On February 12, Pescetti in the Haymarket tried his own *Demetrio.* Handel at Covent Garden replied four days later with *Giustino,* in which, according to Schoelcher, "there was no lack of bears, fantastic animals, and dragons vomiting fire." This, being lighter than *Arminio,* and having in a chorus of sailors the opportunity Handel required for demonstrating his unique powers, made some recuperation possible in the box office. It went so well, in fact, that Handel announced unwisely that he would give it each Wednesday and Friday during Lent. The *Daily Post* of March 11 tells what followed this announcement:

We hear since operas have been forbid being performed at the theatre in Covent-garden on the Wednesdays and Fridays in Lent, Mr. Handel is preparing Dryden's Ode of Alexander's Feast, the oratorios of Esther and Deborah, with several new concertos for the organ and other instruments; also a new entertainment of Music called *Il Trionfo del Tempo, e della Verita,* which performances will be brought on the stage and varied every week.

The first aria in *Giustino* is of peculiar interest. It is *"Un vostro sguardo,"* which Burney described as *"alla moderna,"* by which he meant that it was not composed in what he considered pure Handelian style. It shows, in clearest manner, the tuneful

[13] The cast boasted Strada, the returned Bertolli, Maria Negri, Gizziello, Annibali, Beard, and Reinhold.

influence of Handel's then recent rivals, Hasse and Porpora, as well as of their sweet-melodied predecessors, in particular Leonardo Vinci. The ending of the first section of this aria (which is to be heard in the music Sir Thomas Beecham arranged for the ballet *The Great Elopement*) is the familiar melodic turn attached to the opening words of "Rule, Britannia." But Handel had not borrowed it from Arne's song: Arne's song had not yet been composed. It is the other way round. Arne undoubtedly had *"Un vostro sguardo"* in mind when, in 1740, he composed the masque *Alfred,* in which "Rule, Britannia" is sung.

On March 9, 1737, Handel began his lenten season at Covent Garden with a revival, in slightly revised oratorio form, of *Parnasso in Festa,* the serenata he had arranged three years before for the marriage of the Princess Royal to the Prince of Orange. During three performances of this, "grand concertos" (*concerti grossi*) were played in the intervals between its sections. Then, as well as six singings of *Alexander's Feast,* Handel put on *Il Trionfo del Tempo e del Disinganno,* the serenata he had composed in Italy almost thirty years earlier, and that was now slightly revised and renamed *Il Trionfo del Tempo e della Verità.* By this time he was seriously ill. But these nonoperatic performances were drawing to the box office the funds nothing operatic seemed able to woo, and he continued to drive himself desperately. The first *Il Trionfo* had been a command performance for the Prince and Princess of Wales. He repeated it. He gave *Alexander's Feast* on March 30, oratorios on April 1, 4, 5, 6, and 7. The Prince and Princess, now wholly friendly to Handel, were often in the house, but the serious illness of Queen Caroline gave George II an excuse for staying away. Almost everyone else was there, it seemed. What *Arminio* and *Giustino* could not accomplish was done easily by *Alexander's Feast, Deborah, Esther,* and *Il Trionfo del Tempo e della Verità.* Covent Garden was full every time.

Handel again had success, but it was now too late for him to take pleasure from it. His illness culminated on April 13,

1737, in a nervous collapse and a stroke of paralysis that left him without the power to use his right arm. He was fifty-two years old, and not even his iron constitution could support the incessant driving to which he had been subjecting it. It is likely that a weaker or more nervously attuned man would simply have died. Handel went off to Tunbridge Wells to learn what the waters would do for him, and rallied a little. He did not immediately recoup enough strength to stage *Berenice*, the opera that he had begun on December 18, 1736, and completed six weeks later, on January 27, 1737. Instead, from the very day of his stroke, Covent Garden heard *Dido*, an opera or *pasticcio* whose composer cannot now be determined.

The *Daily Post* for April 30 told London that "Mr. Handel, who has been some time indisposed with the rheumatism, is in so fair a way of recovery, that it is hoped he will be able to accompany the opera of Justin on Wednesday next, the 4th of May; at which time we hear their Majesties will honour that opera with their presence." Part of this hope was fulfilled: Handel led *Giustino* from his harpsichord at Covent Garden on May 4. But the dying Queen was too ill to be present. Handel repeated *Giustino* a week later. And then, amazingly, he found strength enough to stage *Berenice*, being far from the realization that it was to be the last opera he ever brought forth for a company of his own. He had not the wisdom to husband his force or take care of his mind and body, neither of them fully recovered from the aftereffects of the paralytic bolt that had struck him one month before.

The Opera of the Nobility was as sick as Handel or Queen Caroline. Pescetti's *Demetrio*, shored up by intermezzos, was sung thirteen times, then replaced for four performances by Veracini's *Tito* and for a few by a *pasticcio*, *Sabrina*. Colley Cibber wrote, in his *Apology*, that it was during the brief run of *Sabrina* that, despite the addition of an intermezzo, Farinelli "sometimes sung to an audience of five and thirty pounds." A *Demofoonte* was promised for His Majesty's, May 28, but was postponed to May 24 when Farinelli was unable to sing; it does not seem to have been successful. On May 31, June 7, and June 11, Farinelli, in *Sabrina,* sang for the last times in England. Another performance was billed for June 14, but never took place. With that of June 11, therefore, the Opera of the Nobility expired, having cost its chief supporters a final loss of about £12,000. Its chief ornaments — Farinelli, Senesino, and Hasse — left for the Continent, leaving behind them Porpora and the second-rate Pescetti.

A temporary recovery made it possible for Queen Caroline to accompany the King to the May 18 *première* of Handel's *Berenice.*[14] Its wonderful minuet, still familiar today, and the beauty of a brace of its arias were not enough to stem the flood of disaster. After only four singings, *Berenice* had to be removed. Then Handel tried *Dido, Giustino, Alcina* (probably the last opera ever sung by his company), and, on June 25, *Alexander's Feast.* It was all useless. He was now casting good money after bad and coming to the end of both. He closed the Covent Garden theater for the season, and London was without an opera company. London did not care. The public mood was demonstrated when Covent Garden offered *The Dragon of Wantley,* a lineal descendant of *The Beggar's Opera.* Its libretto by Henry Carey was a parody of *Giustino.* Its music was arranged by Lampe, who had been playing the bassoon in Handel's opera orchestra. Its leading role was sung by Waltz, and the demand for places was great enough to warrant a run of sixty-seven performances. The libretto was published without the music, and ran through fourteen editions in twelve months.

The man who had given London thirty-four operas, its first oratorios, and a wealth of instrumental and occasional music over a period of twenty-seven years must have looked to his friends as though this time he was through, defeated at last. He was terribly sick. His limbs and functions were affected. His mind was clouded, if indeed he had not temporarily and

[14] The cast had Strada, Negri, Bertolli, Gizziello, Annibali, Beard, and Reinhold.

intermittently crossed the line from sanity. With difficulties that can be imagined but not determined, he was persuaded to try whether the waters of Aix-la-Chapelle would do completely what those of Tunbridge Wells had accomplished in part. Putting London behind him, he went off to the Continent during the summer of 1737, and none among his friends and enemies knew whether or not he would return or, if he did, what method he could possibly find for making enough money to pay the promissory notes he had been forced to give to his creditors. Pursuing him like a nightmare must have been the name and face of Aurelio del Pò, husband of Strada, the only one of his creditors who had refused a note and was insisting loudly on his pound of flesh. Handel was not actually bankrupt, but he must have seemed so to himself and to others.

III

Handel's fantastically resilient physical constitution aroused wonder in the *Kursaal* at Aix-la-Chapelle. Sir John Hawkins wrote:

He submitted to such sweats, excited by the vapour baths, as astonished every one. After a few essays of this kind, during which his spirits seemed to rise rather than sink under an excessive perspiration, his disorder left him; and in a few hours after the last operation he went to the great church of the city, and got to the organ, on which he played in such a manner that men imputed his cure to a miracle.

Two stories connected with Handel's cure at Aix persist, and though neither of them can be documented conclusively, one of them is almost certainly true. The other — that Handel, hearing from a herald that the future Frederick the Great was en route to the city and wished to meet him, quit the place — it is impossible to believe. Frederick did not visit Aix in 1737, was in fact, not within hailing distance of the famous spa. The believable story is that Handel encountered at the baths one or more prominent burghers of the Baltic town of Elbing, which was shortly to commemorate with appropriate festivities its five-hundredth year of existence. Invited by his new acquaintances to assist a native Elbing musician in a ceremonial cantata for the celebration, Handel is said to have accepted. Certainly the cantata, *Hermann von Balcke,* survived in the Elbing Stadtbibliothek: it has numbers by Johann (or Jean) du Grain and by Handel.

Handel's return from Aix, probably in October, was made by way of Flanders. Stopping at a Flemish town en route, he sought out a church and begged for permission to play the organ. Although he did not reveal his identity, the permission was granted. As soon as Handel began to play, the church organist realized that he was hearing a remarkable performance. It was when Handel dashed off into a fugue, however, that the worthy native organist is said to have rushed upon him, throwing his arms about Handel's exceedingly bulky figure and exclaiming: "You can be no other than the great Handel," thus echoing with a difference Domenico Scarlatti's remark of thirty years before.

The return of the prodigal composer, recovered from the pains of the flesh but not from those of failure and bankruptcy, almost coincided with the beginning of an opera season at His Majesty's Theatre in the Haymarket under the ægis of that other seemingly eternal figure, Heidegger, who began his season on October 29, 1737, with *Arsace*, a *pasticcio* arranged by Pescetti, late of the Opera of the Nobility. Its chief attraction was a *castrato* new to London though already well known for more than a decade on the Continent. This was Gaetano Majorano, called Caffarelli. Heidegger repeated *Arsace* on November 1, following which he began announcing imminent restagings of *Sabrina*, none of which took place.

On November 20, Queen Caroline died, and for a time all theatrical entertainments of any sort were forbidden. On her deathbed this beloved and admirable woman had carried on with her unstable husband one of the most singular colloquies in royal history. Her last plea to this man who had often been flagrantly untrue to her was that he marry again. George was on the verge of tears. "No, no," he said. "I shall have mistresses." And Caroline replied, "*Mon Dieu*, that won't stop you." In his curious, unhelpful way, the King realized the extent of his loss. For a short period his sorrow was so exaggerated as to give courtiers reason for doubting his sanity. He ordered the Queen's vault and coffin opened in the middle of the night, and rode to look upon her body. He shrank back alarmed when, during a card game, queens were dealt to his hand.

Handel, too, had good reason to feel personally bereaved by the death of Caroline of Anspach, whom he first met at Berlin in

1696 when he had been a prodigy of eleven years, she the thir-
teen-year-old guest of the Electress Sophia. When he had lived
at Hanover in 1710 and 1711–12, he had come to know her
better as Georg Augustus' bride of a few years. From the time of
her arrival in England in October 1714 as Princess of Wales
until her illness had made public appearances and affairs a tor-
ture to her, Caroline had been undeviating in her favor to Handel whether he was being supported by the faction favoring her
husband (whom she understood, tolerated, and managed) or
that favoring her son (whom she disliked). Her daughters had
been his pupils and partisans. Now he composed the anthem for
her funeral, completing it on December 12. And when "The
ways of Zion do mourn" was sung in Henry VII's Chapel at
Westminster Abbey on December 17, 1737, it proved to be one
of Handel's noblest and most moving essays at the monumental
manner. It was worthy not only of a woman who had maintained
full human dignity in sore circumstances, but also of the man
who had composed it.

Shortly before the Queen's death, Heidegger had begun to
see that if he was to go on trying to fill His Majesty's for nights
of opera he needed Handel. He was aware, too, that Handel,
still deep under a mound of promissory notes and perhaps
threatened with debtor's prison by the importunate Aurelio del
Pò, needed money. The two needs dovetailed. Heidegger offered Handel £1,000 for two operas and one *pasticcio*, and
Handel accepted the offer. Now he would, after so long a time,
be composing operas for a company in which he had no managerial hand. Taking a version of a much used Apostolo Zeno
libretto, he composed *Faramondo* between November 15 and
December 24. Heidegger brought it to the Haymarket stage on
January 3, 1738.[1] The opera, plainly showing traces of haste and
fatigue on Handel's part, nevertheless contained many passages
in the heroic style with which he had wrought such master-

[1] The cast included Margarita Chimenti, Elisabetta du Parc ("La Francesina"), Merighi, Maria Antonia Marchesini ("La Lucchesina"), Caffarelli, Antonio Lottini, Savage, and Montagnana.

VAUXHALL GARDENS

[*Roubiliac's statue of Handel at the extreme right*]

ROUBILIAC'S VAUXHALL GARDENS HANDEL

[LEFT: *the statue as owned by Novello & Co., Ltd.;* RIGHT: *the terra cotta model in the Fitzwilliam Museum, Cambridge*]

pieces as *Radamisto* and *Orlando*. The most striking passage in *Faramondo*, one that unquestionably sounded far above the heads of the average listener, was the aria *"Voglio che sia."* In it Faramondo is weighing two possible courses of thought, wavering between them. Suddenly he stops singing. The instruments take up the threads of his thought, expressing confusion with remarkable psychological verity. But despite its good moments *Faramondo* is one of Handel's poorest operas. It won him no fresh laurels or new listeners, lasting but eight performances in its first run.

Admirers of Handel arranged with John Walsh for the printing of the score of *Faramondo* in de luxe format. This was announced in the *Daily Post* for January 23, 1738, as follows:

> This day are published proposals for printing by subscription the opera of Faramondo in score, as it is performed at the King's Theatre in the Haymarket, composed by Mr. Handel.
> 1. The work will be printed on good paper.
> 2. The price to subscribers half a guinea, to be paid at the time of subscription.
> 3. The whole will be corrected by the author.
> 4. Those lovers of musick who are willing to subscribe, are desired to send in their names immediately, the work being in such forwardness, that it will be ready to be delivered to subscribers by the 4th of February next. Subscriptions are taken in by John Walsh, and by most musick shops in town.

Among the subscribers listed in the edition itself are Dr. Pepusch and a "Master Pepusch," probably his son by the star of early Handel operas in London, Margarita de l'Épine, whom he had married in 1718. Enjoying the comforts that his wife's fortune had brought him, safely ensconced as organist of Charter House, probably still reaping profits from *The Beggar's Opera*, Pepusch had forgiven Handel for being a man he had derided and wronged.

While Handel pieced together *Alessandro Severo*, the *pasticcio* of his contract with Heidegger, the Haymarket was occupied with eight singings of Pescetti's *La Conquista del Vello d'Oro*.

With many sections of his earlier operas, a fresh and novel overture, and a nosegay of new arias, Handel had *Alessandro Severo*
ready for a *première* on February 25, 1738, initiating a run of
six nights. Two days after completing *Faramondo* — that is,
on December 26, 1737 — Handel had begun the second new opera promised to Heidegger. He labored at this during the runs
of *Faramondo* and *La Conquista del Vello d'Oro*, completing it
on February 14. But it was not mounted immediately after the
withdrawing of *Alessandro Severo*, which was succeeded instead by nine performances of Veracini's *Partenio*. Handel's
new work was *Serse*, the only true comic opera he ever composed.

Serse was first sung at the King's Theatre on April 15, 1738.
This opera would by itself have been sufficient to keep Handel's
name known in the widest sense to this day. For it contains as
its first number a cavatina, originally sung by Caffarelli, to the
phrases beginning *"Ombra mai fù."* This is the melody now
known everywhere as "the Largo from *Xerxes*" or "Handel's
celebrated Largo." So little favor was *Serse* able to win that
spring of 1738 — even with the help of a far from mediocre
cast headed by Caffarelli, La Francesina, La Lucchesina, and
Montagnana (whose voice, true, was by this time described as
a bellow or a roar) — that after five nights it was replaced by
further performances of the season's other works. With one of
Partenio the Heidegger season closed on a sad future on June 6.

How much of a public figure Handel had again become to
the people of London was proved in 1738 (probably during the
first run of *Serse*) when, on May 2, a marble figure of him, seated
and fingering a lyre, was unveiled with special musical accompaniment in Vauxhall Gardens, one of the principal London
pleasure parks. The lessee of the Gardens was Jonathan Tyers,
who had opened it on June 7, 1732. This shrewd businessman
decided that, as his patrons liked hearing Handel's music in the
open air, they would be further pleased to see the Gardens thus
decorated. He thereupon commissioned the full-length likeness from Louis-François Roubiliac. Patronized by Sir Robert

Walpole, Roubiliac was quickly to eclipse the popularity of Rysbraeck and Scheemakers as official sculptor to the nobility. Tyers paid him £300 for the Handel statue. It survives to-day, the property of the music publishers, Novello's; being a flagrant proof of the low state of English sculpture in the days of Hogarth, it is of interest only because of its associations and because Handel's contemporaries thought it a good likeness of him.

This is one of the very few instances of a composer's being honored with a public statue while still alive. Handel's audience in the Gardens (often the scene of frivolous licentiousness) was not, moreover, the sort that demanded only his lighter inspirations. The *Daily Post* for August 21, 1738, for example, records that "the entertainment at . . . Vauxhall . . . concluded with the Coronation Anthem, of Mr. Handel. The company seemed greatly satisfied on that occasion." He also composed, on at least one occasion, pieces especially for Vauxhall Gardens concerts: such is a Hornpipe of 1740.

A scene in Marylebone Gardens, a rival to Vauxhall, is preserved in a *History of the Parish of Marylebone* published in 1833. It is a letter from the grandson of the Reverend J. Fountayne, an acquaintance of Handel:

My grandfather, as I have been told, was an enthusiast in music, and cultivated most of all the friendship of musical men, especially of Handel, who visited him often, and had a great predilection for his society. This leads me to relate an anecdote, which I have on the best authority. While Marylebone Gardens were flourishing, the enchanting music of Handel, and probably of Arne, was often heard from the orchestra there. One evening, as my grandfather and Handel were walking together and alone, a new piece was struck up by the band. "Come, Mr. Fountayne," said Handel, "let us sit down and listen to this piece; I want to know your opinion of it." Down they sat; and after some time the old parson, turning to his companion, said, "It is not worth listening to — it's very poor stuff." "You are right, Mr. Fountayne," said Handel, "it is very poor stuff; I thought so myself when I had finished it." The old gentleman being taken by surprise, was beginning to apologize; but Handel assured him that there was no necessity, that the music was really bad, having been composed hastily, and his time for the production limited; and that the opinion given was as correct as it was honest.

Handel's creditors appear, except for Aurelio del Pò, to have been waiting quietly on the sidelines. The furious husband of the long-faithful Strada continued to make ominous threats, serious in view of the strict legal attitude and the crowding of debtors' prisons. Handel's friends persuaded him to try earning, by a single concert given for his own benefit, enough money to pay off Del Pò in a lump sum. He acceded to this proposal reluctantly, perhaps because the need to stage a benefit for himself seemed to him shameful, perhaps because he feared that a public apparently tiring of his music would not fill the hall. This "oratorio" — it was in reality a potpourri of Handel favorites — was advertised for March 28, 1738, the Tuesday of Holy Week. The pit and the boxes were priced at 10/6 per person. Handel played the organ during the concert, and it was necessary to crowd about five hundred extra seats onto the stage. So great was the admiration for Handel that when he offered the sort of music in which he stood unique the audience that jammed the King's Theatre paid him a profit for that one night of upwards of £1,000. He was able to stop the mouth of the vengeful Del Pò. It was the only bright day for Handel in a season altogether disastrous for Heidegger.

On May 24, 1738, the Princess of Wales gave birth to the boy who was to be George III. On that same day, London newspapers carried the following announcement from Heidegger:

All persons that have subscribed or are willing to subscribe twenty guineas for an Italian opera to be performed next season at the King's Theatre in the Hay-Market, under my direction, are desired to send ten guineas to Mr. Drummond the banker who will give them a receipt, to return the money in case the opera should not go on.

Burney stated, on what authority it is not clear, that Heidegger required a guaranteed subscription of £4,200 before signing on his singers. Either he could not find two hundred persons willing to invest £21 each in an opera venture not to materialize until the following season or his singers made exorbitant salary demands. The June 21 *Daily Post* told something of the story:

On Saturday last, set out for Breda, Signora Strada del Po, to which place she goes in obedience to the commands of her royal highness the princess of Orange, from whence she intends to go to Italy, but before her departure desires the English nobility and gentry, from whom she has received so many signal marks of favour, might be acquainted that it is no way owing to her, that the present scheme for performing operas next winter, in the Hay-market, under the direction of Mr. Heidegger, has miscarried, as has been maliciously reported; she having agreed with Mr. Heidegger above a month ago, as the said gentleman can testify.

Five days later, Heidegger defended himself in an advertisement in the first column of the same newspaper:

Whereas the operas for the ensuing season, at the King's Theatre in the Hay-market, cannot be carried on as was intended, by reason of the subscription not being full, and that I could not agree with the singers, though I offered ONE THOUSAND GUINEAS to *one* of them. I therefore think myself obliged to declare, that I give up the undertaking for next year, and that Mr. Drummond will be ready to repay the money paid in, upon the delivery of his receipt. I also take this opportunity to return my humble thanks to all persons, who were pleased to contribute towards my endeavours of carrying on that entertainment.

Except for four performances by a company apparently scraped together by Pescetti and housed temporarily in Covent Garden from March 10 to April 11, 1739, London heard no more Italian opera or news of it until December 1. No Handel opera was heard in London between May 1738 and November 1740. By the middle of February 1741, too, Handel was to be quit of Italian opera forever except for whatever interest he may have taken in later years in revivals by others of some of the nearly forty operas by means of which he had tried, with fluctuating success and failure, to make a living.

It was during the years of his bankruptcy that Handel first became associated with two charitable causes with which his name was long to be coupled. The first was the "Fund for the support of Decayed Musicians and their Families," organized in 1738 through the efforts of Michael Christian Festing and Maurice Greene. Handel was one of its charter subscribers, some of the others being Purcell's son Edward, William Boyce, Arne, John Beard, Henry Carey, Bernard Gates, Richard Leveridge, Pepusch, Thomas Roseingrave, Reinhold, and John Christopher Smith. As its first money-raising event, the Fund (or Society) presented *Alexander's Feast,* thereby earning enough to guarantee its own continuance. For the rest of his life, Handel gave of his efforts and his money to support the Society. He was to leave it £1,000 in his will. Twenty-five years after his death, the Society was to be awarded another £6,000 from the proceeds of the great Handel Commemoration Festival in Westminster Abbey.

Handel's other important charitable interest was in the asylum or hospital for children founded by Thomas Coram, a retired sea captain and former boatbuilder and farmer of Taunton, Massachusetts. The royal charter for this Foundling Hospital was issued in 1739. It resulted from Captain Coram's sense of shame and horror at the sight of dead and dying children in the streets of London, particularly in the East End. Exposure, desertion, and murder of children were not uncommon in the poorest sections of the city. From about 1722 on, Captain Coram had labored diligently to establish a refuge for these foundlings and orphans. This was slow labor in a society that had little tradition or training in public charity, but he finally won the support of a few fashionable ladies and persuaded them to memorialize the government.

Once the plans for the Foundling Hospital were formalized, subscriptions increased rapidly. The first waifs were cared for in houses temporarily rented in Hatton Garden. Then an estate belonging to the Earl of Salisbury, and lying in Lamb's Conduit Fields west of Gray's-Inn Lane and north of Great Ormond

Street, was acquired. There the long-familiar building was begun in 1742, one wing of it becoming habitable by 1745, the
whole building being opened officially on January 19, 1750.

What the Hospital saved children from can be faintly estimated from the fact that it was considered remarkable, some
years later, that of a total of 1,384 children admitted during its
fifteen first years of operation only 742 had died. M. Dorothy
George has written that, "In the latter part of the [eighteenth]
century it was no longer necessary to receive infants indiscriminately at the Foundling Hospital to prevent their exposure and
desertion or their wholesale slaughter in warehouses or by parish nurses." For some years from 1756 on, the Hospital received
an annual parliamentary grant of £10,000. It became so over-
crowded that less than one third of its children survived, whereupon the grant was stopped. From then on, it was administered
by private charity under carefully plotted restrictions.

Among the notable early supporters of the Foundling Hospital were Handel and Hogarth, both of whom at one time
served on its board of governors. From May 1749 on, Handel
was to give an annual performance for its benefit. From May
1, 1750, on, this was always of *Messiah*, and always returned
the charity from £500 to £1,000. Handel also gave the Hospital an organ. John Christopher Smith the younger became its
organist. In Handel's will, one section of a codicil reads: "I
give a fair copy of the score, and all parts of my oratorio called
the *Messiah* to the Foundling Hospital." [2]

After the close of the Heidegger season on June 6, 1738, Han-

[2] By the custom of long standing, those to whom a composer gave or
sold a score gained with it the right of performance. The Trustees of the
Foundling Hospital, learning in advance of Handel's death of the provision in his will by which a score and parts of *Messiah* were to come to
them after it, attempted to gain the exclusive right to perform the oratorio.
Handel heard that they were about to petition Parliament for that exclusive right. And, becoming justly angry at this ungracious attempt to
exaggerate the extent of his generosity, he is said to have burst out: "The
Devil! For what shall the Foundlings put mine oratorio in the Parliament?
The Devil! Mine Music shall not go to Parliament." Whether because of
his intervention or for some other reason, the Trustees desisted.

del's name was mostly absent from the London newspapers for
the rest of the year. No operas, oratorios, or concerts were heard
at the principal theaters. Except to his close friends, Handel
again might have been dead. But he was in reality not idle:
between July 23 and November 1 he composed two of his
greatest works, *Saul* and *Israel in Egypt*. It has often been
printed that he began *Saul* on July 23 (some have said July 3),
completed it on September 27, rested four days, began *Israel
in Egypt* on October 1, and completed that, after working
twenty-seven days, on October 11. Unfortunately, the mathe-
matics of this tale will not do without explanation, for there are
ten, not twenty-seven, days between October 1 and 11. The
truth is that Handel composed what is now the second part of
Israel in Egypt by October 11, rapidly enough, to be sure, and a
date that jibes with common addition. Then, on October 15, he
began what is now the first part, wrote finis to it about October
20,[3] and then occupied the days from October 20 to November
1 in rounding out and filling in the composition as a whole.[4]

The librettist or librettists of *Saul* and *Israel in Egypt* could
not for a long time be named with certainty. Some attributed
the *Saul* text to Newburgh Hamilton, believing that he had
adapted it from Apostolo Zeno's *Davidde*. Still others had given
it at least in part to Richard Bentley, nephew of the great
scholar, and a neighbor, at Gopsal, of Charles Jennens, at whose
country house Handel was often a guest. But it is now clear,
thanks to a letter discovered in the Aylesford family papers,
that it was described by Jennens as his own work, a description
undoubtedly accepted by Handel. It is, then, probably the oratorio text whose receipt Handel had acknowledged in the letter
he wrote Jennens on July 28, 1735, and to which Jennens referred
in a letter he wrote on September 19, 1738, to the Earl of

[3] This date is uncertain because the page containing it in the score was
badly cut by a bookbinder and part of the dating was thus stripped away.
[4] It was while working on *Saul* and *Israel in Egypt* that Handel first outlined what was to prove his last Italian opera but one, *Imeneo*, which
he did not complete until October 1740; he began it on September 19,
1738.

Guernsey, son to his cousin the Earl of Aylesford. "Mr. Handel's head is more full of maggots than ever," Jennens began. The first "maggot" was "a very queer instrument which he calls carillon (Anglice, a bell) and says some call it a Tubalcain, I suppose because it is both in the make and tone like a set of Hammers striking upon anvils. 'Tis played upon with keys like a Harpsichord and with this Cyclopean instrument he designs to make poor Saul stark mad." The second "maggot" was an organ that Handel had "bespoke of one Moss [Morse] of Barnet" for £500.

His third maggot is a Hallelujah which he has trump'd up at the end of his oratorio since I went into the Country, because he thought the conclusion of the oratorio not Grand enough; tho' if that were the case 'twas his own fault, for the words would have bore as Grand Musick as he could have set 'em to: but this Hallelujah, Grand as it is, comes in very nonsensically, having no manner of relation to what goes before. And this is the more extraordinary, because he refused to set a Hallelujah at the end of the first Chorus in the Oratorio, where I had placed one and where it was to be introduced with the utmost propriety, upon a pretence that it would make the entertainment too long. I could tell you more of his maggots: but it grows late and I must defer the rest till I write next, by which time, I doubt not, more new ones will breed in his Brain.

Jennens apparently failed to appreciate Handel's humorous reference to Tubal-cain (Genesis iv, 22), "instructor of every artificer in brass and iron." Although Handel accepted Jennens' suggestion for the placing of the "Hallelujah," he persisted in his use of the carillon, both in the *sinfonia* in the first act of *Saul* and in the chorus "Welcome, mighty King."

The text of *Israel in Egypt* is made up entirely of excerpts from Exodus and the Psalms. It seems to have been Handel's own work, though it is possible that he had assistance from Jennens, Newburgh Hamilton, Richard Bentley, or someone else. It did not lie complete before Handel when he started to compose. Its final form was not even projected at that hour:

Handel began with what is now the second part, heading it "Moses' Song, Exodus, chapter xv." It was not until that second section was complete that he retraced his steps — perhaps writing or acquiring more text meanwhile — to compose what is now the first part, describing the plagues in Egypt. On the magnificent words he reared an edifice of music so overtoweringly grand, so very Handelian, that Streatfeild well wrote: "Handel might have said of *Israel*, as Wagner said of *Tristan und Isolde*, that it was an extravagance, not to be repeated or imitated, but of all his works it is the most completely out of reach of every other composer who ever lived." The selection of an Everest among the Handelian Himalayas (and some of his greatest works aspire to no such inhuman altitudes) is a pleasant pastime if entertained without grimness. In that selection it has almost always been conventional to name *Messiah* first, *Israel in Egypt* not quite first.

Before January 1, 1739, Handel had leased the King's Theatre in the Haymarket from the temporarily despondent Heidegger. It was there, on January 16, that he presented *Saul* for the first time. The chorus numbered fewer than thirty-five, the band of instrumentalists the same. The remarkable overture for organ and orchestra, a four-movement work exceeding in length any other prelude Handel composed, should have helped the oratorio to success, particularly as it supplied the composer himself with an opportunity to display his wonderful skill at the organ. Not only is the organ written for masterfully and importantly in the composed score — an almost unique procedure in instrumentation at the time — but the second section of the overture ends with the indication *organo ad libitum*. The Dead March, for which Handel is said to have borrowed a pair of large kettledrums from the Tower of London, should also have helped *Saul* to success. It remains as well known today as any purely instrumental section in any of Handel's works. But the public did not respond favorably to *Saul*, which justified only six performances during the 1739 season and did not achieve real popularity until years later.

When Handel realized that *Saul* was no talisman to help him rebuild his fortunes, he temporarily marked time with *Alexander's Feast* and a slightly altered version of *Il Trionfo del Tempo e della Verità*. Then he tried *Israel in Egypt,* presenting it at the King's Theatre on April 4, 1739, preceding it with a version of Queen Caroline's Funeral Anthem revised so as to make its text applicable to the lamentations of the Israelites over the death of Joseph. A public unready to respond to *Saul* could scarcely be expected to do other than it did when confronted with *Israel in Egypt:* tolerate the awesome novelty. This vast epic, with its choruses of a breadth, depth, and height scarcely to be matched in music, was presented only once in more or less the form in which it later became a staple of English musical life. It was repeated on April 11 in a version drastically cut and interspersed with songs in Italian, again preceded by the revised Funeral Anthem. In this altered form, *Israel in Egypt* enlisted enough supporters, some of whom wrote initialed letters of praise to the newspapers, to justify one more performance during 1739. It was revived for a single performance in 1740, and then dropped for sixteen years: Handel performed it twice in 1756, once in 1757, and once in 1758. During the twenty years he lived after composing *Israel in Egypt,* that is, Handel heard it sung but eight times.[5]

The newspapers had announced, during the last week of April, a new "dramatical composition . . . intermixed with choruses, and two concertos on the organ" to be presented at the King's Theatre on Tuesday, May 1, 1739. This piece, *Jupiter in Argos,* was a *pasticcio* of old and new numbers. Autographs of numbers from it survive in the British Museum (Royal Music Library), and the Fitzwilliam Museum (Cambridge), and Sir Newman Flower's collection. The last page of the Fitzwilliam autograph bears the following inscription: *"Fine dell' opera* Ju-

[5] Mention must be made of what may have been a partial singing of *Israel in Egypt* by the Academy of Antient Music on May 10, 1739, when it was announced as "The Song of Moses and the Funeral Anthem for her late Majesty, set to music by Mr. Handel." Some sort of performance of *Israel in Egypt* seems also to have occurred at Oxford about this time.

piter in Argos, April 24, 1739, G. F. Handell." Handel presented this work only twice, ending his season with it on May 5, probably because his losses on the failures of the season had made it impossible for him to invest further funds at this time. Too, international events were readying that would sharply affect the fortunes of all kinds of London entertainment.

Sir Robert Walpole had steered a peaceful course across the tossing waters of European politics for so long that many of the people of England had grown bored. The opposition, with the help of Frederick, Prince of Wales, was in full cry for war against Spain, had been in full cry for some time. The background of this uproar was simple. Contravening the solemn agreements included in the Treaty of Utrecht, British privateers had been trading with Spanish America, dealing largely in slaves abducted from Africa. The Spanish government found protest useless and resorted to violence, boarding privateers, carrying British sailors to Spanish prisons, and endeavoring through a system of *guardacostas* to protect its rights. This angered some Englishmen, and drove to an oratorical frenzy the "Patriots" led by William Pulteney. A final excuse for war was supplied by the comical-tragical incident of Jenkins' ear.

Captain Robert Jenkins, in command of the brig *Rebecca*, was returning from a treaty-breaking trip to the West Indies in 1731 when the crew of a Spanish *guardacosta* stopped the ship, boarded it, rifled its cargo, and (according to Jenkins' story) hanged the Captain from a yard-arm, cut him down when he was all but dead, and then lopped off his ear with a cutlass. The Spanish captain had, Jenkins dramatically asserted, flung the severed ear in his face and told him to take it home and present it to King George. On reaching England, Jenkins managed to relate his gruesome story to the King, who then obtained supposed confirmation of it from his chief commander in the West Indies. Representations were made to Spain, but at first no bellicose excitement rose. Then, in 1738, Jenkins retold the story to a parliamentary committee investigating Spanish "outrages" and produced from a wad of cotton that he always carried about his person a shriveled object he said was his ear.

Waxing oratorical, Jenkins retold the story of the lopping-off of his ear and wound up with: "In that supreme moment I commended my soul to God and my cause to my country." This phrase settled the matter: there had to be war with Spain. Unconsidered then were later doubts of Jenkins' veracity and a belief that he had actually lost his ear while in a pillory. Walpole strove mightily and in vain against a rising fever of jingoism on the part of City merchants, the "Patriots," and the opposition rallying about the Prince of Wales. George II declared war against Spain. The formal proclamation was made at St. James's, Charing Cross, Chancery Lane, Wood Street, and the Royal Exchange on October 23, 1739. Although Walpole was to hold on to power for a short time longer, this actually marked the close of his two decades at the helm. When, in 1742, he was created Earl of Orford, a long era was ending.

Faced with his own depleted resources and a city momentarily fervent for war, Handel acted with wisdom. He took the small theater in Lincoln's-Inn Fields and there, on Thursday, November 22, 1739, brought out his setting of Dryden's *Ode for St. Cecilia's Day*. It was in truth St. Cecilia's Day, and she was honored with a six o'clock performance made up of *Alexander's Feast*, two *concerti grossi*, and an organ concerto in addition to the *Ode*,[6] all at "opera prices." This program was well received, and was repeated on November 27. At this point the company that still hung loosely about Pescetti and the few Italian singers remaining from former opera seasons opened the Little Theatre in the Haymarket. On December 1, with Carestini and "La Muscovita" in the cast, Pescetti's serenata *Diana and Endimion* was launched there for a three-time run. On December 15, the Little Theatre housed what was billed as "SEVERAL CONCERTOS in different instruments intermixed with a

[6] It was in the score of the *Ode for St. Cecilia's Day* that Handel instituted his custom of representing the days of the week in his dates by old astrological signs. These are as follows:

Sun.	Mon.	Tue.	Wed.	Thu.	Fri.	Sat.
☉	☽	♂	☿	♃	♀	♄

These signs Handel continued to use for the rest of his life.

variety of CHOSEN AIRS by the best masters in Italy. The whole divided into three parts. To which, by desire, will be added, the famous SALVE REGINA, composed by the Signor Hasse, and sung by Signor Carestini." By frequent changes of bill and by using the small house, this company was able to survive the rigors of war and the weather, running through to May 31, 1740.[7]

Meanwhile, Handel kept his tiny house in Lincoln's-Inn Fields in operation by repetitions of his two settings of Dryden and with *Acis and Galatea, concerti grossi*, and organ concertos. On Christmas Day, 1739, however, London received the unexpected present of a frost so severe as to rival the renowned one of 1683–4, and Handel had to close his theater until February 21. The cold became so bitter that the Thames froze across. The city took this phenomenon in carnival spirit, and the river ice soon became a village of booths, small houses, and shops. Those who could afford the luxury enjoyed driving by coach on the river from Lambeth to London Bridge. There was music. The people danced. Whole oxen were roasted on the ice. This was no time for sitting still in a poorly built and unheated theater. It was better to go to the "frost fair" on the Thames, where common custom granted license to all shades of pleasure from refined to wild.[8]

On February 4, 1740, the *Daily Post* carried an announcement that *Acis and Galatea* and the *Ode for St. Cecilia's Day* would be sung at the Theatre Royal in Lincoln's-Inn Fields three days later. But on February 6 this was amended: "In consideration of the weather continuing so cold, the serenata called Acis and Galatea . . . will be put off for a few nights further, of which due notice will be given. . . ." The performance actually had to be postponed for two weeks.

Almost as soon as some softening of the weather permitted,

[7] The attractions included a setting (by Pescetti?) of Apostolo Zeno's *Meride e Selinunte*, an opera — mostly by Hasse — called *Olimpia in Ebuda*, and Pescetti's *Busiri*.
[8] William Maitland estimated the population of London at this time at slightly less than 726,000.

Handel sallied out on one more desperate attempt to recapture public favor. Those who wished him ill were becoming bolder. They set street toughs upon gentlefolk daring to go to his theater. They had the posters announcing his performances ripped down. He ignored the rumpus, even when members of his audience were set upon violently and their sedan chairs overturned into snow and mud. From Charles Jennens he obtained a text called *L'Allegro, Il Penseroso ed Il Moderato,* the first two thirds of which were Milton sadly altered, the last third being such pure balderdash that it may have been of Jennens' own penning. In one month, Handel set this gallimaufry to some of his loveliest melodies. His scoring calls for a contrabassoon. This instrument seems not to have been played in England before 1784, and Handel's apparently unanswered calls for it in the Coronation Anthems (1727), *L'Allegro, Il Penseroso ed Il Moderato* (1740), and the *Royal Fireworks Music* (1749) were very early examples of a composer's conceiving a part for it. Handel presented the new composition at Lincoln's-Inn Fields on February 27, 1740. It was a failure, with which he had to admit himself defeated for the time being. Before closing up, however, he gave, on March 28, a benefit performance of the *Ode for St. Cecilia's Day, Acis and Galatea, concerti grossi,* and his B flat Organ Concerto, Opus 7, no. 1, for the Fund for Decayed Musicians.

It was of this period in Handel's career that Burney wrote:

Handel's activity and spirit of enterprize at this time, in his fifty-sixth year, were truly wonderful! opposed and oppressed by the most powerful nobles and gentry of the kingdom! suffering with bodily and mental disease! with rivals innumerable; when a Spanish war was just broke out, which occupied the minds, and absorbed the thoughts of the whole nation! Amidst all these accumulated misfortunes and impediments, he composed his twelve grand concertos, and Dryden's second ode; brought out Saul; Israel in Egypt; Jupiter in Argos; published seven sonatas [Opus 5]; and revived *Il Trionfo del Tempo;* Acis and Galatea; and Alexander's Feast! And yet this seems to have been one of the most idle years of his public life.

While the war became the War of the Austrian Succession, Handel turned a last time, to Italian opera. On October 10, 1740, he completed the two-act *Imeneo*, really an operetta, and notable for little else than the important role played in it by the chorus. On November 8, still at Lincoln's-Inn Fields, he opened what was to prove the last of his operatic seasons. The first attraction was *Parnasso in Festa* "performed in the original oratorio manner, with the addition of scenes, dresses, and concertos on the organ and several other instruments." Then he kept the house shut until St. Cecilia's Day, November 22, when he tried out *Imeneo* on a public no longer interested in him, in his music, or in his mostly second-rate singers, of whom only "La Francesina" was well liked. Two days before that tepidly received *première*, he had completed the last of his more than forty Italian operas. This *Deidamia*, to a Paolo Rolli libretto, was vastly better than *Imeneo*. Indeed, it is one of Handel's most charming lighter operatic scores. In it the chorus is used in an oratoriolike manner. There are two big roles for the bass voice, Fenice and Lycomede, the latter of whom is provided, in his second-act "*Nel riposo*," with an aria of essential Handelian pathos and grandeur. Deidamia's first-act aria, "*Due bell'alme inamorate*," is remarkable for the instrumentation of its accompaniment, which is for cello (originally for a soloist called Caporale), lute, and harpsichord. Not only is this colored by its omission of violin, but also it provides perhaps the latest use in opera in England of the already anachronistic lute.

On December 13, 1740, Handel gave *Imeneo* its second and last performance. Then, on January 10, 1741, again at Lincoln's-Inn Fields, London was offered an opportunity to hear, judge, and react to its last new Handelian opera. The city remained wholly indifferent. *Deidamia* was repeated on January 17 and February 10. With its third singing ended not only Handel's lifetime as a composer of opera, but his decades of work as an operatic impresario as well. The nobility, or most of it, continued opposed to him. The general public appeared to desire nothing but *The Dragon of Wantley* and other spawn of *The*

Willm Hogarth Pinx.^t   Ja.^s Mc Ardell Fecit

Captain Thomas Coram.

Upon whose Petition and Sollicitation The Royal Charter,
for y̆ FOUNDLING HOSPITAL was Granted by his MAJESTY King GEORGE y̆ Second,
17 of October 1739.

CAPTAIN THOMAS CORAM

[*after a painting by Hogarth*]

COVENT GARDEN IN 1741

Beggar's Opera. Convinced of defeat at last, Handel decided to retire from all theatrical activity and devote himself entirely to composition and, it may be, to those instrumental performances for which he was still unrivaled. It was 1741, the very year in which, at Milan in December, Christoph Willibald von Gluck was to present his first opera, *Artaserse.*

After the final singing of *Deidamia,* Handel spaced out the rest of his season with performances of *Parnasso in Festa, Acis and Galatea,* the *Ode for St. Cecilia's Day, L'Allegro,* and *Saul.* On April 8, 1741, at the Lincoln's-Inn Fields Theatre, he gave his "farewell concert," the *Ode* and *L'Allegro.* With that he closed his doors. London was to hear nothing more from him for almost two years, until, on February 18, 1743, he was, at Covent Garden, to show its people his oratorio *Samson,* something really new under the sun.

To the last three years of Handel's operatic career (1738–40) belong, at least by publication, a large percentage of his finest music for instruments alone. His Opus 5, seven sonatas for two violins (or German flutes) and continuo were composed in 1738. Opus 6, twelve great *concerti grossi,* was published by John Walsh in 1740: they had all been completed between September 29 and October 30, 1739. Opus 7, six concertos for organ and orchestra, was likewise published by Walsh in 1740. Because of Handel's habit, the habit of his era, of not writing out everything that he would have played when performing these works, we cannot today tell exactly how they sounded when they were music of exceeding popularity in his own day. But the best of them are music by no means unworthy to be placed alongside the greatest instrumental compositions of Johann Sebastian Bach. They have, furthermore, in brightly rhythmic fast movements and sweet, strong slow movements, the special flavor that marks them as Handelian. For Handel was as able and expressive an absolute musician as he was a programmatic or dramatic one. In his sonatas, concertos, and *concerti grossi* he showed himself one of the sovereign artists of his epoch.

IV

ON Saturday, August 22, 1741, Handel began to compose *Messiah* to a text adapted by Jennens from Job, Psalms, Isaiah, Lamentations, Haggai, Zechariah, Malachi, Matthew, Luke, John, Romans, I Corinthians, Hebrews, and Revelation. He completed Part I in only six days. Nine days later, September 6, he finished the second part. The third part, like the first, occupied him for only six days. For two days beginning on September 12, he worked over details in the scoring. When he completed the whole magnificent fabric on September 14, he had therefore used less than twenty-three days in the creation.

When he had completed *Messiah,* Handel was not tired. Taking up a text that Newburgh Hamilton had founded on Milton's *Samson Agonistes,*[1] he all but completed another oratorio, *Samson* forty-five days after putting the finishing touches on *Messiah.* During this entire period he seems to have been not so much the workmanlike practicing musician who had produced most of his previous works as the rapt, inspired creator. Dr. Allott, Dean of Raphoe, told Miss Hawkins that when Handel was asked about his emotions while composing *Messiah* his reply was: "I did think I did see all Heaven before me, and the great God himself."

It was almost certainly after he had begun working on *Samson* that he received from William Cavendish, Duke of Devonshire, the Lord Lieutenant of Ireland, an invitation to visit Dublin. It is evident that Handel's works were already well known in Ireland. Among the subscribers, for example, listed in the published editions of *Alexander's Feast* and the *Concerti grossi,*

[1] Hamilton also used excerpts from at least six of Milton's shorter poems.

Opus 6, is to be found the following: "The Academy of Musick at Dublin, two copies." Handel accepted the Lord Lieutenant's invitation. He had no plans for any sort of London season, no immediate purpose of performing either *Messiah* or the incomplete *Samson*. He did not have to leave immediately for Dublin, however, and he continued tirelessly at work. On October 29, 1741, he put the *Samson* score aside: it was complete but for three numbers. A few days later, traditionally on November 4 or 5, he set out for Ireland. He had decided to offer the Irish capital, among many others of his works, the *première* of *Messiah;* some members of its cast seem to have accompanied him.

Arrived at Chester, Handel put up for several days at an inn called the Golden Falcon. News of the great composer's arrival spread through the town, and one fifteen-year-old boy went down to the Golden Falcon to take a look at him. Years later, grown up to be Dr. Charles Burney, England's foremost musicologist, he remembered that November of 1741 as follows:

When Handel went through Chester, in his way to Ireland, this year 1741, I was at the Public-School in that city, and very well remember seeing him smoke a pipe over a dish of coffee at the Exchange Coffee-house; for, being extremely anxious to see so extraordinary a man, I watched him narrowly as long as he remained in Chester; which, on account of the wind being unfavourable for his embarking at Parkgate, was several days. During this time, he applied to Mr. Baker, the Organist, my first music-master, to know whether there were any choirmen in the cathedral who could sing *at sight;* as he wished to prove some books that had been hastily transcribed, by trying the choruses which he intended to perform in Ireland. Mr. Baker mentioned some of the most likely singers then in Chester, and among the rest a printer of the name of Janson, who had a good base voice, and was one of the best musicians in the choir. At this time Harry Alcock, a good player, was the first violin at Chester, which was then a very musical place; for besides public performances, Mr. Prebendary Prescott had a weekly concert, at which he was able to muster eighteen or twenty performers, gentlemen, and professors. A time was fixed for this private rehearsal at the *Golden Falcon,* where Handel was quartered; but, alas! on trial of the chorus in the Messiah, *"And with his stripes we are healed,"* — Poor Janson, after repeated attempts, failed so egregiously, that Handel let loose his great bear upon him; and after swearing in four or five languages, cried out in broken English, "You shcauntrel! tit you not dell me dat you could sing at soite?" — "Yes, sir," says the printer, "and so I can, but not at *first sight.*"

Leaving Chester, Handel moved on to Holyhead, at the northwest tip of Wales. There, the terrible weather usual to the Irish Sea in November having moderated slightly, he was finally able to board a Dublin packet by which he arrived in Ireland on November 18. The event was duly recorded as follows in the issue of *Faulkner's Journal* dated the following Saturday, November 21:

And last Wednesday the celebrated Dr. Handell arrived here in the Packet-boat from Holyhead a Gentleman universally known by his excellent Compositions in all kinds of Musick, and particularly for his Te Deum, Jubilate, Anthems, and other compositions in Church Musick (of which for some years past have principally consisted the Entertainments in the Round Church, which have so greatly contributed to support the Charity of Mercer's Hospital), to perform his Oratorios, for which purpose he hath engaged the above Mr. Maclaine [an organist mentioned in the paper's preceding paragraph], his Wife and several others of the best performers in the Musical Way.

Two of Handel's principal singers — Susanna Maria Arne Cibber and Signora Avolio (or Avoglio) — and his friend and first violin, Matthew Dubourg, were either already in Dublin or about to arrive there. The former Susanna Arne, now the unhappy wife of Theophilus Cibber, had behind her a successful stage career that included many performances of Polly Peachum in *The Beggar's Opera.* More immediately important, at the time of Handel's arrival in Dublin she was captivating that city in a drama called *The Conscious Lovers,* at the Theatre Royal. Her presence on Handel's roster would help to guarantee the success of his performances. The theater was ready: it was the Music Hall that William Neal, a music publisher, had built in

Fishamble Street. Neal, a man of important substance, was secretary to the commission that governed Dublin's three chief
charitable organizations, in whose name the Duke of Devonshire had invited Handel to Ireland. It was natural, then, that
Neal should invite Handel to house his forthcoming performances in the new Music Hall, open but little longer than since
Handel had left London.

Faulkner's Journal for December 12, 1741, carried the following advertisement:

On Monday next, being the 14th of December (and every Day following) Attendance will be given, at Mr. Handel's house in Abbey-
street near Lyffey-street, from 9 o'clock in the Morning till 2 in the
Afternoon, in order to receive the Subscription Money for his Six
Musical Entertainments in the New Musick Hall in Fishamble-street,
at which Time each Subscriber will have a Ticket delivered to him,
which entitles him to three Tickets each night, either for Ladies or
Gentlemen.

No single admissions, it appears, were sold at the door. Nor is
the price of a subscription known, though Rockstro believed
that "the price of each place was half a guinea."

Handel gave his first Dublin performance on December 23,
1741, the chief work being *L'Allegro, Il Penseroso ed Il Moderato,* with which were played an organ concerto and two *concerti grossi.* Six days later, Handel wrote a report of his reception
to Charles Jennens:

Dublin Decem^br 29, 1741

S^R

It was with the greatest Pleasure I saw the continuation of Your
kindness by the Lines you was pleased to send me in order to be prefixed to Your Oratorio Messiah, which I set to Musick before I left
England. I am emboldened, Sir, by the generous Concern You please
to take in relation to my affairs, to give you an account of the Success
I have met here. The Nobility did me the Honour to make amongst
themselves a Subscription for 6 Nights, which did fill a Room of 600
Persons. so that I needed not sell one single Ticket at the Door. and
without Vanity the Performance was received with a general Appro-

bation. Sig^ra Avolio, which I brought with me from London pleases extraordinary. I have formed an other Tenor Voice which gives great satisfaction, the Basses and Counter Tenors are very good, and the rest of the Chorus Singers (by my Direction) do exceeding well, as for the Instruments they are really excellent. Mr. Dubourgh being at the Head of them, and the Musick sounds delightfully in this charming Room, which puts me in such spirits (and my Health being so good) that I exert my self on my Organ with more than usual success. I opened with the Allegro, Penseroso, & Moderato, and I assure you that the Words of the Moderato are vastly admired. The Audience being composed (besides the Flower of Ladyes of Distinction and other People of the greatest quality) of so many Bishops, Deans, Heads of the Colledge, the most eminent People in the Law as the Chancellor, Auditor General, &ct. all which are very much taken with the Poetry. So that I am desired to perform it again the next time. I cannot sufficiently express the kind treatment I receive here, but the Politness of this generous Nation cannot be unknown to You, so I let you judge of the satisfaction I enjoy, passing my time with Honnour, profit and pleasure. They propose already to have some more Performances when the 6 Nights of the Subscription are over, and my Lord Duc the Lord Lieutenant (who is allways present with all His Family on those Nights) will easily obtain a longer Permission for me by His Majesty, so that I shall be obliged to make my stay here longer than I thought. One request I must make to you, which is that you would insinuate my most devoted Respects to My Lord and My Lady Shaftesbury. You know how much Their kind Protection is precious to me. Sir Windham Knatchbull will find here my respectfull compliments. You will encrease my obligations if by occasion you will present my humble service to some other Patrons and friends of mine. I expect with Impatience the Favour of your news, concerning Your Health and wellfare, of which I take a real share. as far for the News of your opera's,[2] I need not trouble you for

---

[2] By "your opera's" Handel clearly indicated the operas being given in London. The Earl of Middlesex, aspiring to the role of impresario, had leased the King's Theatre in the Haymarket, and had hired Baldassare Galuppi as chief composer. The chief singer was a soprano *castrato* called Angelo Maria Monticelli. The season ran to June 1, 1742, after which there was one additional season before Galuppi returned to Italy, being replaced that autumn by Giovanni Battista Lampugnani. Of the 1742–3

all this Town is full of their ill success, by a number of Letters from
your quarters to the People of quality here, an I can't help saying but
that it furnishes great Diversion and laughter. The first Opera³ I
heard my self before I left London, and it made me very merry all
along my journey, and of the second Opera, call'd Penelope,⁴ a certain noble man writes very jocosly, il faut que je dise avec Harlequin,
notre Penelope n'est qu'une Sallope. but I think I have trespassed
too much on your Patience, I beg you to be persuaded of the sincere
veneration and esteem with which I have the Honneur to be

Sr

Your

most obliged and most humble servant
George Frideric Handel

Faulkner's Journal for Saturday, December 26, 1741, agreed
with Handel's own estimate of the situation:

Last Wednesday, Mr. Handel had his first oratorio at Mr. Neal's
Musick Hall in Fishamble Street, which was crowded with a more
numerous and polite audience than ever was seen upon the like
occasion. The performance was superior to anything of the kind in
the kingdom before, and our nobility and gentry, to shew their taste
for all kinds of genius, expressed their great satisfaction and have
already given all imaginable encouragement to this grand musick.

Agreeing to certain arrangements before his departure from
England, Handel had attempted to stipulate that the choirs of
Dublin's two cathedrals should be at his disposal, but the au-
thorities had limited his employment of the trained choristers

---

season, Burney wrote: "How much the ballance turned out in favour of
the noble impresario, I am unable to say; if considerable, the honour must
be totally ascribed to the composer and performers, as dancing appears
to have had no share in attracting the public attention."
³ *Alessandro in Persia*, a *pasticcio* arranged by Galuppi. It included arias
by Leonardo Leo, Hasse, Arena, Pescetti, Domenico Scarlatti, and Lampugnani. The libretto had originally been written in 1738, at Lucca, by
the Abbé Francesco Vaneschi, for the use of Pietro Domenico Paradies.
⁴ *Penelope*, composed by Galuppi to a libretto especially prepared by
Paolo Rolli. Discussing it, Burney said: "The genius of Galuppi was not
as yet matured; he now copied the hasty, light, and flimsy style which
reigned in Italy at this time, and which Handel's solidity and science had
taught the English to despise."

2 3 7

to such concerts as were given for charity, stating that the constant use of the choirs in public concerts might lead to unspecified abuses. So he had, for his concerts up to April 12, 1742, the singers of the Philharmonic Society, the Musical Academy — then presided over by Garrett Wellesley, Earl of Mornington, future father of the great Duke of Wellington — and such individual members of the cathedral choirs as joined him of their own accord.

The record convinces that there was an unceasing demand for Handel's "concerts" or "oratorios" — they were indiscriminately referred to as either. The program of December 23, 1741, was repeated, by command of the Duke and Duchess of Devonshire, on January 13, 1742. One week later, with the usual concertos, the chief pieces were *Acis and Galatea* and the *Ode for St. Cecilia's Day*, which were repeated on January 27. For the fifth and sixth performances, on February 3 and 10, *Esther* was sung, the first true oratorio that Handel gave in Ireland. The February 10 performance filled out the first subscription series of six. The second series also consisted of one large vocal work and concertos at each performance. The dates and principal compositions were: February 17 and March 2, *Alexander's Feast;* March 17, *L'Allegro, Il Penseroso ed Il Moderato;* March 24 and 31, *Hymen* (a cantata or serenata version in English of the 1740 opera, *Imeneo*), and April 7, *Esther.* The Duke of Devonshire left Dublin for England on February 16, but it is evident that Handel's musical entertainments were so well established by then as to be able to dispense with patronage from the Lord Lieutenant.

One of the most famous humorous anecdotes about Handel was related by Burney as belonging to a Dublin concert. It is best recounted in Burney's own words:

One night, while Handel was in Dublin, Dubourg having a solo part in a song, and a close to make, *ad libitum,* he wandered about in different keys a great while, and seemed indeed a little bewildered, and uncertain of his original key . . . but, at length, coming to the shake, which was to terminate this long close, Handel, to the great delight of the audience, and augmentation of applause, cried out loud enough to be heard in the most remote parts of the theatre: "You are welcome home, Mr. Dubourg!"

It was on March 27, during Handel's second series of six performances, that the following advertisement first appeared in *Faulkner's Journal* and the *Dublin News-Letter*:

For the Relief of the Prisoners in the several Gaols, and for the Support of Mercer's Hospital, in Stephen's-street, and of the Charitable Infirmary on the Inn's Quay, on Monday the 12th of April, will be performed at the Musick Hall in Fishamble-street, *Mr. Handel's new Grand Oratorio, called the Messiah*, in which the Gentlemen of the Choirs of both Cathedrals will assist, with some Concertos on the Organ, by Mr. Handell. Tickets to be had at the Musick Hall, and at Mr. Neal's in Christ Church Yard, at half-a-guinea each. *N.B.* — No person will be admitted to the Rehearsal without a Rehearsal Ticket, which will be given gratis with the Ticket for the Performance when pay'd for.

The *Dublin News-Letter* added: "Books are also to be had at a British sixpence each."

The "Relief of the Prisoners in the several Gaols" referred to the sponsorship of the society for "the benefit and enlargement of poor distressed prisoners for debt in the several marshalseas of the city of Dublin." *Faulkner's Journal* had announced on March 14, 1741, that the society had, during the year just past (the new year still customarily began on March 25) released 188 "miserable persons of both sexes." Two years later, the society liberated 142 prisoners. The debts for which these 142 men and women had been incarcerated totaled not more than £1,225/17, of which the society paid the creditors £33! The debtors were usually little more pauperized than the creditors.

The public rehearsal, in reality the first singing of *Messiah*, was held on April 8, 1742. *Faulkner's Journal* appeared the following day and included this combined review and notice:

Yesterday Mr. Handel's new Grand Sacred Oratorio, called the *Messiah*, was rehearsed at the Musick Hall in Fishamble Street to a most Grand, Polite, and Crowded Audience; and was performed so well, that it gave universal Satisfaction to all present; and was allowed by the greatest Judges to be the finest Composition of Musick that ever was heard, and the sacred Words as properly adapted for the occasion.

N.B. — At the desire of several persons of Distinction, the above Performance is put off to Tuesday next. The doors will be opened at Eleven, and the Performance begin at Twelve. Many Ladies and Gentlemen who are well-wishers to this Noble and Grand Charity, for which this Oratorio was composed, request it as a favour, that the Ladies who honour this performance with their Presence, would be pleased to come without Hoops, as it will greatly encrease the Charity, by making Room for more company.

Faulkner's was, of course, in error: *Messiah* was not composed with the Dublin charities in mind, however much it benefited them and would in later years benefit London charities. That the performance was put off "to Tuesday next" meant that it was to be given on April 13 rather than, as originally announced, on April 12. On the morning of the performance day, the newspapers repeated the request that ladies attend without hoops, and added that "Gentlemen are desired to come without their Swords." By using the space that hoops and swords might have occupied, the managers were able to increase the Music Hall's capacity from the usual six hundred persons to the seven hundred who actually attended.

The orchestra of those first performances of *Messiah* was led by Dubourg. Mrs. Cibber and Signora Avolio were contralto and soprano soloists respectively. The male solos were sung by James Baileys (tenor), William Lambe and Joseph Ward (altos), and John Hill and John Mason (basses), all from the choirs of Christ Church and St. Patrick's Cathedral. Rockstro believed that Ralph Roseingrave and a Mr. Church — either the choirmaster John Church or the Gloucester Cathedral organist, Richard Church — also took some part. The chorus was made up from the choirs of the two cathedrals. Notations in a copy of the original wordbook that was unearthed in 1891 make it possible that a soprano named Maclaine (whom Streatfeild guessed to be the wife of Maclaine the organist) sang some portions of the solos, including "I know that my Redeemer liveth." Mrs. Cibber and Signora Avolio divided "He shall feed His flock" in a manner that became traditional, though the score originally assigned it to the soprano throughout. Of Mrs. Cibber's rendition of "He was despised," it is recorded that Swift's friend Dr. Patrick Delany, who was shortly to marry Handel's friend Mary Granville, was so moved by it that he shouted out: "Woman, for this thy sins be forgiven thee!"

On Saturday, April 17, *Faulkner's Journal*, the *Dublin News-Letter*, and the *Dublin Gazette* reported the performance in what we call a news release, as it was uniform in the periodicals (only *Faulkner's* carried the final sentence):

On Tuesday last Mr. Handel's Sacred Grand Oratorio, the Messiah, was performed in the New Musick Hall in Fishamble-street; the best Judges allowed it to be the most finished piece of Musick. Words are wanting to express the exquisite Delight it afforded to the admiring crowded Audience. The Sublime, the Grand, and the Tender, adapted to the most elevated, majestick and moving Words, conspired to transport and charm the ravished Heart and Ear. It is but Justice to Mr. Handel that the World should know he generously gave the Money arising from this Grand Performance, to be equally shared by the Society for relieving Prisoners, the Charitable Infirmary, and Mercer's Hospital, for which they will ever gratefully remember his Name; and that the Gentlemen of the two Choirs, Mr. Dubourg, Mrs. Avolio and Mrs. Cibber, who all performed their Parts to Admiration, acted also on the same disinterested Principle, satisfied with the deserved Applause of the Publick, and the conscious Pleasure of promoting such useful and extensive Charity. There were above 700 People in the Room, and the Sum collected for that Noble and Pious Charity amounted to about £400, out of which £127 goes to each of the three great and pious Charities.

After that April 13 singing of *Messiah*, Handel contented himself for more than seven weeks with an occasional concert. Parts of *Scipione*, *Atalanta*, the *Water Musick*, and *Saul* — just possibly, on May 25, all of *Saul* — were given. Only on June 3, "at the particular desire of several of the nobility and gentry," was a second *Messiah* sung "with Concertos on the Organ." By then the Irish summer had become so oppressive that the advertisement stated that "in order to keep the Room as cool as possible, a Pane of Glass will be removed from the top of each of the Windows." Ventilation may have helped, but the press of people in Neal's Musick Hall that June day was a tribute to the compelling power that *Messiah* has exercised from April 8, 1741, to its most recent singing.

The *Messiah* of June 3 was Handel's final Dublin performance, though he seems to have played some part in two benefit concerts given in July. One of these was for Signora Avolio, the other for the former Cecilia Young, who — having married Thomas Augustine Arne in 1736 — was now Mrs. Cibber's sister-in-law. Handel entered into the making of plans for his return to Ireland in 1743. Then, on August 13, he bade farewell to hospitable Dublin and returned, via a packet to Parkgate, to England and London. *Faulkner's Journal,* in its issue dated August 17, had the following item:

Last week, Lady King, widow of the late Rt. Hon. Sir Harry King, Bart., and the celebrated Mr. Handel, so famous for his excellent compositions and fine performances, with which he entertained this town in the most agreeable manner, embarked for England.

The *Dublin News-Letter* added the detail that Lady King and Mr. Handel had "embarked on board one of the Chester traders in order to go to Park Gate."

To a man who for years had been fighting a disastrous battle against a London indifferent on the whole, openly antagonistic in part, and friendly only in small part, the months spent in friendly, unspoiled Dublin must have been refreshment. He had not composed much there, for the only piece that can with fair certainty be dated from his Irish sojourn is a small violin-and-harpsichord work called *Forest Musick*. This contains what is clearly intended to be Irish melody, especially in its second section. But he had regained strength, and he had proved to himself some of the performance values of *Messiah*.

The first word of Handel after his return to Brook Street is a letter he wrote to Jennens:

London Sept: 9th 1742

Dear Sr.

It was indeed Your humble servant which intended You a visit in my way from Ireland to London. for I certainly could have given you a better account by word of mouth, as by writing, how well Your Messiah was received in that country, yet as a Noble Lord, and no less than the Bishop of Elphim [Edward Synge, Bishop of Elphin] (A Nobleman very learned in musick) has given his observations in writing of this Oratorio, I send you here annexed the contents of it in his own words —

I shall send the printed Book of the Messiah to Mr. Sted for you. As for my success in general in that generous and polite Nation, I reserve the account of it till I have the Honour to see you in London. The report that the Direction of the Opera next winter is committed to my care, is groundless. The gentlemen who have undertaken to middle with Harmony can not agree, and are quite in a confusion. Whether I shall do something in the Oratorio way (as several of my friend desire) i can not determine as yet. Certain it is that this time 12 month I shall continue my Oratorio's in Ireland, where they are agoing to make a large subscription allready for that Purpose.

If I had known that My Lord Guernsey [5] was so near when I passed Coventry, You may easily imagine, Sir, that I should not have neglected of paying my Respects to him, since you know the particular esteem I have for his Lordship. I think it a very long time to the month of November next when I can have some hopes of seeing you here in London. Pray let me hear meanwhile of your Health and Wellfare, of which I take a real share beeing with uncommon sincerity and Respect

Your

most obliged humble Servant
George Frideric Handel

[5] This was Heneage Finch, later Earl of Aylesford. A relative of Jennens as mentioned before, he had read a lyric oration, *The Praise of True Magnificence*, at Oxford at the time of Handel's visit there. At Jennens' death, he inherited many of John Christopher Smith's transcriptions of Handel's music.

It is easy to understand Handel's willingness, reasonable to suppose his eagerness, to return to Ireland. But, for reasons that cannot be determined, that second trip was never to take place. Instead, at the age of fifty-eight, Handel was again to be swept into the nerve-racking hubbub and struggle of London. In a sense that is made no clearer by his monument in Westminster Abbey than by his music, chorus after chorus, oratorio after oratorio, decade after decade, and despite whatever temporary oases he may have sought and found at Tunbridge Wells, Aix-la-Chapelle, Halle, or Dublin, there was never any doubt that London was his home.

BOOK IV

SINGERS OF HANDEL'S TIME PERFORMING WILLIAM
DEFESCH'S "JUDITH" (1732)

[*Hogarth*]

HANDEL AND A SCENE FROM "ALEXANDER'S FEAST"

[Engraving by Jacob Houbraken, with ornaments by Hubert Fran-
çois Gravelot, 1738]

I

ON October 12, 1742, Handel finished the last number of his oratorio *Samson*. It is unfortunate that the single term "oratorio" must, by force of custom, be used to indicate works so various in nature as, on one side, *Messiah* and *Israel in Egypt,* and, on the other, *Samson,* some of the earlier works, and all of the subsequent ones. *Israel in Egypt* particularly, and *Messiah* almost as much, are epics on a vast, non-human, universal scale. *Samson* and the others are dramas of a less vast, more human sort. For *Semele,* Handel himself used the phrase "English opera," indicating not only that it was sung in English, but that it was done without the stage action essential to Italian opera. It is a better description of *Semele* than "oratorio." But time has not allowed the phrase to endure despite its useful purpose. Now we must cover with one unsuitable word of disputed provenance works widely disparate in character and style.

In the London *Daily Advertiser* for February 17, 1743, appeared the following notice of Handel's first formal season composed wholly of oratorios:

By Subscription. — At the Theatre Royal, in Covent Garden, tomorrow, the 18th inst., will be performed a new Oratorio called Samson. Tickets will be delivered to subscribers (on paying their subscription money) at Mr. Handel's house, in Brook-street, near Hanover Square. Attendance will be given from nine o'clock in the morning till three in the afternoon. Pit and boxes to be put together, and no person to be admitted without tickets, which will be delivered that day at the office in Covent Garden Theatre, at half-a-guinea each; first gallery, 5s.; upper gallery, 3s. 6d. *Nota.* Each subscriber is to pay six guineas upon taking out his subscription ticket, which entitles him to three box tickets every night of Mr. Handel's first six performances in Lent. And if Mr. Handel should have any more performances after the first six nights, each subscriber may continue on the same conditions.

Alexander Pope, fifty-four years old and at the summit of his remarkable domination over certain realms of taste, had published, in 1742 when he had but two more years to live, the edition of his *Works* that included the fourth book of *The Dunciad*. In it, he — who admittedly had no ear for music — attacked Italian opera and its supporters. By the ironical turn of fate, this onslaught glorified Handel and scathingly belittled those who had driven him to Ireland:

> When lo! a harlot form * soft sliding by,
> With mincing step, small voice, and languid eye:
> Foreign her air, her robe's discordant pride
> In patch-work flutt'ring, and her head aside:
> By singing peers upheld on either hand,
> She triped and laughed, too pretty much to stand;
> Cast on the prostrate Nine a scornful look,
> Then thus in quaint recitativo spoke.
>   "O Cara! Cara! silence all that train:
> Joy to great Chaos! Let division reign: **
> Chromatic tortures soon shall drive them hence,
> Break all their nerves and fritter all their sense:

* (Pope's footnote) The attitude given to this phantom represents the nature and genius of Italian opera; its affected airs, its effeminate sounds, and the practice of patching up these operas with favorite songs, incoherently put together. These things were supported by the subscriptions of the nobility. This circumstance that opera should prepare for the opening of the grand sessions was prophesied of in book iii. ver. 304.

** (Pope's footnote) Alluding to the false taste of playing tricks in music with numberless divisions, to the neglect of that harmony which conforms to the sense, and applies to the passions. Mr. Handel had introduced a great number of hands, and more variety of instruments into the orchestra, and employed even drums and cannon to make a fuller chorus; which proved so much too manly for the fine gentlemen of his age, that he was obliged to remove his music into Ireland. After which they were reduced, for want of composers, to practise the patch-work above mentioned.

One trill shall harmonise joy, grief, and rage,
Wake the dull church, and lull the ranting stage;
To the same notes thy sons shall hum, or snore,
And all thy yawning daughters cry, Encore.
Another Phoebus, thy own Phoebus, reigns,
Joys in my jigs, and dances in my chains.
But soon, ah soon, rebellion will commence,
If music meanly borrows aid from sense.
Strong in new arms, lo! Giant Handel stands,
Like bold Briareus, with a hundred hands;
To stir, to rouse, to shake the soul he comes,
And Jove's own thunders follow Mars's Drums.
Arrest him, empress; or you sleep no more — "
She heard, and drove him to the Hibernian shore.

Pope had asked Dr. Arbuthnot how to evaluate Handel. From
that constant Handelian he had received the reply: "Conceive
the highest that you can of his ability, and they are much beyond anything you can conceive." His consequent championing
of Handel, some dissatisfaction with the miserable operas heard
during Handel's visit to Ireland, and perhaps a genuine taste
for Handel's large settings of English texts, these combined to
assure a successful season. The promised performance of *Samson* began it at Covent Garden on February 18, 1743.[1]

The Samson, John Beard, had added immeasurably to his no-
toriety as a singer by becoming the center of a social scandal.
On January 8, 1739, he had married Lady Henrietta Herbert,
daughter of James, Earl Waldegrave, and widow of Lord Edward Herbert, second son of the Marquess of Powis. Lady
Mary Wortley Montagu, writing acidly to Lady Pomfret about
the ensuing scandal, lighted up the surrounding social scene
with an agility unusual even for her:

Lady Harriet Herbert furnished the tea-tables here with fresh
tattle for the last fortnight. I was one of the first who was informed

---

[1] The principal singers were Catherine (often known as Kitty or "Mrs.")
Clive (Dalila), Mrs. Cibber (Micah), Signora Avolio, John Beard (Samson), and Savage (Manoa); the trumpet soloist was Valentine Snow.

of her adventure by Lady Gage, who was told that morning by a priest, that she had desired him to marry her the next day to Beard, who sings in the farces at Drury Lane. He refused her that good office, and immediately told Lady Gage, who (having been unfortunate in her friends) was frightened at this affair, and asked my advice. I told her honestly, that since the lady was capable of such amours, I did not doubt, if this was broke off, she would bestow her person and fortune on some hackney-coachman or chairman; and that I really saw no method of saving her from ruin, and her family from dishonour, but by poisoning her; and offered to be at the expense of the arsenic, and even to administer it with my own hands, if she would invite her to drink tea with her that evening. But on her not approving that method, she sent to Lady Montacute, Mrs. Durich, and all the relations within reach of messengers. They carried Lady Harriet to Twickenham, though I told them it was a bad air for girls. She is since returned to London, and some people believe her married; others, that she is too much intimidated by Mr. Waldegrave's threats to dare to go through this ceremony; but the secret is now public, and in what manner it will conclude I know not. Her relations have certainly no reason to be amazed at her constitution, but are violently surprised at the mixture of devotion that forces her to have recourse to the church in her necessities; which has not been the road taken by the matrons of her family. Such examples are very detrimental to our whole sex, and are apt to influence the other into a belief that we are unfit to manage either liberty or money.

That Beard was not held in high esteem by all is proved by a letter that Horace Walpole wrote from Arlington Street six days after the first *Samson*. After discussing military operations in Flanders, Walpole commented on the cast and the occasion as follows:

But to come to more *real* contests, Handel has set up an Oratorio against the Opera, and succeeds. He has hired all the goddesses from the farces [Cibber and Clive], and the singers of roast-beef from between the acts at both theatres, with a man with one note in his voice [Beard], and a girl without ever an one [probably Cibber], and so they sing and make brave hallelujahs, and the good company *encore* the recitative, if it happens to have any cadence like what they call a tune.

Sharp as Pope and almost as waspish, but with no better ear or mind for music, Walpole was, like the poet, ready to accept Handel as the overtopping figure in English music. That "the good company" did indeed "*encore* the recitative" is vouched for by seven repetitions that same season of *Samson* alone, and by Walpole himself, who later wrote: "The Oratorios thrive abundantly; for my part they give me an idea of Heaven, where everybody is to sing, whether they have voices or not."

Newburgh Hamilton's fulsome dedication of the text of *Samson* to Frederick, Prince of Wales, did not suffice to keep George II away from the second performance. The *Daily Post* for February 25, 1743, records that forewarned police took the occasion of the royal visit to Covent Garden to arrest there some of the most notorious and talented footpads and pickpockets of London, including two known as The Pigeon and Stink-and-End. The Prince of Wales was pleased by Hamilton's dedication, the King by the music, society by the royal pleasures and its own. Handel's season was a real success. If he had not already abandoned the prospect of returning to Dublin for more performances in Fishamble Street, he probably did so temporarily in view of that success in the larger city. He had decided to try the temper of London audiences toward *Messiah*.

From the moment that Handel announced his intention of making a performance of *Messiah* one of the subscription features at Covent Garden, it was clear that there would be severe ecclesiastical opposition. A secular auditorium was pronounced an unsuitable place for the singing of a musical drama built around the figure of Christ. *Messiah* was therefore billed as *A Sacred Oratorio*, under which name London was to know it for several years. It was first sung at Covent Garden on March 23, 1743, on which occasion (as when it was repeated on March 25 and 29) it attracted little of the praise it had commanded in Dublin. It certainly had not at first the popularity of *Samson*, which far more operatic oratorio had to be sung eight times that season to satisfy its eager public. Those eleven performances, plus the customary concertos and one singing each of *L'Allegro, Il Penseroso ed Il Moderato* and the *Ode for St. Cecilia's Day* filled out Handel's first complete London oratorio season, which closed with a final *Samson* on March 30.

The custom following which *Messiah* audiences stand during the Hallelujah Chorus seems to have been initiated at its first London presentation. In a letter to Sir William Forbes, the Scottish poet and philosopher James Beattie wrote as follows: "When Handel's Messiah was first performed, the audience was exceedingly struck and affected by the music in general, but when the chorus struck up 'For the Lord God Omnipotent' in the Alleluia, they were so transported that they all together, with the King (who happened to be present), started up and remained standing till the chorus ended." To this, Beattie, who had been only seven years old, and a resident of Scotland, when the event occurred, added: "This anecdote I had from Lord Kinnoull." Lord Kinnoul was a friend of Handel's and an intense admirer of *Messiah*. It was to him that the composer is reported to have said — in reply to words of praise for the oratorio: "My lord, I should be sorry if I only entertained them; I wished to make them better." "They" were, for the most part, not "entertained," and it is doubtful that they were made "better." *Messiah* was not heard in London in the season of 1743–4, but twice in that of 1744–5, and then not again until 1749.

The opera company at the Haymarket, still presided over by the Earl of Middlesex, was struggling along as it was to struggle until its collapse on June 16, 1744. It was losing money for its noble patrons and subscribers, and the list of its operas and singers describes it as thoroughly second-rate. One of Burney's remarks about one of the operas is too good to omit. Discussing an opera that Porpora had composed to Apostolo Zeno's *Temistocle,* and that must have been a counter-attraction to the second or third *Samson,* he wrote: "I never saw Music in which shakes were so lavished; Porpora seems to have composed the air: *Contrasto assai,* in a shivering fit."

Despite the lukewarm reception of *A Sacred Oratorio*, Handel had good reason to be happy over his first oratorio season at Covent Garden. He evidently planned another like it to be built around two new oratorios. The first of these was *Semele*, composed to an intended opera libretto written by Congreve in 1707. It was begun on Monday, June 3, 1743, and completed on Monday, July 4. Had military events not interfered, Handel would probably then have proceeded to the preparation of his second novelty for the coming season. The War of the Austrian Succession was continuing in somewhat altered form. Quite unexpectedly, on June 27 at the village of Dettingen, on the River Main near Frankfurt, French armies led jointly by the Duc de Grammont and the Maréchal de Noailles were decisively defeated by the combined Hanoverian and English armies under the somewhat passive personal command of George II. Generals Clayton and Monroy were killed, the Duke of Cumberland was wounded, some 2,000 allied soldiers were lost, and the victory was not followed by its logical developments. But there was no doubt that it was a victory, and the King suddenly became a hero.

It was at once obvious that the King's return to London would desiderate a magnificent public celebration of thanksgiving and praise, particularly if the adherents of the previously unpopular monarch were to sustain and extend the unprecedented personal popularity he had instigated by being at the head of the troops at Dettingen. This meant music by Handel. On Sunday, July 17, therefore, he began to compose the *Dettingen Te Deum* [2]; thirteen days later he started the *Anthem* ("The king shall rejoice," Psalms XX and XXI) to accompany it. Both were couched in what has been called his "big bow-wow manner," familiar in the Coronation Anthems, the *Utrecht Te Deum* and *Jubilate*, and the Funeral Anthem for Queen Caroline. The King and the Duke of Cumberland returned to London in No-

[2] Handel set the *Hymn of St. Ambrose* at least five times — in two of the Chandos Anthems, the *Utrecht Te Deum*, the Funeral Anthem for Queen Caroline, and the *Dettingen Te Deum*.

vember, progressing through a city illuminated in their honor. Rumors that Louis XV was lending his powerful support to another attempt by the Stuarts to conquer England and place Prince Charles Edward the Young Pretender on the throne failed to hush the excitement.

The *Dettingen Te Deum* and *Anthem* were given public rehearsal in the Chapel Royal at St. James's in both September and November. The occasion for which they had been designed, the solemn thanksgiving for the victory at Dettingen, was unrolled in the presence of the royal family at St. James's on November 27. The majestic and overawing strains of Handel's music were received with almost universal approbation.

The *Dettingen Te Deum* is one of the works on which charges of wholesale plagiarism against Handel have been based. The music of ten of its members is very like that to be found in a *Te Deum* that has been attributed to Francesco Antonio Urio, an Italian priest who published music between 1690 and 1706. Chrysander printed the Urio *Te Deum*. If it was in truth by Urio, then Handel was a plagiarist to about the same extent as Shakespeare, and with about the same results as to the fate of his sources and the magnificence of the use he made of them. But though there is no remaining doubt that Handel borrowed other men's music unceremoniously, there can be considerable doubt as to the true authorship of the "Urio" *Te Deum*. Let us see.

Most of the choruses in *Israel in Egypt,* in turn, are adapted from a *Magnificat* that has been attributed to another Italian priest, Dionigi Erba, who is said to have served as a choirmaster in Milan toward the end of the seventeenth century. There is, again, no doubt of the similarity, in some cases the identity, of Handel's choruses in *Israel in Egypt* and those in Erba's *Magnificat*. But there can be considerable doubt as to the true authorship of the "Erba" *Magnificat*. Again, let us see.

Sedley Taylor, in *The Indebtedness of Handel to Works by Other Composers,* published in 1906, made a strong case for Handel's having lifted from Urio and Erba, among many others.

But Percy Robinson, in his *Handel and His Orbit*, published in 1908, advanced a theory about these two obscure gentlemen, a theory, be it said, that is plausible, but that if correct does not by any means exculpate Handel of all plagiarism. Robinson pointed out that the "Urio" *Te Deum* and the "Erba" *Magnificat* were in themselves both curiously Handelian, and might from internal evidence be early works by Handel. Further, he said with truth that there is a village called Urio a few miles north of Como on the west shore of the west arm of Lake Como and a town called Erba a few miles east of Como. Handel could easily have visited these places in 1709, possibly in company with Agostino Steffani. While visiting them, he might himself have composed the "Urio" *Te Deum* and the "Erba" *Magnificat*, placing the names of the towns on them to the future confusion of musical historians, and then laying them aside until he made use of some of their contents in various later works. The fact that a priest named Urio certainly, and a priest named Erba possibly, existed and composed would not render this historical possibility impossible.

Except to the strictest moralist and the professional attributor, the facts in these cases are of little importance. Handel did borrow. So did Bach and Shakespeare. They nearly always not only improved beyond recognition what they took, but more often than not saved it from complete and eternal obscurity. It has never been claimed that Handel took a whole piece, as Bononcini did, and passed it off entire and alone as his own work.

Between the composition of the Dettingen ceremonial pieces and their performance, Handel completed, in September 1743, to a text arranged by James Miller,[3] his second proposed novelty for the coming season, the oratorio *Joseph and His Brethren*. Despite all his activity, or perhaps because of it, Handel was still unwell. "Mr. Handel has a palsy and cannot compose," wrote Horace Walpole at this time. Handel did not soon pro-

---

[3] Sometimes referred to as the Reverend James Miller, the author of a tragedy called *Mahomet*, as well as farces and comedies, was a fellow of Wadham College, Oxford.

duce *Semele, Joseph and His Brethren,* or anything else: he
had no season at all between March 30, 1743, and February 10,
1744. On the latter date he began to repeat the previous season
of twelve performances during Lent.

Handel's success during the 1742–3 season did not mean that
whole segments of high society were not still rampant against
him. They included many who felt with reason that his oratorios
detracted from the audiences for Middlesex's operas in the Haymarket. Cabals and intrigues of many varieties proliferated, and
with the natural result: both Middlesex's venture and Handel's
began sliding down the greased slope to bankruptcy. Handel
opened his Lenten season, the subscription price of which was
£4/4, on February 10, 1744, with the *première* of *Semele.* This
superbly beautiful work, in reality an actionless opera rather
than an oratorio, was a mild success, receiving only four performances that season. Not even the heavenly persuasions of
the *alla Hornpipe* chorus "Now Love, that everlasting boy,"
Juno's "Above measure," Semele's "O sleep, why dost thou leave
me?" and Jupiter's exquisite and eternally fresh "Where'er you
walk" could prevail against the inflamed and silly passions of
court politics and social jealousy.

After the first *Semele,* Mrs. Delany wrote in a letter: "There
was no disturbance at the play-house." She clearly had feared,
as Streatfeild has pointed out, that "a chorus of cat-calls might
reasonably be expected at the production of a new oratorio."
The "Goths," as she called members of the cabals arrayed
against her composer-hero, held their tongues. But less than two
weeks later, she wrote: "Semele has a strong party against it,
viz., the fine ladies petits maitres, and ignoramus's. All the
opera people are enraged at Handel, but Lady Cobham, Lady
Westmoreland, and Lady Chesterfield never fail it." Both the
King and the Prince of Wales continued their now undeviating
loyalty to Handel. Indeed, the King was often, it was said, all
but alone in Covent Garden when a pro-Middlesex hostess succeeded, by entertaining lavishly on the night of a Handel oratorio, in keeping most of society away. Lord Chesterfield walked

out of Covent Garden one night before the performance of an oratorio was over. "What, my Lord, are you dismissed?" he was asked by an acquaintance. "Is there not an oratorio?" And Chesterfield replied: "Yes, they are now performing, but I thought it best to retire, lest I should disturb the King in his privacies."

On January 1, 1743, the Middlesex company had presented at the King's Theatre in the Haymarket Galuppi's setting of a Vaneschi libretto, *Enrico*. Its principal attraction was the appearance of three new singers, of whom the most important turned out to be Signora Galli, who was to be for decades a familiar figure on the English musical stage. She made the first of her many appearances in a Handel work when *Joseph and His Brethren* was sung at Covent Garden for the first time on March 2, 1744, others in the cast being Sullivan (Joseph), La Francesina (Asenath), and Beard. Galli did not conquer in these early appearances: her vogue was to come later. *Joseph and His Brethren* was no more of a drawing-card than *Semele*, like which it was sung only four times that season. It is no peer to the strength of *Samson* or the sweet delights of *Semele*. But like them, like so many others among Handel's compositions, it would supply today's music-lovers with welcome relief from routine performances of *Messiah*.

Handel patched out his season at Covent Garden with two singings each of *Saul* and *Samson*. It had been a thin season, but no thinner than the one at the King's Theatre, which closed with a performance of Lampugnani's *Alceste* on June 16, 1744. After that there was no opera in London [4] until January 7, 1746, when the King's Theatre was to reopen with Gluck's *La Caduta de' Giganti*. During this 1743-4 season, the Middlesex company had, curiously enough, presented Handel's *Alessandro*, announcing it as "Roxana, or Alexander in India, composed by

[4] Except for nine or ten performances at the Little Theatre in the Haymarket, given from April 7, 1745, on. These were under the direction of Geminiani, and were patronized by Prince Ferdinand Philip Lobkowitz and Count Saint-Germain. The piece was a *pasticcio* called *L'Incostanza Delusa*.

Mr. Handel, with dances and other decorations, entirely new."
As presented, it contained at least nine arias that not only were
not by Handel, but had no possible connection with the story.
It also omitted a dozen arias from the original opera. Both
additions and subtractions were passed over without so much
as a footnote.

The temporary failure of the Middlesex enterprise found
Handel already dickering with Jennens over the text of a new
oratorio. It was to be one of the works he would present when,
staking most, if not all, of his available funds, he would take
over the King's Theatre the following November, announcing a
series of twenty-four concerts. On June 9, 1744, he wrote as follows to Jennens:

London Juin 9th 1744

Dear Sir,

It gave me great Pleasure to hear Your safe arrival in the Country
and that Your Health was much improved. I hope it is by this time
firmly establichd, and I wish You with all my Heart the Continuation of it, and all the Prosperity.

As you do me the Honour to encourage my Musicall Undertak-
ings, and even to promote them with a particular Kindness, I take
the Liberty to trouble You with an account of what Engagement I
have hitherto concluded. I have taken the Opera House in the
Haymarketh. engaged, as Singers, Sigra Francesina, Miss Robinson, Beard, Reinhold, Mr Gates with his Boyes's and several of the
best Chorus Singers from the Choirs, and I have some hopes that
Mrs Cibber will sing for me. She sent me word from Bath (where
she is now) that she would perform for me next winter with great
pleasure if it did not interfere with her playing, but I think I can
obtain Mr Riches's permission (with whom she is engaged to play in
Covent Garden House) since so obligingly he has gave Leave to Mr
Beard and Mr Reinhold.

Now I should be extreamly glad to receive the first Act, or what
is ready of the new Oratorio [Belshazzar] with which you intend to
favour me, that I might employ all my attention and time, in order
to answer in some measure the obligation I lay under. this new favour

will greatly increase my obligations. I remain with all possible gratitude and Respect

S^r

Your

most obliged and most humble
Servant
George Frideric Handel

Handel was not waiting to set to work on the next season's
new compositions until the specified text should arrive from
Jennens. On July 19, 1744, he began to set, under the title of
Hercules, the Reverend Thomas Broughton's adaptation of
Sophocles' *The Women of Trachis.* This, announced in the *General Advertiser* of January 1, 1745, as a "musical drama," was
later referred to by Handel himself as an oratorio. One month
after beginning it, Handel again addressed Jennens:

July 19, 1744

Dear Sir

At my arrival in London, which was Yesterday, I immediately
perused the Act of the Oratorio [*Belshazzar*] with which you favour'd me, and, the little time only I had it, gives me great Pleasure. Your reasons for the Length of the first act are intirely satisfac-
tory to me, and it is likewise my opinion to have the following Acts
short.[5] I shall be very glad and much obliged to you, if you will soon
favour me with the remaining Acts. Be pleased to point out these
passages in the Messiah which you think require altering — [6]

[5] Far from keeping the other acts short, Jennens made them so long
that Handel refused to set them intact, cutting more than one hundred
(but not enough) of the lines. The handbook containing the text, which
was printed inviolate at Jennens' insistence, has a note. This reads: "*N.B.*
— The oratorio being thought too long, several things are marked with
a black line drawn down the margin, as omitted in the performance."
[6] Jennens (who, be it remembered, had merely compiled the text of
Messiah) had evidently complained about some of the music to Handel
as well as to others. To one of his friends he had written: "I shall shew
you a collection I gave Handel, call'd Messiah, which I value highly. He
has made a fine entertainment of it, though not near so good as he might
and ought to have done. I have with great difficulty made him correct
some of the grossest faults in the composition, but he retained his overture

I desire my humble Respects and thanks to My Lord Guernsey for his many Civility's to me, and believe me to be with the greatest Respect

Sr

Your

most obedient and most humble

Servant

George Frideric Handel

The first act of *Hercules* was completed on July 30, the second on August 11, the last on August 17. Four days later, Handel once more addressed Jennens:

London

Agosty 21

1744

Dear Sir

The Second Act of the Oratorio [*Belshazzar*] I have received safe, and own my self highly obliged to You for it. I am greatly pleased with it, and shall use my best endeavours to do it justice. I can only say that I impatiently wait for the third Act and desire to believe me to be with great Respect

Sr

Your

most obliged and most humble

Servant

George Frideric Handel

More than three weeks later, still not having received the text of the third act, Handel wrote as follows to Jennens, who lingered at his house at Gopsal, near Atherstone, Leicestershire:

---

obstinately, in which there are some passages far unworthy of Handel, but much more unworthy of the Messiah." It is possible that Handel accepted from Jennens minor criticism of his treatment of syllabic values and accents, exceedingly unlikely that he would have allowed that vain and nonmusical man to point out "the grossest faults" in the music, had it contained any.

2 6 0

London
Septbr. 13
1744

Dear Sr

Your most excellent Oratorio has given me great Delight in setting
it to Musick and still engages me warmly. It is indeed a noble piece,
very grand and uncommon; it has furnished me with Expressions,
and has given me Opportunity to some very particular Ideas, besides
so many great Chorus. I intreat you heartly to favour me soon with
the last Act, which I expect with anxiety, that I may regulate my
self the better as to the Length of it. I profess my self highly obliged
to you, for so generous a Present, and desire you to believe me to be
with great esteem and Respect

Sr.
Your
most obliged and most humble
Servant
George Frideric Handel

When the long-delayed text finally arrived, Handel was ap-
palled by its enormous length. He conveved his reaction to
Jennens:

London
Octobr. 2.
1744.

Dear Sir

I received the 3d Act, with a great deal of pleasure, as you can
imagine, and you may believe that I think it a very fine and sublime
Oratorio, only it is realy to long, if I should extend the musick, it
would last 4 Hours and more.

I retrench'd already a great deal of the Musick, that I might preserve the Poetry as much as I could, yet still it may be shortned.
The Anthems come in very properly, but would not the Words (tell it
out among the Heathen that the Lord is King) sufficient for one
Chorus? The Anthem (I will magnify thee O God my King, and
will praise thy name for ever and ever. (vers) the Lord preserveth
all them that love him, but scattreth abroad all the ungodly. (vers
and chorus) my mouth shall speak the Praise of the Lord and let all

flesh give thanks unto His holy name for ever and ever Amen) conclude well the Oratorio. I hope you will make a visit to London next
Winter. I have a good set of singers. S. Francesina performs Nicotris,
Miss Robinson,[7] Cyrus, Mrs. Cibber, Daniel, Mr. Beard (who is recovered) Belshazzar, Mr. Reinhold, Tobias, and a good Number of
Choir Singers for the Chorus's. I propose 24 Nights to perform this
season on Saturdays, but in Lent on Wednesdays or Frydays. I shall
open on 3d of Novembr with . . . yah! I wish you heartily the continuation of your health, and professing my grateful acknowledg-
ments for your generous favours, and I am with great esteem and
Respect

Sr

Your

most obliged and most humble servant
George Frideric Handel.

The *Daily Advertiser* of October 20, 1744, carried the following notice, which shows that the plans Handel had mentioned to Jennens had been matured:

By particular desire; Mr. Handel proposes to perform, by subscription, twenty-four times during the winter season, at the King's
Theatre, in the Haymarket, and engages to exhibit two new performances and several of his former oratorios. The first performance
will be on Saturday, the 3d of November, and will continue every
Saturday till Lent, and then on Wednesdays and Fridays. Each subscriber is to pay eight guineas at the time he subscribes, which entitles him to one box ticket for each performance. Subscriptions are
taken in at Mr. Handel's house, in Brook-street, near Hanover
Square; at Mr. Walsh's in Katherine-street, in the Strand; and at
White's Chocolate House, in St. James's-street. Those gentlemen and
ladies who have already favoured Mr. Handel in the subscription,
are designed to send for their tickets at his house, in Brook-street,

[7] In *The Letters and Writings of George Frideric Handel*, Dr. Erich
Müller identified this "Miss Robinson" as Anastasia Robinson, who by
1744 was about forty-six years old and Dowager Countess of Peterborough. This identification I find it wholly impossible to accept despite
the fact that I am unable to make another. I do not believe that the
Countess of Peterborough ever sang in public after 1724.

MRS. CIBBER

[after a painting by Hudson]

THE ROYAL FIREWORKS STRUCTURE IN THE GREEN PARK

where attendance will be given every day (Sunday excepted), from nine o'clock in the morning till three in the afternoon.

Handel opened his 1743–4 season with a revival of *Deborah* on November 3, 1744. Two days later, in what can only have been comment on an exceedingly scattered house, the *General Advertiser* said: "As the greatest part of Mr. Handel's sub-scribers are not in town, he is requested not to perform till Saturday, the 24th instant; but the subscription is still continued to be taken in at Mr. Handel's house," as before. On November 24, *Deborah* was repeated "with a concerto on the organ." One week later, Handel revived *Semele* "after the manner of an oratorio," and "with additions and alterations"; this was repeated on December 8. Then there was an unexplained hiatus until January 5, 1745, when *Hercules* was sung for the first time.

Hercules stands high among the Handel works of such remarkable quality that the present-day failure to revive them is inexplicable. Here, as often elsewhere, Handel is scarcely inferior to Mozart in his musical delineation of individual psychology. Such a searchingly dramatic chorus as "Jealousy, infernal pest" is not as characteristic of this operalike oratorio as the finest of its individual arias, superbly turned and miraculously apt melodies that create beyond the possibility of mistake the mental states of Dejanira, Iole, Hercules, and Hyllus. Dejanira is caught up in a very hurricane of passion, reaching its sovereign culmination in her extraordinary *scena*, "Where shall I fly?" But the finest number in *Hercules* is one of the greatest dramatic arias in all music, the gentle Iole's bloodcurdling "My father." No change of musical style, no memory of the violent operatic emotions of Wagner, Verdi, and Strauss, can wholly rob the modern listener of the ability to react to Handel in this vein with the balance of musical and dramatic emotion it requires for full appreciation. In this vein he remains unique.

But *Hercules,* for all its shuddering vitality and variegated beauty, did not fill the King's Theatre. After a repetition of this "new musical drama" on January 12,[8] there was another lapse

[8] *See* letters, pages 313–15.

until March 1, when the offering was *Samson*. A cold snap then added to Handel's worries, for when *Samson* was to be repeated on March 8 there was public announcement that "proper care will be taken to make the house warm." The season froze. Handel threw in revivals of *Saul, Alexander's Feast,* and *Joseph and His Brethren.* On March 27, he brought up *Belshazzar* as perhaps his last hope of salvaging the season: it was liked only enough to warrant three performances. Nor did *The Sacred Oratorio* (as *Messiah* was still called) serve much better to replenish depleted coffers. On April 23, with the sixteenth of the season's proposed twenty-four performances, Handel had to look defeat in the eyes and close up for the time being.

Both *Belshazzar* and *Hercules* contain short instrumental passages of program music that, while they fit flawlessly into their context, can be extracted to show how advanced an instrumentalist and scene-painter Handel could be without the use of text. In *Belshazzar*, in the vast, controlledly chaotic scene of the handwriting on the wall, there is a brief purely instrumental section marked *"allegro postillons."* Nobody has been able to interpret the *Mene, mene,* and a decision has been made to send for wise men who may reveal its meaning. Belshazzar orders messengers to speed off in search of them, and it is the departure and swiftness of these messengers that the instruments depict with a verisimilitude that even Richard Strauss did not better and a beauty he seldom approached. In *Hercules*, a *sinfonia* precedes Act III by way of invoking the agonies of the hero: it is as close to speech, to painting, and to drama as music can come and remain music. Like the *Belshazzar "allegro postillons,"* it is also very euphonious and beautiful.

On May 10, 1745, a curious concert took place at "Mr. Hickford's Room" in Brewer Street for the benefit of "Miss Davis," an eight- or nine-year-old Irish prodigy. The child was announced to perform "on a Harpsichord of Mr. Rutgerus Plenius's making, Inventor of the new deserv'd famous Lyrichord." The lyrichord was one of several abortive attempts to make piano-like instruments capable of sustaining sound. Its inventor, Roger Plenius, who had patented it in 1741, has been credited with being the first man to attempt building a harpsichord in England. The music to be played at Miss Davis's benefit was announced in the *Daily Advertiser* of May 10 as "Several favourite Organ Concertos and Overtures of Mr. Handel's . . . with two remarkable Songs, Composed by Mr. Handel, entirely for the Harpsichord, accompanied by Miss Davis, with some select Songs to be perform'd by Mrs. Davis, a Scholar of Bononcini's." This was not little Miss Davis's first public appearance or her first performance of music by Handel: in Dublin in 1742 she had accompanied her mother "to a Song of Mr. Handel's, composed entirely to shew the Harpsichord; the Vocal Parts to be performed by Mrs. Davis, and her sister Miss Clegg,[9] who never performed in publick before, some new Songs out of the last Operas, and three of the most favourite Duetts of Mr. Handel's to be performed by Mrs. Davis and her Sister. . . ."

From some time before May 1743, Handel's wavering health had been worse than usual. After the close of the unsuccessful 1744–5 season, he was affected in body and mind as much as he had been in 1737, when he had been forced to visit Aix-la-Chapelle. He was in no condition to face the senselessly concentrated fury of his noble opponents and the rowdies they stirred into pulling down his placards and interfering noisily with his oratorios. He went somewhere to rest, probably to Tunbridge Wells. In August 1745, however, he was again in London, as is proved by the following excerpt from a letter dated August 29, 1745, from William Harris, one of three brothers friendly to Handel, to his sister-in-law, Mrs. Thomas Harris.

I met Mr. Handel a few days since in the street, and stopped and put him in mind who I was, upon which it would have diverted you to have seen his antic motions. He seemed highly pleased and was full of inquiry after you and the Councillor [Thomas Harris]. I told him I was very confident that you expected a visit from him this summer. He talked much of his precarious state of health, yet he looks well enough. I believe you will have him with you ere long.

[9] Otto Erich Deutsch speculates that Mrs. Davis and Miss Clegg may have been sisters of another child prodigy, the noted violinist John Clegg (1714–50?).

Nothing in the contents or tone of William Harris' letter, written to a sister-in-law then living on Salisbury Downs, indicates that he was at all aware that Scotland, England, even London itself, were at that hour in acute danger from the last flaring up of the Stuarts, their final and bloodiest attempt to regain power. On August 12, 1745, Charles Edward Louis Philip Casimir Stuart, the Young Pretender, had arrived off Erisca in the Hebrides. A little later he was on the mainland in Inverness-shire. At first almost failing to win enough immediate support to remain, Charles Edward slowly, and then rapidly, rallied the Highlanders to the old and storied Stuart banner. Before the resulting march on London was to reach its greatest southward extent, before the Duke of Cumberland was to crush the Stuart cause forever at the bloody battle of Culloden and in the bloodier terror with which he followed it, England and London were to become terrified indeed. They were to have little enough time for an ill and aging composer. But the war was to supply Handel with the "occasion" for his *Occasional Oratorio,* the Battle of Culloden with that for *Judas Maccabaeus.* And it turned out that the *Occasional Oratorio* and *Judas Maccabaeus* were to mark the final veering in Handel's long, tempest-ridden career. With them his triumph was to begin, the last uninterrupted apotheosis, rising in a crescendo that would not attain its full volume until the Handel Festival at London's Crystal Palace in 1894, one hundred and fifty years later.

Dr. Charles Burney, who was nineteen years old in 1745, gave one of the few reliable glimpses of Handel at this period when he wrote:

Handel at this time "did bestride our musical world like a Colossus." He had done with operas; and after his return from Ireland, applied himself wholly to the composition of sacred Music. In 1745, I performed in his band, sometimes on the violin, and sometimes on the tenor [viola], and by attending the rehearsals, generally at his own house in Lower Brook-street, and sometimes at Carlton-house, at the desire of his constant patron the late prince of Wales, father to his present Majesty [George III], I gratified my eager curiosity in seeing and examining the person and manners of so extraordinary a man, as well as in hearing him perform on the organ. He was a blunt and peremptory disciplinarian on these occasions, but had a humour and wit in delivering his instructions, and even in chiding and finding fault, that was peculiar to himself, and extremely diverting to all but those on whom his lash was laid.

II

THE EARL of Middlesex decided to reopen the King's Theatre in the Haymarket for more productions of Italian opera during the 1745–6 season. Either he or members of his co-directing board sent an invitation to young Christoph Willibald von Gluck, who since 1741 had successfully composed nine or ten operas for Milan, Venice, and Turin. Gluck arrived in London during the autumn of 1745, and was shortly at work compiling *La Caduta de' Giganti,* a *pièce d'occasion* intended to celebrate the ebbing of the Jacobite tide, which had risen close to engulfing London itself. Sometime during this autumn or early winter, Gluck was presented to Handel, whom he always admired extravagantly. *La Caduta de' Giganti,* produced at the King's Theatre on January 7, 1746, was sung five times. It was considered a failure, particularly by Gluck himself. He tucked a score of it under his arm and called on Handel to ask the older man to criticize it for him.

"You have taken far too much trouble over your opera," was Handel's embittered comment. "Here in England that is mere waste of time. What the English like is something that they can beat time to, something that hits them straight on the eardrum." It is certain that Handel was more concerned with the failures of his own operas than with the quality of Gluck's. He seems to have liked Gluck personally, but to have had insight into Gluck's shortcomings, particularly evident in such early works as *La Caduta de' Giganti,* of which the best that Burney could find to say was that "something might be expected from a young man able to produce this opera, imperfect as it was." Handel is supposed to have said that Gluck "knaws no more of contrapunto as mein cook." This is not as cruel as it sounds, for "my cook" would be Gustavus Waltz, who indeed knew something of counterpoint, a department of musical craft in which Gluck never became a notable master.

Gluck's opinion of Handel the musician did not suffer at all from his contact with the man. Nearly half a century later, Gluck — a famous and successful composer — entertained Michael Kelly, the accomplished tenor and friend of Mozart. In his *Reminiscences,* this amiable Irishman wrote as follows of part of that meeting with Gluck:

One morning, after I had been singing with him, he said, "Follow me upstairs, Sir, and I will introduce you to one whom all my life I have made my study and endeavoured to imitate." I followed him into his bedroom, and opposite to the head of the bed saw a full-length picture of Handel in a rich frame. "There, Sir," said he, "is the portrait of the inspired master of our art. When I open my eyes in the morning I look upon him with reverential awe and acknowledge him as such, and the highest praise is due to your country for having distinguished and cherished his gigantic genius."

While in England, Gluck produced another *pasticcio, Artamene,* and took part in two concerts, one with Handel, one playing on the musical glasses, or glass harmonica. An advertisement for this latter curious occasion reads

A Concerto upon Twenty-six Drinking-Glasses, tuned with Spring-Water, accompanied with the whole Band, being a new instrument of his own Invention; upon which he performs whatever may be done on a Violin or Harpsichord, and thereby hopes to satisfy the Curious, as well as Lovers of Musick.

Gluck's veracity in claiming to have invented an instrument that had been heard in England years earlier and in claiming to be able to perform with only twenty-six tones what could be played on a violin or harpsichord need not be questioned here. What is interesting is that he enlisted Handel's aid for his concert of March 25, 1746: Handel then performed one of his organ concertos.

Meanwhile the southward invasion of the Highlanders in support of Charles Edward Stuart (who had proclaimed his father James III of England and James VIII of Scotland) had begun to retreat to the north. And Handel had cast together a hodgepodge of Psalm texts and songs, set the whole to new and mostly inferior examples of his music combined with borrowings from the Coronation Anthems, *Israel in Egypt,* and a quotation of Arne's "Rule, Britannia," and called the whole extended and planless anthem *Occasional Oratorio.* He prefaced it with a magnificent overture containing a march movement that has had a long separate existence of its own. This overture is very close to the modern conception of program music, being clearly and unmistakably a condensed chronicle of the military aspects of the Jacobite rebellion.

Not having given his subscribers of the previous season the twenty-four performances due them, Handel leased Covent Garden for the Lenten season of 1746. Each of the disappointed subscribers was handed three tickets for each of three free performances, a singular placation in view of the fact that all three were singings of the *Occasional Oratorio.* This received its *première* on February 14, 1746, with "La Francesina," Reinhold, and Beard, and was repeated on February 19 and 26. Whether or not Handel was able to sell any tickets for these performances is not known. That they were not highly profitable may be indicated by the facts that the third of them closed this brief season and that he did not hold another until the next Lent.

On April 16, 1746, in a desolate spot of Inverness-shire known as Culloden, English troops under the command of the Duke of Cumberland, George I's grandson, soundly thrashed the Highland followers of Charles Edward Stuart, Queen Anne's nephew. The Duke became a wildly honored national hero: the English, affectionately accepting his nickname of Billy the Butcher, were not inclined to be too horrified at the terror he at once instituted throughout the Highlands. Frederick, Prince of Wales, Cumberland's elder brother, suggested to Handel that he prepare to celebrate the Duke's triumphal return to London with an ora-

HANDEL'S WILL

LAST PAGE OF MANUSCRIPT OF *JEPHTHA*

[*inscribed* "G. F. Handel, aetatis 66. Finis. Friday (*sign*) Agost. 30. 1751."]

torio based on the exploits of Judas Maccabaeus. Handel carried this proposal to a new friend, the Reverend Thomas Morell, and this antiquarian scholar agreed to provide the text. Handel began to set his *Judas Maccabaeus* on Monday, July 8, or Tuesday, July 9, 1746, and completed it less than five weeks later, on Sunday, August 11. As finished on that date, it was almost the work as we could know it today if we would, the chief difference being that it did not yet contain "See the conquering Hero comes," which was to be transferred to it later from the still unwritten *Joshua*, or "Sion now her head shall raise," the last great chorus Handel was to compose, which was to be added to it years later.

After Handel's death, Morell wrote a letter containing the following remarks on writing *Judas Maccabaeus* for Handel:

As to myself, great lover as I am of music, I should never have thought of such an undertaking . . . had not Mr. Handel applied to me when at Kew in 1746 and added to his request the honour of a recommendation from Prince Frederick. Upon this I thought I could do as well as some who had gone before me, and within two or three days carried him the first act of *Judas Maccabaeus*, which he approved of. "Well," says he, "and how are you to go on?" "Why, we are to suppose an engagement, and that the Israelites have conquered, and so begin with a chorus as 'Fallen is the foe,' or something like it." "No, I will have this," and began working it, as it is, upon the harpsichord. "Well, go on." "I will bring you more tomorrow." "No, something now." "So fall thy foes, O Lord —" "That will do," and immediately carried on the composition as we have it in that admirable chorus. That incomparable air, "Wise men, flattering, may deceive us" (which was the last he composed,[1] as "Sion now his head shall raise" was his last chorus) was designed for *Belshazzar*, but that not being performed, he happily flung it into *Judas Maccabaeus*. N. B. — The plan of *Judas Maccabaeus* was designed as a compliment to the Duke of Cumberland, upon his returning victorious from Scotland. I had introduced several incidents more apropos, but it was thought they would make it too long, and they were there-

---

[1] Morell was evidently unaware that this was only a slightly altered version of "*Se vuoi pace*" from *Agrippina*.

fore omitted. The Duke, however, made me a handsome present by the hands of Mr. Poyntz. The success of the oratorio was very great, and I have often wished that at first I had asked in jest for the benefit of the 30th night instead of a 3d. I am sure he would have given it to me; on which night there was above £400 in the house. He left me a legacy, however, of £200.

Handel had long since freed himself, with varying results, from entire dependence on the shifting tempers of kingly and noble patrons. Now he took another step toward economic independence. Instead of selling subscriptions to his Lenten oratorio season of 1747, he threw down the gauntlet, selling all places for every performance to the public on an individual-performance basis. This action was in part responsible for the fact that his fortunes now began perceptibly to improve, that he was to know, despite occasional failures, no more chaotic and crushing seasons for the rest of his life. Another reason for the happy result of his first non-subscription season was *Judas Maccabaeus* itself, an oratorio of noisy and otherwise obvious charms that is not always Handel at his best but is always music for the largest public. The season was made up of six performances of *Judas Maccabaeus*, the first on April 1, 1747, two of *Joseph and His Brethren,* and three of the *Occasional Oratorio.* Galli achieved a resounding success in *Judas Maccabaeus,* in which, according to one account, she had to compete with real firearms, used to lend verisimilitude to the battle music.

It had not been Handel's intention to delay presenting *Judas Maccabaeus* until April 1. He was deterred from giving it earlier by what he considered excessive public unrest over and interest in one of the most touted *causes célèbres* of the era, the trial of Simon Fraser, Lord Lovat, subject of one of Hogarth's most revealing portraits. This octogenarian Scottish chief had greeted Charles Edward Stuart's landing with his customary ambiguity. He dealt in apparent impartiality with both sides for a time, but at last — so old and infirm that he had to be carried everywhere on a litter — he fell quite afoul of the legal government, was arrested on an island in Loch Morar, and was taken prisoner to

London. His trial for treason lasted from March 14 to 19, 1747, and was handily the most discussed news in the cities of England. Handel, not wishing public attention distracted from the first singing of his uproarious tribute to the Duke of Cumberland, waited until the trial was completed and the sentence of death pronounced. Eight days after that April 1 *première* of *Judas Maccabaeus*, Lord Lovat was executed. It was said that his last breath was expended in a (for him) ambiguous quotation from Horace: *"Dulce et decorum est pro patria mori."*

The hero of Morell's *Judas Maccabaeus* was, of course, the great Jewish military leader who, from 166 to 161 B.C., battled against the Syrian attempt, organized by the Seleucid King Antiochus IV (Epiphanes), to Hellenize Judaea. The Hellenizers attempted to uproot Judaism, hoping to supplant it with a recrudescence of ancient Greek paganism. In 162 B.C., Judas Maccabaeus forced Lysias, Regent of Judaea, to guarantee religious freedom to the Jews. After his victory, many of the Hasidim ("pious" or "faithful") laid down their arms, preferring peace to further struggle for political independence, which was carried on by Judas Maccabaeus and his most ardent followers. He won another important military victory at Adasa in 161 B.C., defeating the enemy brilliantly but not decisively, with the result that within a few weeks there had to be another battle at Elasa, in which he was killed.

Judas Maccabaeus, then, was a great hero to the Jews. As such, as a Jew presented in an entirely favorable light, he was also a hero all but unique on the English stage. When Handel's musical glorification of his exploits first reached Covent Garden in 1747, there were probably not above 5,000 Jews in England. But all except a handful of that 5,000 lived in London, where they had enjoyed considerable freedom for nearly a century. Some of them had become well-to-do merchants. Pleased and heartened by the light in which one of their national heroes was being presented to the English public, many Jews hurried to patronize Covent Garden, appreciably swelling the box office for *Judas Maccabaeus*. Their recruitment helped Handel pre-

sent that oratorio six times during its first season, about forty
times before his death twelve years later.

Morell and Handel saw at once the desirability of Jewish
patronage at Covent Garden. Morell's next text for Handel was
Alexander Balus, a sequel to *Judas Maccabaeus*. It deals with
the love of Alexander Balas for a daughter of Ptolemy Philo-
metor, King of Egypt. Judas Maccabaeus' brother and successor, Jonathan, who supported Alexander Balas' claim to the
Syrian throne against Demetrius Soter, is presented as digni-
fied and admirable. He might have pleased London's Jews as
much as his brother, had either Morell's or Handel's delineation of him contained the bumptious vitality of the earlier portrait. Begun on June 1, 1747, Handel's *Alexander Balus* was
completed not quite five weeks later, on July 4.

Morell's letter, already quoted in part, continues:

The next year [after *Judas Maccabaeus*] he desired another, and
I gave him *Alexander Balus*, which follows the history of the fore-
going in the Maccabees. In the first part there is a very pleasing air,
accompanied with the harp, "Hark, hark, he strikes the golden lyre!"
in the second two charming duets, "O what pleasure past expressing,"
and "Hail, wedded love, mysterious law." The third begins with an
incomparable air in the affetuoso style, intermixed with the chorus
recitative that follows it. And as to the last air I cannot help telling
you that when Mr. Handel first read it he cried out, "Damn your
iambics!" "Don't put yourself in a passion, they are easily trochees."
"Trochees, what are trochees?" "Why, the very reverse of iambics,
by leaving out a syllable in every line, as instead of 'Convey me to
some peaceful shore,' 'Lead me to some peaceful shore.'" "That is
what I want." "I will step into the parlour and alter them immediately." I went down and returned with them altered in about three
minutes, when he would have them as they were, and had set them
most delightfully, accompanied with only a quaver and a rest of
three quavers.

Alexander Balus is one more Handel work that cries out for
present-day revival. Here what lends unique value to the oratorio is not so much the individual choruses and arias as the

overall atmosphere, surprisingly but penetratingly Oriental.
That alternately spiced and somber Easternness is in the wonderful chorus beginning "O calumny," in Cleopatra's "Hark,
hark, he strikes the golden lyre," with its picturesque accompaniment of harp, mandolin, and flutes, and even in Alexander
Balus' passionately seductive love song, "O Mithra." Handel,
who so often succeeded in his oratorios in establishing a Hebraic
or early Christian atmosphere, and whose operas with pseudo-
classical librettos are often wholly lighted by the Italian, German, and even English skies of his own day, has in *Alexander
Balus* evoked the pagan Near East with delicate and convincing
strokes. Its love music conveys the very essence of a dream of
that lost, enchanting world.

The astonishing popularity that Handel's works had begun to
display in Covent Garden did not pass unnoticed by the Earl of
Middlesex and his committee of noble friends. To open their
1747–8 season, they had someone concoct for them a *pasticcio*
consisting largely of popular numbers from several Handel operas — *Riccardo Primo, Radamisto, Tamerlano, Siroe,* and *Admeto* at least — called it *Lucio Vero,* and presented it in the
Haymarket on November 4, 1747. "I well remember," Burney
wrote later, "the richness of the harmony and ingenuity of the
contrivance of several songs . . . very striking, compared with
the light melodies and their accompaniments of what I had
heard at the Opera-house before." Handel's star was now high
in the ascendant: *Lucio Vero,* which profited him not at all
except in reclaim, won numerous performances during November and December, more during January and March 1748. One
singer in this *pasticcio* was Giulia Frasi, who was much applauded by the public. She had arrived on the London scene
from Italy with Galli. After her success in *Lucio Vero,* Handel
hired her, became friendly with her, and made use of her talents
for many of the rest of the performances he gave during his
remaining lifetime.

The report of the *General Advertiser* for November 13, 1747,
on the first public rehearsal of *Lucio Vero* is interesting both

because of its language, which demonstrates points in the history of publicity, and for what it tells of the position of Handel in London:

Yesterday was rehearsed, at the King's Theatre in the Haymarket, the opera of Lucius Verus. This drama consists of airs borrowed entirely from Mr. Handel's favourite operas, and so may (probably) be justly styled the most exquisite composition of harmony ever offered to the publick. Those lovers of musick among us whose ears have been charmed with Faustina, Faranello, Senesini, Cuzzoni, and other great performers, will now have an opportunity of reviving their former delight; which, if not so transporting as then, may yet prove a very high entertainment. Mr. Handel is acknowledged (universally) so great a master of the lyre, that nothing urged in favour of his capital performances can reasonably be considered as a puff.

But Handel himself was not resting on his acknowledged laurels. Although he had *Alexander Balus* ready for the lenten season of 1748, he did not favor his sixty-two years and rest on the assumption that he could space out that season with one new oratorio and repetitions of *Judas Maccabaeus*. Instead, having tapped Morell for one more Biblical history, he began, fifteen days after finishing *Alexander Balus*, to compose the new text, *Joshua*. This he completed in thirty-one days, on Wednesday, August 19, 1747. He had thus composed two full-length oratorios, and with little borrowing from earlier works, in exactly seventy-nine days, during at least fifteen of which, and probably more, he had not touched either.

Handel's lenten season of 1748 at Covent Garden was made up of thirteen performances, six of *Judas Maccabaeus*, four of *Joshua* (the first on March 9), and three of *Alexander Balus* (the first on March 23). The last was not a drawing-card despite its extraordinary music. Handel himself revived it only once; it has rarely been heard since 1754. *Joshua*, containing, be it recalled, "See the conquering Hero comes," addressed to Othniel returning from the conquest of Debir, was little more successful. It, too, had great beauties: the pastoral loveliness of "While Kedron's brook" and "As cheers the sun," Caleb's

evocative "Shall I in Mamre's fertile plain," and "Glory to God,"
the stupendous chorus describing the collapse of the walls of
Jericho. Two of its most familiar numbers Handel had adapted
from earlier works by himself. For "Heroes when with glory
burning" he had reached back to a gavotte song he had composed nearly forty years earlier for his Venetian opera of 1709,
Agrippina; the infectiously joyful "O had I Jubal's lyre" was
adapted from an even earlier work, his setting of the Psalm
Laudate pueri, composed in 1707.

William Shield, violist and theatrical composer who was a
friend of Haydn's, told the following anecdote in his *Introduction to Harmony:*

Traveling from London to Taplow with the father of modern harmony [Haydn], and having, during the preceding evening, observed
his countenance expressing rapturous astonishment during the concert of ancient music, I embraced the favorable opportunity of in-
quiring how he estimated the chorus in *Joshua,* "The nations trem-
ble." The reply was, "He had long been acquainted with music, but
never knew half its powers before he heard it, and he was perfectly
certain that only one inspired author ever did, or ever would, pen so
sublime a composition."

Following what might have developed into an unchanging
routine had he been younger, Handel occupied himself during
the late spring and summer of 1748 in the preparation of two
new oratorios for the lenten season of 1749. Neither of the texts
he used can be attributed certainly, though there is some possibility that the first was again the handiwork of Morell. This
was *Solomon,* begun on May 5, 1748, and completed on June
13, in thirty-nine days, that is, despite its great length. The second was *Susanna,* begun on July 11, finished on August 24. Well
past his sixty-third birthday, it had taken Handel one hundred
and eleven days, during at least twenty-eight of which he did
not work on them, to complete two tremendous oratorios. Furthermore, they are two masterpieces.

The two new settings of texts based on the Old Testament

were offered to the Covent Garden public in reverse order as
to date of composition, *Susanna* on February 10, 1749, *Solomon*
on March 17. The season's tally was: *Susanna,* four performances; *Solomon,* three; *Samson,* four; *Messiah,* now so desig-
nated, one; and *Hercules,* two.

Handel's responsiveness to the character of his texts cannot
be illustrated more clearly than in a contrast of *Susanna* and
Solomon. Solomon is a full-blooded example of his "big bow-
wow" manner. It gives the incorrect impression of being made
up entirely of one series of grand, orientally splendid choruses
limning, stroke after stroke, the complex palace life of an East-
ern monarch. This is a false impression, for the many stupendous choruses are set off by, made to seem more gigantic by,
smaller passages of wonderful tenderness toward human and
natural fragilities. There are the exquisite songs of love, "With
thee the unsheltered moor I'd tread" and the sensuously seductive "nightingale" chorus, "May no rash intruder"; there are
"How green our fertile pastures" and "Beneath the vine and
fig-tree's shade," both evoking intimate, calm aspects of nature.
But these are overtopped, cast altogether into shadow, by the
surge and huge Hebraic majesty of the choruses.

Susanna is a smaller drama. It has better delineated individual characters, sly touches of irony and humor. One of its choruses, to be sure — "Righteous Heaven" — is not dwarfed by
anything in *Israel in Egypt, Messiah,* or *Solomon.* But the per-
vading tone of *Susanna* is set by the delicate beauty of one of
the loveliest songs ever composed, "Ask if yon damask rose be
sweet," in which (as has often been pointed out) the influence
of Purcell is manifest. *Susanna,* too, has "Would custom melt"
and "Ye verdant hills," which Streatfeild well described as having "almost a feeling of folk music." *Susanna* is Handel display-
ing the tenderest side of his nature, his affectionate humor and
sweet passion; *Solomon* is a masterpiece of the only composer
who has ever matched Bach in the majesty and scope of his
largest works.

III

DURING 1749, Handel was called upon to act in his official capacity as purveyor of ceremonial music to the English nation. On April 24 of the preceding year, at Aix-la-Chapelle, a congress had been convoked to settle what (from England's point of view) had begun as the War of Jenkins's Ear and had developed into the War of the Austrian Succession. By May 20, 1748, the contracting parties, who by then included the Republic of Genoa, the Duchy of Modena, and the Kingdom of Sardinia, as well as Spain, England, France, Bohemia, Hungary, and Holland, reached a temporary agreement. The definitive treaty was signed on October 7, 1748. The English, who in reality received by it very little return for their pains except a guarantee of the Protestant succession, the return of Madras, and a renewal of the unworkable 1713 treaty with Spain, were enormously pleased to have the peace formalized. They decided to go on a national spree of celebration, the culmination of which was set for April 27, 1749.

In November 1748, in London's Green Park, hard by St. James's Palace and about five hundred feet from the Queen's Library, workmen began to erect a setting for a tremendous display of fireworks. This edifice was designed by the French architect and scenic artist Jean-Nicholas Servan, known as the Chevalier Servandoni, who had supervised scenery and stage machinery at the Paris Opéra (then in the Palais Royal) for eighteen years. It was a "machine" built of wood in an adaptation of Doric-temple style. When it was finished on April 26, 1749, it stood 410 feet long and 114 feet high. It consisted of an intricately elaborate central structure bearing the arms of the Duke of Montagu (in charge of the celebration as well, probably, as of paying for most of it), figures of appropriate Greek gods, a bas-relief of George II, and a pole bearing aloft — to perhaps a height of two hundred feet above the turf — a huge conventional representation of the Sun. The building had steps, pillars, and passageways. In two directions from it there were extended walks laid above arched colonnades and ending in smaller pedimented structures.

To celebrate properly this egregiously ugly building, the general, if temporary, prosperity of the realm, and (very incidentally) the Peace of Aix-la-Chapelle, nothing would do but music by Handel especially composed for outdoor performance. By April 21, 1749 — perhaps earlier — Handel had ready the score of what is now usually called the *Royal Fireworks Music*. On that day a crowd, stated by the *Gentleman's Magazine* to have numbered 12,000, paid 2/6 [1] each to hear the music rehearsed at the Spring Gardens in Vauxhall. While the band of one hundred musicians went through the overture and five movements of the suite, this thronging concourse formed such a traffic jam on London Bridge that not a carriage could get through for three hours. "The footmen were so numerous as to obstruct the passage," the *Gentleman's Magazine* stated, "so that a scuffle ensued, in which some gentlemen were wounded."

On April 27 itself, all entrances to the Green Park were thrown wide. It was feared that they would not supply ingress enough for the crowds expected, and some sixteen yards of the Park's wall itself were therefore pulled down. By evening a tremendous portion of London's populace was either in the Green Park or crowding adjacent points of vantage. In the Queen's Library were members of the royal family, including the King and the

[1] The *Gentleman's Magazine* put the price of admission to this rehearsal at 9/6, but, as Schoelcher pointed out, this high price scarcely squares with an audience of 12,000. Also, it would give an approximate return of £5,700, a quite incredible figure. "The *General Advertiser*," Schoelcher pointed out, "puts the tickets at 2s. 6d., which is far more reconcilable with an audience of 12,000 persons. Even that would bring £1,500, which is, after all, a good round sum."

Duke of Cumberland; also the Dukes of Bedford, Richmond, and Montagu. The Prince and Princess of Wales watched from the house of the impresario Duke of Middlesex in near-by Arlington Street, not having been invited to the Library.

The overture to the *Royal Fireworks Music* led off the festivities. It was played on twenty-four oboes, twelve bassoons, nine trumpets, nine horns, one contrabassoon, three pairs of kettledrums, and one serpent. The last was a bass cornet almost eight feet long, with a two-octave compass rising from the B flat or C below the bass staff. It had a bent mouthpiece, and was folded back on itself three times besides ending in an almost complete circle. When a man played it while standing, it reached halfway down his thigh and looked very much indeed like a rigid serpent. A possibly apocryphal story was told of Handel's first view of this instrument. "What the Devil be that?" he asked. "It is a new instrument called the serpent," was the answer. "Oh! the serpent," Handel commented. "Aye, but it not be the serpent what seduced Eve." [2]

When the overture was concluded, the Royal Salute was given by one hundred and one brass cannon: seventy-one six-pounders, twenty twelve-pounders, and ten twenty-four-pounders. The din must have been apocalyptic. Suddenly the whole of Servandoni's temple was outlined in pyrotechnic light. Then the entire band, which with the strings mounted to one hundred players, gave the bourrée and *Largo alla Siciliana* of Handel's suite, and a set piece of fireworks represented Peace. This was followed by an allegro to accompany a set piece for Rejoicing. By this time, the fireworks had begun to get out of hand as fireworks do, and it is doubtful that many in that unnumbered crush were able to hear the two final minuets. From atop the temple the huge sun flamed out across the Park and the city. And then catastrophe burst: the building itself roared into sheets of flame.

[2] Of Handel's humor, Burney wrote: "Had he been as great a master of the English language as Swift, his *bons mots* would have been as frequent, and somewhat of the same kind."

All reports indicate that a brisk wind was blowing across the Green Park. Flaming boards and pieces of decoration, perhaps even half-spent rockets, fell among the people, who began to rush heedlessly and dangerously against the banked masses of their fellows. The Queen's Library itself was momentarily endangered. Flying into a rage, the Chevalier Servandoni began to denounce the Duke of Montagu for the failure of the occasion and the untimely incineration of his temple.[3] His temper rushed up until he drew his sword and lunged threateningly at Montagu, and had to be arrested, being held until he won pardon from the Duke of Cumberland the next day. The panicky surging of the crowd continued, and Horace Walpole wrote that many people were injured, two of them fatally. Except for having supplied the musical world with one of Handel's instrumental works, the Green Park celebration turned out as much a costly failure as the Peace of Aix-la-Chapelle itself was to prove.

On May 27, 1749, with a band considerably reduced from that in the Green Park, Handel repeated the *Royal Fireworks Music* in the Chapel of the Foundling Hospital in Hatton Garden during a benefit concert, the proceeds of which were to be used largely for completing the Chapel. It was played in the presence of the Prince and Princess of Wales and an audience of more than one thousand, each of whom had paid 10/6 for his ticket. George II had subscribed £2,000 to the charitable cause, an anonymous donor £50. The total receipts therefore amounted to more than £2,575. On May 7, Handel had visited the committee governing the hospital, making the offer to give this performance. It was as a result of that offer that he was made a member of the Board of Governors and Guardians of the institution. Besides the *Royal Fireworks Music*, the May 27 benefit performance was made up of an anthem (in all likelihood the *Dettingen Anthem*, "The King shall rejoice"), parts

---

[3] Most of Servandoni's works were, by their very nature, little less temporary than the Green Park temple. He did, however, design the façade and the chief altar decorations of the Parisian Church of Saint-Sulpice.

of *Solomon* relating to the dedication of the Temple in Jerusalem, and "several pieces composed for the occasion, the words taken from Scripture, and applicable to the Charity, and its benefactors." This last, "Blessed are they that consider the poor," has become known as the *Foundling Hospital Anthem*.

One month and one day after the concert in the Foundling Hospital Chapel, Handel began to set the last but one of his oratorios. The text was a *Theodora* that Morell had based on Corneille's *Théodore, vierge et martyre*. Its composition occupied him from June 28 to July 31, 1749. What he did during the rest of that summer is not known. If he went abroad or otherwise left London, he was nevertheless back in the city by the end of September, for it was then that he wrote to Charles Jennens a letter of particular interest, in which he outlined the opinions of one of the greatest organists of all times as to the proper design of an organ:

London. Set. 30.
1749

Sir

Yesterday I received Your letter, in answer to which I hereunder specify my Opinion of an Organ which I think will answer the Ends you propose, being every thing that is necessary for a good and grand Organ, without reed Stops, which I have omitted, because they are continually wanting to be tuned, which in the Country is very inconvenient, and should it remain useless on that account, it would still be very expensive althou' that may not be your consideration. I very well approve of Mr Bridge [4] who without any objection is a very good Organ builder, and I shall willingly (when he has finished it) give you my Opinion of it. I have referr'd you to the Flute Stop in Mr. Freemans Organ being excellent in this kind, but as I do not referr you in that Organ. The System of the Organ I advise is. Vizt The Compass to be up to D and down to Gamut,

full Octave,   Church Work,

One Row of Keys, whole Stops and none in halves.

---

[4] Richard Bridge (*fl.* 1729–57) constructed some of the finest organs of the period during which Handel lived in England.

Stops

An Open Diapason — of Metal throughout to be in Front.
A Stopt Diapason — the Treble Metal and the Bass Wood.
A Principal   — of Metal throughout.
A Twelfth   — of Metal throughout.
A Fifteenth   — of Metal throughout.
A Great Tierce   — of Metal throughout.
A Flute Stop   — such a one is in Freemans Organ.

I am glad of the Oppurtunity to show you my attention, wishing you all Health and Happiness,

I remain with great Sincerity and Respect
Sir
Your
most obedient and most humble
Servant
George Frideric Handel.

Whether or not Handel went down to Jennens' house at Gopsal in Leicestershire and remained as his guest to try Bridge's organ after its installation we do not know. It is likely: he had often been Jennens' guest before.

In answer to a commission from John Rich, and possibly, as Sir John Hawkins believed, in payment of a debt to that lessee of Covent Garden, Handel completed, on January 8, 1750, incidental music for a performance of Smollett's English adaptation of the *Alcestis* of Euripides. He already knew the play, for the *Admeto* he had produced in 1727 was likewise based on it. Servandoni, the same who had built the Doric temple in the Green Park, was to design the scenery for what was clearly intended to be a very handsome mounting of Smollett's work. The music survives in score, though Smollett's text has disappeared. It indicates that roles were to be sung and acted by Mrs. Arne, one of her sisters (of whom Isabella married Lampe, Esther a man named Jones), the tenor Lowe, and Gustavus Waltz. Samuel Arnold, who in 1790 published the mutilated score, believed that a Mrs. Faulkner was also supposed to sing in it. But Smollett's *Alcestis* with Handel's incidental music was not performed. Nature intervened.

Shortly after noon on February 8, 1750, London and Westminster were shaken by a sharp earth tremor. In Leadenhall
Street, Billiter Street, and Horselydown, chimneys toppled to
the ground. In Southwark, the hayloft of a slaughterhouse was
demolished. The West End trembled through its houses, furniture, and pewter. From Westminster Hall, barristers and
judges rushed into the streets in fear that the building would
crush them. Superstitious people were doubly alarmed when
they learned that the quake had scarcely been noticed outside
the city: it clearly manifested divine wrath at the vicious life
of the metropolis.

Within a few weeks, of course, the alarm was quieted. Then,
on March 8, at 5:30 in the morning, the city shuddered again.
Once more pewter rattled, china and glass were shattered,
chimneys and roof tiles were dropped crazily into the streets,
and big ones fell from the west towers of Westminster Abbey.
One young lady was reported to have been thrown out of bed
so violently as to shatter her arm. Superstitious people were now
in a state of high panic. Wild stories began to circulate the more
rapidly when it was learned that, again, the quake had scarcely
been felt outside the city. It was said that lightning had ripped
the sky on all sides at the time of the tremor, that in St. James's
Park not only had the ground moved visibly, but fishes had
leaped high out of the water. It was obvious that Providence
was issuing punctual warnings to the vice-ridden inhabitants
of the city. The Bishop of London indited a pamphlet accepting this idea and exhorting Londoners to improve themselves
while there was still time; he found more than 40,000 takers.
People began to leave for the country, apparently on the theory
that it was their neighbors who were wicked.

Next a private in the Horse Guards discovered that a predic-
tion made millennia earlier had announced that the third of
three quakes occurring one month apart would utterly demolish
London and Westminster and all who lived therein. Stark terror spread as that appointed date — April 8, 1750 — drew near.
People snatched at every excuse for going into the country.

"They say they are not frightened, but that it is such fine weather, Lord, one can't help going into the country," Horace Walpole noted. By the night of April 7–8, many thousands had sought near-by fields. Lodgings were so scarce in the country-side that many of the wealthy had to pass the night in their coaches on the roads. "All night long," Sir Walter Besant said, "they sat thus, waiting in terror and suspense, expecting every moment the thunder and rumblings and roarings and the agitation of the world, when the proud pinnacles and spires of London should topple and fall and lie levelled in one common ruin."

Exactly nothing happened in London on the night of April 7–8, 1750. Very many relieved and shamefaced people went back to their business and their vices. The unfortunate prognosticator of doom was imprisoned as a false prophet. Life in Westminster and London took on its customary motion and noise. Whatever else the great two-month scare had accomplished (aside from numerous temporary repentings), it had effectively interfered with good attendance at theatricals and musical entertainments. It explains why John Rich did not produce Smollett's *Alcestis* with Handel's music at Covent Garden.

Handel was not one of the terrorized. Sixteen days after the first earthquake, he addressed the keeper of His Majesty's Ordnance Office as follows:

Saturday
Febr 24
1750.

Sr

I having received the Permission of the Artillery Kettle Drums for my use in the Oratorio's in this season;

I beg you would conseign them to the Bearer of this Mr. Frideric Smith

I am

Your very humble Servant
G. F. Handel.

And he went right ahead with his spring oratorio season. He appears to have begun it with two performances of *Saul* and four of *Judas Maccabaeus*. Then, on March 16, "with a new concerto on the organ," he gave the *première* of *Theodora*. It was not well attended, surely as much because of the Horse Guardsman's prophecy as because of any intrinsic lack of charm. Handel performed it three times that season. Then he brought on two singings of *Samson*, and with one of *Messiah* (thus announced in London under the title always used since then) on April 12 — four days after divine wrath had failed to crumple the city — brought the naturally indifferent season to an end.

On the night of the second performance of *Theodora*, the house was particularly thin. Turning to one of his guests, Handel said: "Will you be here next Friday night? I will play it to you." This wry humor was wrenched from him because he valued *Theodora* very high among all his many works. According to the *Biographia Dramatica*, he was once asked "whether he did not consider the grand [Hallelujah] Chorus in *The Messiah* as his masterpiece. 'No,' said he, 'I think the chorus, "He saw the lovely youth," at the end of the second part in *Theodora* far beyond it.'" Writing in 1784, Burney footnoted a remark about the intermittent lack of popularity suffered by the oratorios with the following, in which the curious pronunciation he attributed to Handel is left because he did, after all, more than once hear him talk:

In 1749 [*sic!*], *Theodora* was so very unfortunately abandoned, that he was glad if any professors, who did not perform, would accept of tickets or orders for admission. Two gentlemen of that description, now living, having applied to Handel, after the disgrace of *Theodora*, for an order to hear the *Messiah*, he cried out, "Oh your sarvant, Mien-herren! you are tamnaple tainty! you would not co to *Teodora* — der was room enough to tance dere, when dat was perform."

Sometimes, however, I have heard him, as pleasantly as philosophically, console hi[s] friends, when, previous to the curtain being

2 8 7

drawn up, they have lamented that the house was so empty, by saying, "Nevre moind; di moosic vil sound de petter."

On another occasion, someone told Handel that Sir T. Hankey had said that if *Theodora* were sung again he would book all the boxes. Thereupon Handel exploded: "He is a fool; the Jews will not come to it as to *Judas* because it is a Christian story; and the ladies will not come because it is a virtuous one."

Theodora (with *Messiah* Handel's only English oratorio to a Christian text) includes many numbers of exceeding power and beauty. Unfortunately, they do not compensate wholly for Morell's dull text. Musically it is very fine, but it has not the human vitality of such a work as *Alexander Balus*. Its best moments, aside from "He saw the lovely youth," which Handel had evaluated properly, are in Theodora's "Angels ever bright and fair"; the choral paean to Venus, "Queen of summer, queen of love," with its clear memories of Purcell; and Irene's "Defend her, Heaven." The whole score is worked out with the most minute care. Every resource of musical learning and invention is brought to bear on hundreds of characteristic touches and programmatic strokes.

In 1749, Handel had presented to the Foundling Hospital Chapel an organ, built apparently not by Richard Bridge, but by the "Moss" [Morse] of Barnet whom he had mentioned to Jennens in 1738. He meant to dedicate it when, on May 1, 1750, he presided over the first of nine annual benefit performances of *Messiah* that he was to supervise in the Chapel, but it was not completed in time. This was announced in the *General Advertiser* of Friday, April 21, 1750, as follows:

Hospital for the Maintenance and Education of Exposed and Deserted Young Children, in Lamb's Conduit Fields, April 18, 1750.

George Frederic Handel, Esq., having presented this Hospital with a very fine organ for the chapel thereof, and repeated his offer of assistance to promote this charity, on Tuesday, the first day of May, 1750, at twelve o'clock at noon, Mr. Handel will open the said organ, and the sacred oratorio called *Messiah* will be performed under his direction. Tickets for this performance are ready to be delivered by the Steward at the Hospital; at Batson's Coffee House, in Cornhill; and White's Chocolate House, in St. James's-street, at half a guinea each. N.B. — There will be no collection. By order of the General Committee.   Harman Verelst, Secretary.

The same publication, two weeks later, three days after the performance — that is, on May 4 — published another advertisement, dated May 2, 1750:

A computation was made of what number of persons the chapel of this hospital would conveniently hold, and no greater number of tickets were delivered to hear the performance there on the 1st instant. But so many persons of distinction coming unprovided with tickets, and pressing to pay for tickets, caused a greater number to be admitted than were expected; and some that *had* tickets, not finding room, went away. To prevent any disappointment to such persons, and for the further promotion of this charity, this is to give notice that George Frederic Handel, Esq., has generously offered that the sacred oratorio called *Messiah* shall be performed again under his direction, in the chapel of this hospital, on Tuesday, the 15th instant, at twelve of the clock at noon; and the tickets delivered out, and not brought in on the 1st instant, will then be received. The tickets will be delivered from Monday the 7th to the 14th, and not after.[5]

A benefit concert given on May 18, 1750, seems to have been the occasion on which Francesca Cuzzoni made a vain bid to recapture English music-lovers. It was more than twenty-seven years since she had made her London debut in Handel's *Ottone,* sixteen since she had bade farewell to his company. She was now fully fifty years old. She had never been beautiful, and by 1750 she had lost (besides the husband she had been tried for poisoning) both her fortune and her voice. Her attempt to shine again was a failure. Three months after it, Horace Walpole noted that she had been arrested because of a debt of £30,

[5] According to Burney, the *Messiah* benefits under Handel's hand earned the Hospital £6,935, those for the eighteen years after his death (conducted first by John Christopher Smith and then by Charles John Stanley) a further £3,364, for a total of £10,299 in twenty-eight years.

and that the Prince of Wales had bailed her out of debtor's prison. ("Who will do as much for him?" Walpole characteristically added.) She went on to Holland and was soon forgotten. She made the aging pauper's futile attempts to rise above poverty, but in 1770, forty-seven years after she had first sung for Handel, she died in obscurity at Bologna.

Handel was not going to die in poverty and obscurity. In the summer of 1750, deciding to visit Germany again, he drew up his will. He was, after all, sixty-five years old. That main body of his will, later to be amended in four codicils, reads as follows:

In the Name of God Amen.
I George Frideric Handel considering the Uncertainty of human Life doe make this my Will in manner following
viz.
I give and bequeath unto my Servant Peter le Blond, my Clothes and Linnen, and three hundred Pounds sterl: and to my other Servants a year Wages.
I give and bequeath to Mr Christopher Smith [here "Senior" is crossed out] my large Harpsicord, my little House Organ, my Musick Books, and five hundred Pounds Sterl:
Item I give and bequeath to Mr James Hunter five hundred Pounds Sterl:
I give and bequeath to my Cousin Christian Gottlieb Handel of Coppenhagen one hundred Pounds Sterl:
Item I give and bequeath to my Cousin Magister Christian August Rotth of Halle in Saxony one hundred Pounds Sterl:
Item I give and bequeath to my cousin the Widow of George Taust, Pastor of Giebichenstein near Halle in Saxony three hundred Pounds sterl. and to Her six Children each two hundred Pounds sterl:
All the next and residue of my Estate in [here "South Sea Annuity's" is crossed out] Bank annuity's or what soever Kind or Nature.
I give and bequeath unto my Dear Niece Johanna Friderica Floerken of Gotha in Saxony (born Michäelsen in Halle) whom I make my sole Exec. of this my last Will.
In wittness whereof I have here unto set my hand this 1 Day of June 1750.
George Frideric Handel

Of the people mentioned in the body of Handel's will, some cannot now be identified. Peter le Blond died before March 22, 1757. Christopher Smith was John Christopher Smith the younger, the son of Handel's old schoolmate. James Hunter is identified as "a scarlet-dyer at Old Ford." Christian Gottlieb Händel was a grandson of the composer's half-brother Karl. Christian Roth seems to have been the son of a sister of Handel's father's first wife. "My cousin the Widow of George Taust" was clearly not Handel's cousin, but his aunt by marriage, the widow of his mother's brother. Johanna Friederika Flörke was the daughter of Handel's sister Dorothea Sophia by Michael Dietrich Michaelsen: she had married Johann Ernst Flörke. Her descendants, of whom many must survive, would be the closest collateral descendants of Handel himself. She had eight children, at least six grandchildren, and more than fifteen great-grandchildren. It is interesting to note that the total of the specified money bequests in the will is £3,000.

By June 1750, it had become clear to Handel that the Smollett *Alcestis* was not going to be performed with the incidental music he had composed for it. On June 28, he therefore began to adapt much of that music to a text called *The Choice of Hercules,* taken in large part from Spenser's *Polymete.* He completed the new work, which he himself labeled "A Musical Interlude," on July 5, whether in England or on the Continent is not clear. The most remarkable thing about *The Choice of Hercules* is not to be found by looking at its score alone. Only when that score is placed beside what remains of the *Alcestis* score can we discern the almost magical rightness with which Handel was able to fit old music to new words and situations. As Rockstro said, ". . . except for the dates in Handel's own handwriting, we should have been entirely without a guide as to the priority of either Composition."

The date of Handel's trip to the Continent is not known. He may have been still in London or at Halle visiting the Flörkes when, on July 28, 1750, Johann Sebastian Bach, aged sixty-five like Handel himself, died at Leipzig. Bach had held the highest opinion of his great contemporary. But if Handel heard of Bach's death at all, there is little probability that he thought of that happening as more than the passing of a worthy local church musician. Bach's renown was still severely limited. It was to be eclipsed in Germany by that of his son Carl Philipp Emanuel, in England by that of his son Johann Christian. If Handel visited Halle's Liebfrauenkirche, where Zachau, now dead thirty-eight years, had taught him the techniques of music, he may have heard at the organ there still another of Bach's sons the greatly gifted, unstable Wilhelm Friedemann.

In London, on August 21, the *General Advertiser* carried the only remaining piece of information about Handel's last visit to his natal land: "Mr. Handel, who went to Germany to visit his Friends some Time since, and, between the Hague and Haarlem had the Misfortune to be overturned, by which he was terribly hurt, is now out of Danger." The jolting, not to mention the possible serious injury, that might be sustained by a passenger in a mid-eighteenth-century post chaise would not have been minor for a young man in good health. Handel was sixty-five, and for years had not been well. His eyes in particular had begun to bother him. And now he had been "terribly hurt." His friends in England must have wondered, when they read the *General Advertiser* notice, whether or not he would return to them.

Return Handel did, though a rapidly aging man. It has often been stated that he was back in London during the autumn of 1750. This is mere conjecture. The only certainty is that he had returned there by December.[6] In January 1751 he there began to set, to another text by Morell, the oratorio *Jephtha*. The first date in this manuscript — it is midway in the overture — is January 21, 1751; the date at the end is August 30. *Jephtha* was to be not only Handel's last oratorio, but also his last large composition of any sort, the 1751 English version of *Il Trionfo del Tempo e della Verità* excepted.

In earlier years it had not taken Handel more than seven

6 See letter to Telemann in Appendix A (p. 316).

months to compose an oratorio. But in writing *Jephtha* he was more than once interrupted by infirmity, as is proved by a combination of the dates in the manuscript and outside evidence. Having composed some of the first part and all of the second part by February 23, Handel put the manuscript aside for four months. The character of his autographing — as shown by a comparison of that in *Jephtha* with that in earlier scores and by a comparison of different sections within *Jephtha* itself — clearly demonstrates the gradual failure of his eyesight.

It was probably on March 13, 1751, that the Countess of Shaftesbury wrote to her cousin James Harris:

My constancy to poor Handel got the better of . . . my indolence, and I went last Friday to 'Alexander's Feast'; but it was such a melancholy pleasure, as drew tears of sorrow to see the great though unhappy Handel, dejected, wan, and dark, sitting by, not playing on the harpsichord, and to think how his light had been spent by *being overplied in music's cause.* I was sorry to find the audience so insipid and tasteless (I may add unkind) not to give the poor man the comfort of applause; but affectation and conceit cannot discern or attend to merit.

It was not only Handel's eyes that troubled him during the first part of 1751: there is good reason for believing that his mind was troubled, much as it had been twice before. It is certain that he took a cure at Cheltenham. On Saturday, June 15, the *General Advertiser* announced that: "On Thursday last Mr. Handel arrived in town from Cheltenham Wells, where he had been to make use of the waters." For what it is worth, there is a remarkable difference between contiguous parts of the score of *Jephtha:* the recitative "Deeper and deeper still," composed in February, is written straight out, almost without erasure or blottings-out; "Waft her, angels," the aria now often senselessly attached to it, composed between June 18 and July 17, is a veritable rebus of excisions, second thoughts, and signs of general dissatisfaction and lack of ease.

At Covent Garden, on February 26, 1752, Handel gave the

first performance of *Jephtha.*[7] The season was filled out with two singings of *Joshua,* one of *Hercules,* three of *Samson,* two of *Judas Maccabaeus,* two of *Messiah,* and two repetitions of *Jephtha,* which was better liked than *Theodora* had been. During the course of this season, Handel's sight became so dim that he was unable to read notes at the organ: he could play only by memory or extemporaneously.

Consulting a Guy's Hospital chirurgeon named Samuel Sharp, Handel had learned that his eyes were afflicted with incipient *"gutta serena,"* what we now call cataracts. Sir John Hawkins later wrote that this diagnosis cast Handel down to the depths, "scarce leaving him patience to wait for that crisis in his disorder in which he might hope for relief." His eyes pained him, and there is little doubt that he was simultaneously suffering from other weaknesses and ailments. He was sixty-six years old, and he now underwent three "treatments" or operations, all without the modern anodyne of anesthesia, each consisting of piercing the balls of his eyes with a needle. One of these operations was performed by the private surgeon of the Princess of Wales, William Bromfield. Another, it appears, was the bungling work of that curious peripatetic figure, the "Chevalier" John Taylor, "Opthalmiater," a quack who had operated unsuccessfully on Bach's eyes in January 1750, and who seems also to have tried his uncertain science on Edward Gibbon.

On November 4, 1752, the *General Advertiser* sounded hopeful:

Yesterday George Frederic Handel, esq., was couch'd by Wm. Bromfield, esq., surgeon to her Royal Highness the Princess of Wales, when it was thought there was all imaginable hopes of success by the operation, which must give the greatest pleasure to all lovers of music.

Whether the surgeon's drastic incisions gave Handel temporary surcease from darkness and pain cannot be determined. Indeed, the exact degree of his blindness from November 1751,

[7] The leading roles were distributed as follows: Iphis, Giulia Frasi; Storge, Signora Galli; Jephtha, Beard; Hamor, Charlotte Brent; Zebul, Mr. Wass.

when Mrs. Delany wrote that "poor Handel has lost the sight
of one of his eyes," to the end of his life is difficult to judge.
A London newspaper for January 27, 1753, reported: "Mr.
Handel has at length, unhappily, quite lost his sight. Upon his
being couch'd some time since, he saw so well that his friends
flattered themselves his sight was restored for a continuance;
but a few days have entirely put an end to their hopes." Opinions have varied and fluctuated: the most accurate guess that
can be made on the basis of meager and often contradictory evidence is that his sight troubled him always during the final eight
years of his life, that at times he could see dimly or even well,
at others scarcely or not at all.

It seems to have been during the first onslaughts of his blindness that Handel had a violent quarrel with his old friend John
Christopher Smith the elder. They were on the street in Tunbridge Wells when loud words began to fly between them.
Things came to such a crisis that Smith, forgetting or momentarily not caring that the blind, infirm, and enormously fat Handel could scarcely move without assistance, left him on the
street and returned to London. It was probably because of this
break that Handel crossed out "Senior" after "Mr Christopher
Smith" in his will, and sent to France for the younger Smith,
asking him to return to England immediately to assist him in
preparing a season for 1753. Surgeon Sharp had recommended
to him that he ask aid from John Stanley, the blind organist
whose inability to read scores had forced him to develop a phenomenal memory. "Mr. Sharp," Handel replied, "have you
never read the Scriptures? Do you not remember, if the blind
lead the blind, they both fall into the ditch." Stanley, nevertheless, was to work with Smith both before and after Handel's
death. With Smith's arrival from France to become his general
factotum and amanuensis began the final period, glorious and
unhappy, of Handel's life.

IV

THE YEAR 1751 had witnessed the death of two men of first importance in England during Handel's lifetime. On March 20, Frederick, Prince of Wales, at loggerheads with his father to the end, had died at the age of forty-four. It is probable that Handel would unthinkingly have forgotten the intermittent enmity with which Frederick had plagued him and his musical enterprises, and would have saluted his passing with a grand and appropriate anthem had the King so ordered things. But George II loved Frederick no more dead than alive, and the Prince's burial in Westminster Abbey was no more ceremonial than minimum decency demanded. Behind him Frederick left his wife, two daughters, and four sons, the eldest of whom would, one year after Handel's death, ascend the English throne as George III.

The other death occurred on December 12, 1751, when Henry St. John, Viscount Bolingbroke, died at the age of seventy-three. This had been a powerful man when Handel had first visited England more than forty years earlier. How far away those years of the last of the Stuart rulers must have seemed to Handel! He had been twenty-five then, a promising, even a successful, young composer — but with most of his more than forty Italian operas, the finest of his instrumental pieces, and all of his more than twenty-five English oratorios ahead of him. When Bolingbroke had shared power with the Earl of Oxford, Aaron Hill had been manager of the Queen's Theatre and *Rinaldo* had become the rage of musical London. And now the old dodger and quarreler, brilliant and wrongheaded to the end, spending his last years writing defenses of his ideas and actions, had died.

Of the men London had known best in that period, in fact, Handel himself was now one of the last on the scene.[1]

And on March 9, 1753, punctual despite the decay of his body and the dimming of his eyes, Handel began his oratorio season, which was to include two combined performances of *The Choice of Hercules* and *Alexander's Feast*, two of *Jephtha*, three of *Judas Maccabaeus*, three of *Samson*, and one of *Messiah*. At most of the performances Handel himself still presided at the organ, John Christopher Smith or John Stanley lifting that burden from him only later on. His words about the blind leading the blind must have come back to him when Stanley took his place at a Haymarket performance of *Alexander's Feast*. The *Public Advertiser* for March 2, 1753, carries the following notice:

. . . This Day will be performed ALEXANDER'S FEAST. By Mr. *Handel*. With a Concerto on the Organ, by Mr. *Stanley*, who is to conduct this Performance. . . .

In *Anecdotes of G. F. Handel and J. C. Smith*, published in 1799, William Coxe wrote as follows:

When Smith played the Organ at the Theatre, during the first year of Handel's blindness, *Samson* was performed, and Beard sang, with great feeling,
> *Total eclipse — no sun, no moon,*
> *All dark, amid the blaze of noon.*

The recollection that Handel had set this air to Music, with the view of the blind Composer then sitting by the Organ, affected the

---

[1] The Earl of Oxford had died in 1724, ten years after Queen Anne, two years after Marlborough, and the same year as the once notorious Sacheverell. Thomas Britton had, by 1751, been gone from the London scene for thirty-seven years, Addison for thirty-two, and Steele for twenty-two. Others whom Handel outlived included Aaron Hill (1750), George I (1727), Pope (1744), Gay (1732), Pepusch (1752), Arbuthnot (1735), Sir Robert Walpole (1745), Duke of Chandos (1744), Earl of Burlington (1753), Heidegger (1749), Swift (1745), and Anastasia Robinson (1755). Of the two great composers who had been born the same year as Handel, Bach had died in 1750, while Domenico Scarlatti, dying in 1757, was to predecease his friend by two years.

audience so forcibly, that many persons present were moved even to tears.

It was heavy irony indeed that Handel's setting of lines by the great poet who also suffered blindness should have turned out at last descriptive of his own situation.

Like Stanley, however, Handel was able to direct without seeing. Even during the 1753 season, when his health otherwise seems to have been particularly bad, he was nonetheless often seated at the console. In the *General Advertiser* for May 2, 1753, the following appeared:

Yesterday, the sacred oratorio called Messiah was performed in the Chapel of the Foundling Hospital, under the direction of the inimitable composer thereof, G. F. Handel, Esq., who, in the organ concerto, played himself a voluntary on the fine organ he gave to the Chapel.

Now the years began to acquire a pattern that Handel could not have altered had he wished to alter it. He mostly stayed close in his Brook Street house, alone or working with Smith at corrections and additions to his most popular oratorios. Somehow or other the two men worked out a method by which Handel could dictate the music still welling in his undimmed creative imagination. At times he was even able to scribble in a hand that varied from almost complete illegibility to a quavering approximation to his earlier script. He appeared occasionally at a private musical event, helped a friend design an organ. Each year he presided at the Foundling Hospital benefit performance of *Messiah*. Each year he took some part in the annual season of his oratorios.

On September 20, 1754, Handel wrote to Telemann — himself now seventy-three years old — the last of his surviving letters:

at London this 20 Sepr.[2]
1754

Sir

It is some time since I had a provision of exotic plants prepared to send to You, when Captain Jean Carsten (whom I had spoken to so

[2] There was by this time no longer any need to give double dates at the

that You should get them) told me that he had learned that you were defunct. You do not doubt that this report afflicted me extremely. You will Judge then of the Joy with which I have learned that you find yourself in perfect Health. The same Captain Jean Carsten who has just arrived here on his return from your region, sends me this good news through a friend, and also that you have Consigned to him a List of exotic plants to procure for you, I have embraced this occasion with great pleasure, and I have made an Effort to find these plants, and you will have almost all of them; As Captain Carsten needs not to leave here until the coming month of December, he has had the kindness to Offer to send them to you by the first Ship leaving here, and you will find on the Note herewith both the name of the Captain and of the ship. I hope that this little present which I have dared to offer you will be agreeable to you; I beg you to be kind enough to give me news of your Health which I hope is very perfect, and I also wish you every Kind of prosperity, who am with inviolable esteem

Sir

Your very humble and very obedient
Servant
G: F. Händel.

---

head of a letter. Pope Gregory XIII had, in 1528, reformed the old calendar, issuing regulations by which its incorrectness could be remedied. Sweden, Russia, and England, for varying reasons, failed to adopt the Gregorian reforms (Russia held longest to the Julian calendar, with the result that its dates became wrong by one more day each century). At last, when England's calendar had fallen behind that of most of the rest of the world by eleven days, Lord Chesterfield and the mathematical-minded Lord Macclesfield, assisted by the mathematician Bradley, had persuaded the Pelham ministry to usher the reform through Parliament. It was ordered that January 1, rather than March 25, was to be considered the first day of the year. The difference of eleven days from the Gregorian calendar was to be made up by a Draconian measure: the day following September 2, 1752, was to be called September 14, 1752. This wholly sensible measure was naturally opposed with violence. The Duke of Newcastle begged Chesterfield not to stir up the public by "new-fangled things." He was correct in his way, for there was considerable popular resistance to the reform. Many people continued to use Julian and Gregorian dates together, and it was many years before Julian dates altogether disappeared.

299

Handel seems not to have varied his enforcedly lethargic pattern of living in 1755. Nor did he mark his seventieth birthday, February 23 of that year, in any special manner, so far as can be determined. He was understandably subject to periods of black depression, one of the worst of which occurred during 1756, the year of the birth, at Salzburg, of Wolfgang Amadeus Mozart. Yet it must have been in 1756 that Handel, through Smith, worked on the adaptation and setting of the English translation — by Morell — of the serenata he had called *Il Trionfo del Tempo e del Disinganno* when he had composed it in Italy about 1708 to Cardinal Panfili's text, but had renamed *Il Trionfo del Tempo e della Verità* when he had revised it, still in Italian, in 1737. For this English version, with the character of Deceit added, with most of the recitative re-composed to fit English words, and with nine entirely new numbers and eight newly introduced from other compositions, was to be produced, the last of Handel's works, in 1757.

On August 6, 1756, too, Handel added the first codicil to his will. From a bankrupt he had become, if not rich, at least well-to-do, and he was facing death close by. That first codicil reads as follows:

I, George Frideric Handel, make this codicil to my will.
I give unto my servant Peter le Blond two hundred pounds additional to the legacy already given him in my will.
I give to Mr Christopher Smith fifteen hundred pounds additional to the legacy already given him in my will.
I give to my cousin Christian Gottlieb Handel, of Coppenhagen, two hundred pounds additional to the legacy given him in my will.
My cousin, Magister Christian August Roth, being dead, I give to his widow two hundred pounds, and if she shall die before me, I give the said two hundred pounds to her children.
The widow of George Taust and one of her children being dead, I give to her 5 remaining children three hundred pounds apiece, instead of the legacy given to them by my will.
I give to Dr. [Thomas] Morell, of Turnham Green, two hundred pounds.

I give to Mr. Newburgh Hamilton, of Old Bond-Street, who has assisted me in adjusting words for some of my compositions, one hundred pounds.

I make George Aymant, Esquire, of Lawrence Pountney Hill, London, merchant, co-executor with my niece, mentioned in my will, and give him two hundred pounds, which I desire him to accept for the care and trouble he shall take in my affairs.

In witness whereof I Have hereunto set my hand and seal, this sixth day of August, one thousand seven hundred and fifty-six.

George Frideric Handel.

On the day and year above written, this codicil was read over to the said George Frideric Handel, and was by him signed and published in our presence.

Thos. Harris.
John Hetherington

This codicil added £2,500 to the £3,000 provided in the body of the will itself. On March 22, 1757 — eleven days after he had presented *The Triumph of Time and Truth* to his now enormous and faithful public — Handel had to add a second codicil to his will, death having again robbed him:

I, George Frideric Handel, do make this further codicil to my will. My old servant, Peter le Blond, being lately dead, I give to his nephew, John Duburk, the sum of five hundred pounds.

I give to my servant, Thomas Bramwell, the sum of thirty pounds, in case he shall be living with me at the time of my death, and not otherways.

In witness whereof I have hereunto set my hand, the twenty-second day of March, one thousand seven hundred and fifty-seven.

George Frideric Handel.

[Here follows the witnesses' attestation, identical with that on the first codicil.]

On August 4, 1757, the third and semi-final codicil was added:

I, George Frideric Handel, do make this further codicil to my will. My cousin, Christian Gottlieb Handel, being dead, I give to his sister, Christiana Susanna Handelin, at Goslar, three hundred pounds;

and to his sister [Rahel Sophia], living at Pless, near Teschen, in Silesia, three hundred pounds.

I give to John Rich, Esquire, my great organ that stands at the Theater Royal, in Covent Garden.

I give to Charles Jennens, Esquire, two pictures, the old man's head and the old woman's head, done by Denner.[3]

I give to [here something has become illegible] Granville,[4] Esquire, of Holles-street, the landskip, a view of the Rhine, done by Rembrandt, and another, by the same hand, which he made me a present some time ago.

I give a fair copy of the score, and all parts of my oratorio called the *Messiah* to the Foundling Hospital.

In witness whereof I have hereunto set my hand, this fourth day of August, one thousand seven hundred and fifty-seven.

George Frideric Handel.

[Here follows the witnesses' attestation, identical with that on the first codicil except that John Hetherington was replaced by John Maxwell.]

During 1758 Handel continued his recent manner of life almost unchanged by rapidly deteriorating health. He still occasionally appeared at concerts. He did not forget the Foundling Hospital. He went through the rigors of his annual oratorio season. For a performance of *Judas Maccabaeus* during 1758, he dictated to Smith the magnificent chorus "Sion now her head shall raise." This is based on, of all things, a melody by his ancient rival Giovanni Battista Bononcini, whose death, probably at Venice, had occurred about the time of Bach's. By the end of 1758 it must have been clear to Handel — and to Smith and whoever visited the house in Brook Street — that he was a dying man. His legendary appetite had deserted him. He had clear, expressed premonitions of death. It must have seemed likely that his last public appearance was behind him, that there

[3] Balthasar Denner or Dennar was a German painter. He did several portraits of Handel. Little else is known of him except that he was born at Hamburg in 1685 and died in Rostock in 1749.

[4] Probably Mrs. Delany's brother Bernard Granville, whom Handel had helped to choose an organ in 1756.

"THE SHARP FAMILY"

[from a painting by Zoffany]

Although from a period (late 1770's) after Handel's death, this painting illustrates his last period well. The third man from the left holds a serpent; other instruments represented include a harpsichord, horns, a double flageolet, and a theorbo.

HANDEL

[*statue by Roubiliac on the tomb in Westminster Abbey*]

would either be no Handel oratorio season in 1759 or at best a season without Handel.

But the enormously fat, terribly weary, blind old man had still somewhere in him some of the energy that had carried him to many lands, to many climaxes of fame and despair over seventy-four years. He passed his seventy-fourth birthday on February 23, 1759. During the season,[5] which began (on March 2) promptly and like the others, he gave two performances of *Solomon*, and one of *Susanna*, each of which contained new numbers, pieces recently dictated to Smith. He actually conducted three singings of *Samson*, two of *Judas Maccabaeus*, and three of *Messiah*. On April 6, he led *Messiah* at Covent Garden. Preparing to leave the theater when it was over, he fainted. When they had carried him to Brook Street, friends or servants called in a Dr. Warren. Two days more and it would be Palm Sunday. When the dying man regained consciousness, he said: "I want to die on Good Friday in the hope of rejoining the good God, my sweet Lord and Saviour, on the day of his Resurrection." Then he lay waiting, alternating between consciousness and coma.

On April 11, the Wednesday of Holy Week, Handel was conscious and possessed sufficient strength to add a final codicil to his will. It shows again, and under the most difficult circumstances, his charity and his unwavering thoughtfulness to those who had befriended and served him:

I, George Frideric Handel make this further codicil.
I give to the governors or trustees of the Society for the Support of Decayed Musicians and their Families one thousand pounds, to be disposed of in the most beneficial manner for the objects of that charity:
I give to George Aymant, Esquire, one of my executors, two hundred pounds additional to what I have before given him.
I give to Thomas Harris, Esquire, of Lincolns Inn Fields, three hundred pounds;

[5] Handel's profit from this season was estimated for Bernard Granville as £1,950.

I give to Mr. John Hetherington, of First Fruits Office, in the Middle Temple, one hundred pounds;

I give to Mr. James Smyth, of Bond Street, perfumer, five hundred pounds;

I give to Mr. Mathew Dubourg, musician, one hundred pounds;

I give to my servant, Thomas Bramwell, seventy pounds additional to what I have before given him;

I give to Benjamin Martyn,[6] Esquire, of New Bond-street, fifty guineas;

I give to Mr. John Belchar,[7] of Sun Court, Threadneedle-street, surgeon, fifty guineas;

I give all my wearing-apparel to my servant, John de Bourk;

I give to Mr. John Cowland,[8] of New Bond-street, apothecary, fifty pounds;

I hope I have the permission of the Dean and Chapter of Westminster to be buried in Westminster Abbey, in a private manner, at the discretion of my executor, Mr. Aymand; and I desire that my said executor may have leave to erect a monument for me there, and that any sum not exceeding six hundred pounds, be expended for that purpose, at the discretion of my said executor.

I give to Mrs. Palmer,[8] of Chelsea, widow of Mr. Palmer,[8] of Chelsea, formerly of Chapel-street, one hundred pounds;

I give to my maid-servants each one year's wages over and above what shall be due to them at the time of my death;

I give to Mrs. Mayne,[8] of Kensington, widow, sister of the late Mr. Batt,[8] fifty guineas;

I give to Mrs. Downalan,[9] of Charles-street, Berkeley Square, fifty guineas;

I give to Mr Reiche, Secretary of the affairs of Hanover, two hundred pounds.

In witness whereof I have hereunto set my hand and seal, this eleventh day of April, 1759.

G. F. Handel.

[6] Benjamin Martyn was a writer who served as secretary to the company organized for founding the American colony of Georgia. His connection with Handel is unknown.

[7] John Belcher, also a friend of Alexander Pope.

[8] Nothing is known of this person.

[9] This is evidently the Miss Donnellan at whose home, according to a letter of Mrs. Delany's, Handel played the harpsichord as late as 1755.

This codicil was read over to the said George Frideric Handel, and by him signed and sealed, in the presence, on the day and year above written, of us,

A. J. Rudd.

J. Christopher Smith.

Handel lingered on through Maundy Thursday and Good Friday, the seventeenth anniversary of the first public performance of *Messiah*. During the night of Friday–Saturday, April 13–14, 1759, he died quietly. Dr. Warren told Burney that the actual death happened as Handel had wished, before midnight, that is, and therefore on Good Friday. But there is no indication that Warren was actually present when Handel died. James Smyth, a close friend of Handel's last years, wrote to Bernard Granville that their great acquaintance had died on Saturday, April 14, at eight o'clock in the morning. But Smyth almost certainly was not present either. At any rate, the tenth annual benefit performance of *Messiah* at the Foundling Hospital, already announced for May 3 at twelve of the clock, would not be given "under the direction of G. F. Handel, Esq." as promised, but, for the first time, under that of John Christopher Smith.

The funeral of George Frideric Handel took place in Westminster Abbey about eight o'clock on the evening of Friday, April 20, 1759. The *Universal Chronicle* for April 28, 1759, described the scene:

Friday night about Eight o'clock, the remains of the late Mr Handel were deposited at the foot of the Duke of Argyll's Monument in Westminster Abbey; and though he had mention'd being privately interr'd, yet from the Respect due to so celebrated a Man, the Bishop, Prebends, and the whole Choir attended to pay the last Honours due to his Memory; the Bishop himself performed the Service.[10] A Monument is also to be erected for him, which there is no doubt but that his Works will even outlive. There was almost the greatest Concourse of People of all Ranks ever seen upon such, or indeed upon any other Occasion.

[10] The sermon was preached by Dr. Zachary Pearce, Bishop of Rochester and Dean of Westminster.

3 0 5

By one of the most curious vagaries of official taste in all history, the music performed at Handel's funeral was not by Handel. A brief announcement in the issue of the *Public Advertiser* for April 20, 1759, makes it completely certain that what the combined voices of the Gentlemen of the Chapels Royal, the Choirs of St. Paul's Cathedral and St. Peter's (i.e., Westminster) sang was a Funeral Anthem by Dr. Croft, who also lay buried in the Abbey.

And thus it was that the son of Georg Händel, barber-surgeon of Halle in Saxony, came to rest among the great in England's official pantheon. In the many years that have passed since the night of his funeral, the people of England have honored him by more than the hideous memorial statue by Roubiliac that was erected in the Abbey. They have remembered Handel imperfectly and only in part. But they have loved his music as they were allowed to know it better than the music of any other man. For good or for bad, Handel was the greatest of English composers. In the Abbey and in the throats of Englishmen he has been best memorialized. Germany, where he was born, came late to the feast of Handel. Other countries, the United States included, have heard him even more fractionally than England.

Many readjustments to the art of music could be made in that curious and infuriating anomaly which passes by the name of "the standard repertoire." None among them could refresh music and the minds of music-lovers more welcomely than a renascence of Handel. The last century has witnessed the rebirth of Johann Sebastian Bach. Mozart has been swept to the skies. How long must we look sharply to find one small, hopeful sign that those who control the programs of public music will offer us the whole variegated and wonderful repertoire of vocal, instrumental, choral, and operatic music that lies — some of it unheard for more than a century — in the volumes of the *Gesellschaft* and other editions of Handel?

For to represent Handel as the composer of little else than *Messiah*, an occasional operatic aria, the *Water Musick*, one or two *concerti grossi*, and endless malformations of "the Largo" is tantamount to representing Bach by nothing but the B-minor Mass, an occasional cantata aria, one or two Brandenburg Concertos, and arrangements of the "Air for the G String." A musical world that has come to know a great deal more than that of Bach (though still, when the cantatas are considered, not nearly enough) will be able, tomorrow or the day after, to rescue Handel from Roubiliac and annual outrages on *Messiah*. When that rediscovery of Handel takes place, his whole voice will break on the musical world at once familiar and new, one of the most majestic, tender, and human voices ever lifted in praise of life, of love, of beauty, and of the art of music.

APPENDIX A

LETTERS OF HANDEL NOT INCLUDED IN

THE TEXT

[Fragment of a letter sent to Johann Mattheson in Hamburg]

March 18, 1704

It would give me great delight to enjoy your charming conversation, and this wish will soon come true, when the time arrives that your presence is discovered to be absolutely necessary at the Opera. Please also, I ask humbly, tell me of the time of your departure so that I may have the chance to show you my respect by coming to meet you with Mlle Sbülens [1]. . .

✿꒰✿꒰✿꒰✿꒰✿

[Addressee unknown]

The 13 March 1715

Pray pay Mr Phillip Cooke my Dividend being Fifteen pounds on Five hundred pounds, which is all my stock in the South Sea Company books & for half a Year due at Christmas last & this shall be Your Sufficcient Warraant from

S^r
Your very humble Servan^t
George Frideric Handel

[1] It is now impossible to identify Mlle Sbülens. She may well have been a daughter or other relation to the Hamburg merchant Johann Wilhelm Sbülen mentioned in Handel's letters of August 10, 1731 (see p. 155) and August 28, 1736 (see p. 205).

[*To Mr. John G——*]

this 29 June 1716, London

Sir

What Ever my Dividend is on five hundred pounds South Sea Stock that The South Sea Company pays att the opening of their Books next August pray pay Itt to Mr. Thomas Carbonnel or order and you will oblige

Sir

Your H[umble] Servt
George Frideric Handel.

ᛟᛟᛟᛟᛟᛟᛟᛟᛟ

[*To Johann Mattheson*]

at London
February 24, 1719

Monsieur,

Through the Letter that I have just received from you, dated the 21 of the current month I find myself so obliged to satisfy you more particularly than I have done in my earlier letters on the two points under discussion that I cannot dispense with stating that I find my opinion generally confirming yours, so well deduced and proved in your book touching on Solmization and the Greek Modes.[2] It appears to me that the question is reduced to this: If one should prefer a Method easy and of great perfection to another that is accompanied by great difficulties, capable not only of disgusting Music students but also of making them consume precious time that could better be employed in deepening this art and cultivating their genius? It is not that I wish to claim that it is not possible to get anything useful from Solmization: but as it is possible to acquire the same knowledge in much less time by the method being used at present with so much success, I cannot see why we should not choose the road that leads most easily and in the shortest time to the goal we seek. As for the Greek Modes, I find, Monsieur, that you have said all that can be said about them. Knowledge of them is doubtless necessary to those wishing to practice and perform ancient Music that has been composed following the Modes; but as we have been freed from the strait boundaries of ancient Music, I cannot see of what utility

[2] *Das beschützte Orchester* (Hamburg, 1717).

the Greek Modes can be for modern Music. There you have, Monsieur, my sentiments, you will oblige me by letting me know if they correspond to what you awaited from me.

As to the second point, you yourself can judge that it demands much concentration, of which I am not the master among pressing occupations that I have before me. When I shall be a little less pressed, I shall review the principal Epochs I have had in the course of my Profession, in order to make you see the esteem and particular consideration with which I have the honor to be

Monsieur

your very humble and very

obedient servant

G. F. Handel.

✿✿✿✿✿✿✿✿✿

[*Letter dedicating* Radamisto *to George I*]

[London, late 1720]

TO THE
KING'S
Most Excellent Majesty.
Sir,

The Protection which Your Majesty has been graciously pleased to allow both to the Art of Musick in general, and to one of the lowest, tho' not the least Dutiful of Your Majesty's Servants, has embolden'd me to present to Your Majesty, with all due Humility and Respect, this my first Essay to that Design. I have been still the more encouraged to this, by the particular Approbation Your Majesty has been pleased to give to the Musick of this Drama : Which may I be permitted to say, I value not so much as it is the Judgment of a great Monarch, as of One of a most Refined Taste in the Art : My Endeavours to improve which, is the only Merit that can be pretended by me, except that of being with the utmost Humility,

SIR

Your Majesty's,

Most Devoted,

Most Obedient,

And most Faithful

Subject and Servant

George-Frederic Handel.

APPENDIX A

London, the $\frac{21}{10}$ August, 1733

Sir and most Honored Brother

I received your esteemed letter of the past month containing the enclosure from our dear relatives at Gotha, and I reply to it by this post. With all my heart I rejoice that they and all their dear relatives are so well, and I hope that they will constantly remain so. Again I see what great pains you have taken over the income and expenditure from July 1 last year, 1732, to July 30, 1733, related to the house my Mother left, and I must mention my profound gratitude to you for this.

You mention that it would be necessary for me to see the house myself, but much as I should like to pay you a visit, I must refrain from that pleasure because of the press of events, but I shall give you my opinion on it in writing.

It was very good of you, my Honored Brother, to recall my mother's final wish concerning her tombstone, and I hope that you will carry it out.

I see from the accounts you sent that Frau Händelin,[3] who lives in the house, pays six Reichsthaler rent per year; I should in the future prefer her not to pay anything, and she can remain in it as long as she wishes. I return to you herewith the account, with my signature as you wished, and I shall not overlook my obligations with respect to this. My humblest greetings to your dear Wife. Kindly greetings to the esteemed Taust family, and to all our dear friends. I shall soon be a bother to my esteemed Brother again, but I hope that you will pardon me, for I know you and your kindness. I beg you to believe that I shall always remain, in sincere affection, my especially esteemed Brother's always willing and obedient

Servant

George Friedrich Händel

[3] This may have been either the wife or the daughter-in-law of Handel's half-brother Karl.

APPENDIX A

[*To Sir Wyndham Knatchbull, Bart., of Mersham le Hatch near Ashford, Kent*]

August 27, 1734.

Sir,

At my arrival in Town from the Country, I found my self honored of your kind invitation.

I am sorry that by the situation of my affairs I see my self deprived of receiving that pleasure being engaged with Mr. Rich to carry on the Operas in Covent Garden.

I hope at your return to Town, Sir, I shall make up this loss. Meanwhile I beg you to be persuaded of the sincere respect with which

I am

Sir

your

most obedient and most humble

Servant

George Frideric Handel.

❂❂❂❂❂❂❂

To the Right Honourable
the Earl of Shaftesbury
A. Giles's.   London June 29th 1736.
My Lord.

At my return to Town from the Country (where I made a longer stay than I intended) I found myself honoured with Your Lordships Letter. I am extremely obliged to Your Lordship for sending me that Part of My Lord Your Fathers Letter relating to Musick.[4] His notions are very just. I am highly delighted with them, and can not enough admire 'em. Your Lordships kind remembrance of me makes me sensible to the utmost degree, and it is with the profoundest respect that I am

My Lord

Your Lordships

Most obedient and most humble servant

George Frideric Handel.

---

[4] Anthony Ashley Cooper, Earl of Shaftesbury, wrote a *Letter relating to Musick*. Handel's correspondent was his son, the Fourth Earl.

APPENDIX A

In the London *Daily Post* for October 4, 1738, the following announcement appeared:

This Day is published, Price 3s.

Six Concerto's for the Harpsichord, or Organ.

Compos'd by Mr. *Handel.*

** These Six Concerto's were publish'd by Mr. Walsh from my own Copy corrected by my self, and to him only I have given my Right therein.

George Frideric Handel.

Printed for and sold by John Walsh. . . .

In a few Days will be published,

The Instrumental Parts to the above Six Organ Concerto's.

❈❈❈❈❈❈❈❈

To

—— Chetwin Esq^{r 5}

in Cork Street

      P   sent [6]

Jany 10, 1742–3 [7]

S^r

The following Oratorio of Samson is Intended to be perform'd at the Theatre Royal in Cov^t Garden with your permission I am

S^r

Y^r humble Servt

Jno Rich

George Frideric Handel

❈❈❈❈❈❈❈❈

[*To the* Daily Advertiser, *where it was published January 17, 1745*]

Sir.

Having for a Series of Years received the greatest Obligations from the Nobility and Gentry of this Nation, I have always retained a deep Impression of their Goodness. As I perceived, that joining

---

[5] William Chetwynd, an inspector of plays. His permission was required for any staging.

[6] This cryptic inscription has been interpreted to mean that the requested permission was sent (that is, received).

[7] Old style dateline, probably required on official documents. We should call it simply January 10, 1743.

3 1 3

good Sense and significant Words to Musick, was the best Method of recommending *this* to an English Audience; I have directed my Studies that way, and endeavour'd to shew, that the English Language, which is so expressive of the sublimest Sentiments is the best adapted of any to the full and solemn Kind of Musick. I have the Mortification now to find, that my Labours to please are become ineffectual, when my Expences are considerably greater. To what Cause I must impute the loss of the publick Favour I am ignorant, but the Loss itself I shall always lament. In the mean time, I am assur'd that a Nation, whose Characteristick is Good Nature, would be affected with the Ruin of any Man, which was owing to his Endeavours to entertain them. I am likewise persuaded, that I shall have the Forgiveness of those Noble Persons, who have honour'd me with their Patronage, and their Subscription this Winter, if I beg their Permission to stop short, before my losses are too great to support, if I proceed no farther in my Undertaking; and if I intreat them to withdraw three Fourths of their Subscription, one Fourth Part only of my Proposal having been perform'd.

I am, Sir,

Your very humble Servant,

G. F. Handel

Attendance will be given at Mr. Handel's House in Brook's Street, near Hanover Square, from Nine in the Morning till Two in the Afternoon, on Monday, Tuesday, and Wednesday next, in order to pay back the Subscription Money, on returning the Subscription Ticket.

✦✧✦✧✦✧✦✧✦

[*To the* Daily Advertiser, *where it was published January 25, 1745*]

Sir,

The new Proofs which I have receiv'd of the Generosity of my Subscribers,[8] in refusing upon their own Motives to withdraw their Subscriptions call upon me for the earliest Return, and the warmest Expressions of my Gratitude; but natural [as] it is to feel, proper as

[8] The generosity to which Handel referred is indicated by the following letter published in the *Daily Advertiser* of January 18, 1745:

it is to have, I find this extremely difficult to express. Indeed, I ought not to content myself with bare Expressions of it; therefore, though I am not able to fulfil the whole of my Engagement, I shall think it my Duty to perform what Part of it I can, and shall in some Time proceed with the Oratorios, let the *Risque* which I may run be what it will.

I am, Sir,
Your very humble Servant,
G. F. Handel

❦❦❦❦❦❦❦❦❦

[*To a Mrs. Brerewood*]

March. 15. 1748.

Madame

I gave Ordres that you and Mr Brerewood should be free of the House in my Oratorios all this season. I am glad of this Opportunity to shew you the true Esteem and Regard with which I am

Madam
Your
very humble Servant
G. F. Handel

❦❦❦❦❦❦❦❦❦

Probably dating from 1749 is an inscription in Handel's own writing (Sir Newman Flower called it an "ageing scrawl") on a copy of the *Theodora* text in Thomas Morell's autograph: "I intend to produce this Oratorio at the Theatre Royal, Covent Garden. GEORGE FRIDERIC HANDEL."

To the Author.
Sir,
Upon Reading Mr. Handel's Letter in your Paper this Morning I was sensibly touch'd with that great Master's Misfortunes, failing in his Endeavours to entertain the Publick; whose Neglect in not attending his admirable Performances can no otherwise be made up with Justice to the Character of the Nation, and the Merit of the Man, than by the Subscribers generously declining to withdraw the Remainder of their Subscription.

I would lament the Loss of the Publick in Mr. Handel, in Strains equal to his if I was able, but our Concern will be best express'd by our Generosity.

We are, Sir,
Your obedient Servants,
Subscribers.

St. James's
Jan. 17, 1744–5

APPENDIX A

[To Georg Philipp Telemann]

at London this $\frac{25}{14}$ of Decembr

1750.

Monsieur

I was on the point of leaving The Hague for London when Your most agreeable Letter was presented to me by Mr. Passerini.[9] I had just enough time to hear his Wife sing. Your Support and recommendation sufficed not only to excite my curiosity, but also to make me show her all my approbation, as I was quickly convinced that she has rare merit. They are going to Scotland to fill the promise of an Engagement for a six-month season of Concerts. There She could perfect herself in the English language, and then (as they intend to sojourn for a while in London) I shall not fail to render to Them all the services they may need from me.

Furthermore, I was deeply touched by Your polite expressions, so full of Friendship; Your obliging ways and Your Reputation have made too great an impression on my Heart and my Spirit for me not to Reciprocate Your gentility. Be certain that You will always find in me a full return of sincerity and veritable Esteem.

I thank You for the beautiful Work *du Sisteme d'intervalle,*[10] which you have had the kindness to send me; it is worthy of Your Endeavors and Your Knowledge.

I felicitate you on the perfect Health that You enjoy at a somewhat advanced Age, and from a good Heart I wish you the Continuation of every sort of prosperity for many years in the future. If the passion for exotic Plants & should be able to prolong Your days and sustain the Vivacity natural to you, I offer with real pleasure to contribute to it in some manner. I make You, then, a Present, and I send You (through the address herewith) a Box of Flowers that the Connoisseurs of these Plants assure me are choice and of Charming rarity; if they tell me the truth, You will have the best Plants of all England; the season is still right for having Flowers; You will be the best Judge; I await Your decision in this regard. Meanwhile, do

[9] In 1752 a musician by this name played the viola d'amore and the violin in London. Nothing else is known of him, nothing at all of his songstress wife.

[10] Apparently this was *"Das neue musicalische System,"* an article by Telemann that appeared in Lorenz Christoph Mizler's *Die neu eröffnete musikalische Bibliothek,* a pioneering musical periodical.

not make me languish too long for Your agreeable Reply to this
letter, as I am with the most sensible Friendship and perfect passion
Monsieur
Your
very humble and very obedient
Servant
George Frideric Handel.

APPENDIX B

A BRIEF ANALYSIS OF HANDEL'S *ORLANDO* (1732)

A PREFATORY WORD

Scholars can make, and have made, plausible genealogies for opera that date it back as far as the Greek drama. It can be connected even more persuasively with the mystery plays and miracle plays of the Middle Ages and the masques of the Renaissance. If a point is to be selected as the one at which a single first work recognizable as an opera and nothing else can be dated, however, that point must be the daybreak of the seventeenth century. Then a group of mixed professional and amateur musicians (it included Giovanni Bardi, a Florentine noble, as well as Vincenzo Galilei, father of the martyred astronomer) created the first true opera in the process of trying to give rebirth to drama produced in the Greek manner, with music. As a result of the tendencies and aesthetic beliefs that had led immediately up to them, the first operas — Jacopo Peri's lost *Dafne* and the surviving *Euridice* he composed with Giulio Caccini — were works of thin musical interest, all but entirely dominated by their librettos, plays with a large amount of interwoven incidental music. Caccini (1548?–1618) and Peri (1561–1633) deserve honor as the originators of modern opera; nothing in their surviving music marks them as composers in any way equal to the great religious musicians of their day.

Surprisingly soon after 1600, dozens of musicians were trying their unaccustomed hands at the magical new art of opera. The first man of musical genius to touch it was Claudio Monteverdi (1567–1643), whose masterpieces — from the *Orfeo* of 1607 to such works of his old age as *Il Ritorno d'Ulisse* and *L'Incoronazione di Poppea* — show the flawless balance between text and music that has been achieved only a few times in opera's long history. But the seeds of opera's decay from the high estate to which Monteverdi had borne it were being sown before he had begun to compose, while Caccini and Peri were still lonely pioneers. Too soon it had become obvious that the immediate appeal of opera could be enormously increased by exploiting the popularity and individual capabilities of certain singers. Caccini's daughter Francesca (known as "La Cecchina") was not only a composer of considerable abilities, but also the first *prima donna*. From her success and that of her contemporaries and successors among sopranos — from their success, not in fitting themselves into the texture of an operatic performance, but in standing out from it — grew one of opera's historic weaknesses. The fact that male singers soon became even more popular than (and as) sopranos simply multiplied the weakness.

Alessandro Scarlatti (1659–1725), whose works Handel unquestionably knew and studied and imitated, was a very great composer. It is only from an ideal comparison, then, that it is fair to say that his constant use of the *aria da capo* — one in which, usually after a middle section, the opening section is repeated — helped to stultify the dramatic flow of opera. However beautiful Scarlatti's arias may have been, however successful as singable entities his operas may have been, the result of his dominance was as detrimental to the dramatic component of opera as Peri and Caccini's insistence on the dramatic component had been detrimental to opera as an equal marriage of text and music.

Another great composer, Jean-Baptiste Lully (1632–87), pouring out operas for the court of Louis XIV, added to opera another element so carried to extremes as to weaken the entire structure of the art. This was the "machine" or scenic effect. Lully's operas abound in magnificent music to be sung, magnificent music to be danced. They have, on occasion, psychological verisimilitude of the most penetrating sort. But they are primarily vehicles for elaborate stage displays. Worse, they are often vehicles for such magnificence at the expense of opera's true inner nature, the balanced amalgam of drama and music.

Handel, then, could not inherit a living operatic art in healthy condition. Nor was he by character a conscious innovator or reformer, the sort of man who might have looked ailing opera in the eye and told it how to become well and hale. Not in Germany, where only a broadly vulgar type of half-spoken, half-sung *Singspiel* was native, could he have found a good tradition for serious opera. By his day in Italy, too, the golden mean of Monteverdi was mostly forgotten in a flood of operas pandering to the eternal Italian taste for song at the expense of all else. He never visited France, but in London he encountered the "machine" opera well advanced. He was to fill some forty operas with wonderful music without ever achieving the artistic unity and persuasiveness such a smaller, minor master as Bizet was to achieve in *Carmen*.

It remained for the suddenly wise Gluck (1714–87) — with the very important help of his environment and his wiser librettist, Calzabigi (1714–95) — to attempt to return opera to the balance Monteverdi had won for it. (The fact that Gluck and Calzabigi said they were doing something else is unimportant.) It remained for Mozart (1756–91) to solve with the simplicity of genius the problems Gluck and Calzabigi had recognized, and to create in *Le Nozze di Figaro* and *Don Giovanni* operatic models everyone can enjoy and no composer can use. Handel's achievement was of another sort, on another level, in another world. His operas fail if measured by the highest standards. All of them, nonetheless, have pages of regal, of pastoral, of amorous, of enchanted loveliness. And a few of them are — or would be if we would perform them — operatic evenings or afternoons only the handful of great operatic masters have known how to surpass.

THE ANALYSIS

Orlando has five characters: Orlando (contralto), described simply as "heroe"; Angelica, Queen of the Catai (soprano), "lover of Medoro"; Medoro (alto), "prince, lover of Angelica"; Dorinda (soprano), "shepherdess," and Zoroastro (bass), "sorcerer, friend of Orlando." It is in three acts. It opens with an overture in F sharp minor that runs to one hundred and twenty-eight measures. This is scored for violins *divisi in tre*, oboes *divisi in due*, violas, and *"bassi"* (cellos, basses, and figured harpsichord). The first eighteen measures, in bright, rapid style 4/4 time, are repeated, leading the second time directly into a seventy-measure allegro in 3/4 time. Not repeated, this allegro in turn leads to nine measures of 4/4 time marked *"Lentement."* This comes to a full close, but is followed by thirty measures of an allegro jig in which the viola and *bassi* parts are in 4/4 time, the violin in 12/8. This, of which only the first ten measures are repeated, also comes to a full close.

Act I is divided into twelve short scenes. The first, accompanied by strings and harpsichord, is for Zoroastro (Montagnana), who is discovered resting on a rock from which he contemplates the movements of the stars. "Plain with a mountain view. On the summit of the mountain, Atlas, who supports the sky on his shoulders. Many genii are seated about the foot of the mountain." The sorcerer, in a largo accompanied recitative (or *aria parlante*) that begins *"Gieroglifici eterni,"* apostrophizes the heavenly bodies. In Scene 2, Orlando (Senesino) enters, and to the accompaniment of the *bassi* (and at times solely the cellos) sings a largo cavatina, *"Stimulato dalla gloria."* He and Zoroastro converse in recitative with harpsichord accompaniment. "The Sorcerer makes a sign with his wand, and the genii disappear from the mountain. In their place appears the Palace of Love, with a figure of a boy seated on the throne, having at his feet certain sleeping heroes of antiquity." Then begins Zoroastro's second aria, *"Lascia amor,"* which makes use of eight-part harmony (voice, oboe 1 and 2, bassoons, violins 1 and 2, viola, and *bassi*). Marked *allegro ma non troppo,* this *da capo* aria has a relatively simple vocal line thrown against complex figurations in the accompaniment. It closes the second scene. The third scene is Orlando's alone. After nineteen measures of recitative starting *"Immagini funeste"* and marked *largo e piano,* he sings the andante aria *"Non fù già,"* again with eight-part harmony (two horns, oboe 1 and 2, violins 1 and 2, viola, *bassi,* and voice).

Scene 4 provides another new stage picture. Dorinda (Celeste) is discovered in a "glade with shepherds' cottages." She sings a brief recitative — *"Quanto diletto"* — to the four-part accompaniment of violins 1 and 2, viola, and *bassi.* "The noise of weapons is heard from within. Orlando, sword in hand, brings with him a princess liberated from the hands of her enemies." Orlando has a recitative beginning *"Itene pur tremendo,"* much like Dorinda's and with the same accompaniment. This leads to Dorinda's *"Ho un certo rossore,"* an *aria da capo* in three-part harmony (*tutti unisoni, bassi,* and voice). Scene

5 follows without change of setting. Angelica (Strada) has a brief, harpsichord-accompanied recitative, "*M'hai vinto al fin'*," leading into an aria beginning "*Ritornava al suo bel viso.*" This is marked "*largo, e staccato, mà piano,*" and is accompanied by violins 1 and 2, viola, and *bassi*. When her voice breaks off, a solo violin makes up the missing fifth voice in the harmony, whereupon Medoro (Bertolli) enters with a dialogue-like continuation of the same aria.

In Scene 6, Angelica and Medoro converse in recitative accompanied by harpsichord, and Angelica (with *violini unisoni* and *bassi*) sings the *aria da capo* "*Chi possessore è del mio core.*" Scene 7 shows Dorinda and Medoro conversing in recitative with harpsichord. Then Medoro has an *aria da capo* in slow tempo (violins and *bassi*), "*Se il cor mai tidira.*" Scene 8 is a soliloquy for Dorinda: recitative with harpsichord ("*Povera me!*"), followed by a four-part allegro *aria da capo* (*tutti unisoni*, viola, *bassi*), "*O care parolette.*" Scene 9 is begun with harpsichord-accompanied recitative for Zoroastro, Medoro, and Angelica. In the midst of it, "The Sorcerer leaves, making a sign with his wand; from underground there rises a great fountain that hides Medoro, the scene changing into a delightful garden." The scene ends with Angelica's slow *aria da capo* (violins 1 and 2, viola, *bassi*), "*Se fedel vuoi ch'io ti creda.*"

Scene 10 is Orlando's. After a brief recitative (harpsichord) beginning "*T'ubbidirò,*" he sings an allegro *aria da capo*, "*Fammi combattere*" (*tutti*, viola, *bassi*), during sections of which a solo violin substitutes for the *tutti*. Scene 11 is a brief recitative dialogue (harpsichord) for Medoro and Angelica, "*Angelica, deh! lascia. . . .*" Dorinda enters, and in Scene 12 the three converse in recitative (harpsichord) that leads to a terzetto marked *andante larghetto* (*tutti unisoni*, *bassi*, three voices). This "*Consolati, o bella,*" again *da capo*, closes the act.

Act II has eleven scenes divided between two settings: "Forest" and "Prospect of distant sea; on one side a laurel grove, on the other the mouth of a grotto." Scene 1 is a slow aria for Dorinda. Scene 2, beginning with dialogue recitative for Orlando and Dorinda, develops into a slow *aria da capo* for Dorinda. Scene 3 is Orlando's, recitative followed by an *aria da capo*. Scene 4 (second setting) opens with recitative for Zoroastro, Angelica, and Medoro, and concludes with Zoroastro's remarkable, expressive *aria da capo*, "*Tra caligni profonde.*" Scene 5, after recitative for Medoro and Angelica, changes to *siciliano* rhythm for Medoro's *aria da capo,* "*Verdi allori.*" Scene 6 is Angelica's, recitative followed by an allegro *aria da capo.* Scene 7 is recitative for Orlando. At its close, he enters the grotto, and Scene 8 begins with recitative for Angelica, leading into another *aria da capo* for her, this time a larghetto, "*Verdi piante.*" The rest of this scene and all of the very brief ninth scene are recitative for Orlando, Angelica, and Medoro. Scene 10, again short, consists wholly of recitative for Orlando and Angelica.

Scene 11 of the second act is the most remarkable in the opera. It is a mad scene for Orlando. Beginning in 4/4 time, it passes with little pause into 5/8 measures — at the time of its composition an exceedingly rare, if not unprecedented signature in opera. What is more, the 4/4 returns for two measures only to be interrupted by the 5/8 for one, in a manner Stravinsky was to make familiar to the twentieth century. Before this long and tremendous theatrical scene closes, in fact, Orlando has sung in "*tempo di Gavotta*" (₵) and 6/8 time as well! It works up to a striking climax, with Orlando crying "*Ma sì, pupille, sì, sì, piangete, sì, sì, sì, pupille, sì, sì, piangete, sì, piangete, sì.*" "Orlando throws himself furiously into the grotto, which bursts open, revealing the Sorcerer, with Orlando in his arms, in his car, which flies through the air."

Act III of *Orlando* has ten scenes, all set in an "enclosure of palms." It opens with a four-part *sinfonia* (violin 1, oboes 1 and 2; violin 2; viola; *tutti bassi*) of eighteen measures, not repeated. There follows recitative for Medoro and Dorinda, leading to an *andante allegro aria da capo* for Medoro. Scene 2, very brief, is recitative for Dorinda. Scene 3 opens with recitative for Orlando and Dorinda. This is followed by a sort of duet for Dorinda and Orlando, the latter still mad and raging in fragments of melody (some of it, so strong was the custom and so telling here, *da capo*). The scene ends with an instrumental ritornello. Scene 4, after recitative for Angelica and Dorinda, leads to another *aria da capo* for Angelica. The fifth scene is Dorinda's, recitative and the aria "*Amor è qual vento,*" remarkable for one of Handel's few uses of the diminished-seventh chord. Scene 6 is Zoroastro's, recitative followed by one of Handel's master arias for bass, "*Sorge infausta,*" sung *da capo.* Scene 7 is recitative for Angelica and Dorinda, leading without interruption into Scene 8. This, after recitative for Orlando and Angelica, contains a dialogue duet for them, *"Finchè prendi,"* which has a richly instrumented accompaniment, and is not *da capo.* They break off into recitative for four measures. "He throws her furiously into the grotto, which is suddenly changed into a beautiful temple of Mars, in which Angelica is seated on a high place and guarded by genii." Orlando (Orlando *furioso,* for such is the tempo mark) then sings an accompanied recitative. This in turn leads to his four-part invocation to sleep, *"Già l'ebro mio ciglio"* (*"violette marine per le Signori Castrucci"* [1] and *bassi*). In Scene 9 Zoroastro undertakes to cure Orlando's madness. This is recitative, first with harpsichord, then accompanied. "He makes a sign with his wand, and four genii come through the air with an eagle carrying a golden vase in its beak. Zoroastro takes the vase, and the eagle flies away with the genii through the air." Then follows a delightful instrumental interlude *"andante, e pianissimo."* "The Sorcerer approaches Orlando, when Dorinda appears." Dorinda and Zoroastro converse in recitative. "Zoroastro throws the liquid over Orlando's face, and then leaves. Orlando returns to sanity." Orlando and Dorinda talk in recitative, and Orlando sings an aria, *"Per far, mia diletta."* In the final scene, the five principal characters converse in recitative, which leads to the "chorus" (quintet) finale, *"Trionfa oggi 'l mio cor,"* which is accompanied by oboes 1 and 2; violin 1; violin 2; viola; *tutti bassi.*

[1] The *violetta marina* was introduced into England by Castrucci in 1732. It was a highpitched *viola d'amore,* like which it had sympathetic strings under the fingerboard and was held like a violin rather than vertically, neck upward, like a viol. It had no frets. That it earned some enduring popularity in England seems to be indicated by the fact that Leopold Mozart later referred to it as the "English *violet.*"

BIBLIOGRAPHY

(This is a list of a few of the many books consulted — and suggested for further reading. No periodical articles are included: they are extremely numerous and can best be learned about through the catalogue of a large library in which they are obtainable.)

ABRAHAM, GERALD, editor: *Handel, a Symposium.* London, New York, Toronto, 1954.

BAIRSTOW, E. C.: *Handel's Oratorio "The Messiah."* London, 1928.

BESANT, SIR WALTER: *London in the Eighteenth Century.* New York, 1903.

BURNEY, CHARLES: *A General History of Music from the Earliest Ages to the Present Period (1789).* Edited by Frank Mercer. London, New York, 1936, 2 v.

—— *An account of the musical performances in Westminster-abbey, and the Pantheon, May 26th, 27th, 29th; and June the 3d and 5th, 1784. In commemoration of Handel.* London, 1785.

—— *The present state of music in France and Italy; or a journal of a tour through those countries.* London, 1771.

BURNEY, FANNY: *Diary and letters of Madame D'Arblay.* London, 1904–05, 6 v.

CHRYSANDER, FRIEDRICH: *G. F. Händel.* Leipzig, 1858, 1860, 1867, 3 v. (never completed).

CIBBER, COLLEY: *An apology for the life of Colley Cibber.* London, 1740.

CLARK, RICHARD: *Reminiscences of Handel, His Grace the Duke of Chandos, Powells the harpers, the Harmonious Blacksmith, and others.* London, 1836.

CLARKE, ELIZA: *Handel.* London, Paris, New York & Melbourne, 1885.

COXE, W[ILLIAM]: *Anecdotes of George Frederick Handel and J. C. Smith.* London, 1799.

BIBLIOGRAPHY

DAVEY, HENRY: *Handel.* New York, 1913.

DEAN, WINTON: *Handel's Dramatic Oratorios and Masques.* London, New York, Toronto, 1959.

DELANY, MARY: *Autobiography and correspondence of Mary Granville, Mrs. Delany.* Edited by Lady Llanover. London, 1861–62, 6 v.

DENT, EDWARD J.: *Handel.* London, 1934.

DEUTSCH, OTTO ERICH: *Handel, a Documentary Biography.* New York, n. d. [195?].

FASSINI, SESTO: *Il Melodramma italiano a Londra nella prima metà del settecento.* Turin, 1914.

Festschrift der Händelfestspiele, Leipzig, 1954; 1955.

FLOWER, SIR NEWMAN: *George Frideric Handel: His Personality and His Times.* London, Toronto, Melbourne, Sydney, 1947.

FULLER–MAITLAND, J. A.: *The Age of Bach and Handel (Oxford History of Music,* v. IV). Oxford, 1921.

GEORGE, M. DOROTHY: *London Life in the Eighteenth Century.* London and New York, 1925.

GREEN, J. R.: *A Short History of the English People.* New York, 1895.

HADDEN, J. CUTHBERT: *Handel, a Biography.* London, 1888.

HALLE STADTARCHIV: *Georg Friedrich Händel; Abstammung und Jugendwelt. Festschrift zur 250. Wiederkehr des Geburtstages Georg Friedrich Händel.* Halle, 1935.

HANDEL, GEORGE FRIDERIC: *The Letters and Writings of George Frideric Handel.* Edited by Erich H. Müller. London, Toronto, Melbourne and Sydney, 1935.

HÄNDEL-FESTKOMITEE: *Wege zu Händel.* Halle, 1953.

Händel-Jahrbuch: 1 (VII), 1955; 2 (VIII), 1956; 3 (IX), 1957. *See also* Taut, Kurt.

HAWKINS, SIR JOHN: *A general history of the science and practice of music.* London, 1776, 5 v.

HERVEY, JOHN, BARON: *Some Materials Towards Memoirs of the Reign of King George II.* Edited by Romney Sedgwick. London, 1931, 3 v.

HILL, AARON: *The dramatic works of Aaron Hill.* London, 1760, 2 v.

HITZIG, WILHELM: *Georg Friedrich Händel, 1685–1759; sein Leben in Bildern.* Leipzig, 1935.

KRONENBERGER, LOUIS: *Kings and Desperate Men.* New York, 1942.

LÁNG, PAUL HENRY: *Music in Western Civilization.* New York, 1941.

LARSEN, JENS PETER: *Handel's Messiah: Origins, Composition, Sources.* New York, 1957.

LECKY, WILLIAM EDWARD HARTPOLE: *A History of England in the Eighteenth Century.* New York, 1888, 8 v.

LEICHTENTRITT, HUGO: *Händel.* Stuttgart, Berlin, 1924.

LOEWENBERG, ALFRED: *Annals of Opera, 1597–1940.* Genève, 1955, 2 v.

MACFARREN, SIR GEORGE ALEXANDER: *Centenary commemoration. 1859. A sketch of the life of Handel with . . . notices of the works selected for each day's performance at the centenary festival in the Crystal palace.* London [1859?].

MAINWARING, JOHN: *Memoirs of the life of the late George Frederic Handel. To which is added, A Catalogue of his Works, and Observations upon them.* London, 1760.

MARSHALL, FLORENCE ASHTON [Mrs. Julian]: *Handel.* London, 1883.

MATTHESON, JOHANN: *Grundlage einer Ehrenpforte.* Hamburg, 1740.

MELVILLE, LEWIS: *The First George in Hanover and England.* New York, 1909.

MICHEL BRENET (MARIE BOBILIER): *Hændel, biographie critique.* Paris, 1912.

MÜLLER-BLATTAU, JOSEPH: *Georg Friedrich Händel.* Potsdam, 1933.

MYERS, ROBERT MANSON: *Handel's Messiah, a Touchstone of Taste.* New York, 1948.

NIETSCHMANN, HERMANN OTTO: *Georg Friedrich Händel. Ein*

Künstlerleben, von Armin Stein (pseudonym). Halle, 1882–83, 2 v.

RAMSAY, EDWARD BANNERMAN BURNETT: *Two Lectures on the Genius of Handel and the Distinctive Character of His Sacred Compositions.* Edinburgh and London, 1862.

REISSMANN, A.: *Georg Friedrich Händel; sein Leben und seine Werke.* Berlin and Leipzig, 1882.

ROBINSON, PERCY: *Handel and his Orbit.* London, 1908.

ROCKSTRO, WILLIAM SMITH: *The Life of George Frederick Handel.* London, 1883.

ROLLAND, ROMAIN: *Hændel.* Paris, 1910.

—— *Voyage musical aux pays du passé.* Paris, 1919.

SCHOELCHER, VICTOR: *The Life of Handel.* Translated from the French by James Lowe. New York, 1857.

SIEGMUND-SCHULTZE, WALTHER: *Georg Friedrich Händel.* Leipzig, 1954.

SITWELL, SACHEVERELL: *A Background for Domenico Scarlatti.* London, 1935.

SMITH, WILLIAM C.: *Concerning Handel, His Life and Works.* London, 1948.

STREATFEILD, RICHARD ALEXANDER: *Handel.* New York, 1909.

TAUT, KURT: *Verzeichnis des Schrifttums über Georg Friedrich Händel (Händel-Jahrbuch. VI Jahrgang).*

TAYLOR, SEDLEY: *The indebtedness of Handel to works by other composers.* Cambridge, 1906.

TOWNSEND, HORATIO: *An Account of Handel's Visit to Dublin.* London, 1852.

VERNON LEE (VIOLET PAGET): *Studies of the Eighteenth Century in Italy.* London, 1880.

VOLBACH, FRITZ: *Georg Friedrich Händel.* Berlin, 1898.

WILLIAMS, CHARLES FRANCIS ABDY: *Handel.* Revised edition, edited by Eric Blom. London, New York, 1935.

YOUNG, PERCY M.: *Handel.* London and New York, 1947. *The Oratorios of Handel.* New York, 1950.

General Index

i

GENERAL INDEX

GENERAL INDEX

GENERAL INDEX

Index of Works by Handel
Referred to in the Text

I. OPERAS AND PASTICCI

(N.B. Only the *pasticci* almost certainly arranged by Handel are indexed here; others may be found in the general index under their titles.)

INDEX OF WORKS

A NOTE ON THE AUTHOR

Herbert Weinstock was born in Milwaukee, Wisconsin, on November 16, 1905. After attending the University of Chicago briefly and operating his own bookshop in Milwaukee for three years, in 1930 he moved to New York, where he has lived ever since except for numerous trips to Mexico and Europe. He has been Executive Editor of Alfred A. Knopf, Inc., since 1943; program annotator for the Little Orchestra Society since 1950; and a recordings reviewer for the Saturday Review. *His published books are:* Tchaikovsky (*1943*); Handel (*1946; revised 1959*); Chopin: The Man and His Music (*1949*); Music as an Art (*1953*); *and two collaborations with Wallace Brockway —* Men of Music (*1939; revised 1950*) *and* The Opera (*1941*). *Mr. Weinstock translated Carlos Chávez's* Toward a New Music (*1937*) *and was co-editor, with Hubert Herring, of* Renascent Mexico (*1935*). *He has contributed articles on musical subjects to periodicals, the* Encyclopedia Americana, *and the* World Book Encyclopedia.

A NOTE ON THE TYPE USED IN THIS BOOK

The text of this book is set in CALEDONIA, *a Linotype face designed by W. A. Dwiggins. Caledonia belongs to the family of printing types called "modern face" by printers — a term used to mark the change in style of type-letters that occurred about 1800. Caledonia borders on the general design of Scotch Modern, but is more freely drawn than that letter.*

The book was composed, printed, and bound by The Plimpton Press, Norwood, Massachusetts. The binding is based on designs by W. A. Dwiggins.